ERIC A. SEIBERT

ENJOYING
the OLD
TESTAMENT

A CREATIVE
GUIDE TO
ENCOUNTERING
SCRIPTURE

ivp
Academic

An imprint of InterVarsity Press
Downers Grove, Illinois

InterVarsity Press
P.O. Box 1400, Downers Grove, IL 60515-1426
ivpress.com
email@ivpress.com

InterVarsity Press® is the book-publishing division of InterVarsity Christian Fellowship/USA®, a movement of students and faculty active on campus at hundreds of universities, colleges, and schools of nursing in the United States of America, and a member movement of the International Fellowship of Evangelical Students. For information about local and regional activities, visit intervarsity.org.

Scripture quotations, unless otherwise noted, are from the New Revised Standard Version Bible, copyright © 1989 National Council of the Churches of Christ in the United States of America. Used by permission. All rights reserved worldwide.

Cover design and image composite: David Fassett
Interior design: Daniel van Loon
Images: state park: © Adam-Springer / iStock / Getty Images Plus
> *blue watercolor background: © andipantz / iStock / Getty Images Plus*
> *splashing sea: © Ariel Nuez / EyeEm*
> *Iceland river delta: © Justinreznick / E+ / Getty Images*
> *night sky illustration: © Khaneeros / iStock / Getty Images Plus*
> *space nebula: © maciek905 / iStock / Getty Images Plus*
> *space galaxy: © maraqu / iStock / Getty Images Plus*
> *canyon walls: © Marcus Lindstrom / E+ / Getty Images*
> *stained glass window © Pascal Deloche / Godong / Stone / Getty Images*
> *national park lake: © Paul Biris / Moment Open / Getty Images*
> *oil paint abstract: © photominus / iStock / Getty Images Plus*
> *rock surface: © The Real Tokyo Life / Moment / Getty Images*
> *abstract liquid background: © Vuk Ostojic / Moment / Getty Images*

ISBN 978-1-5140-0120-2 (print)
ISBN 978-1-5410-0121-9 (digital)

Printed in the United States of America ♾

InterVarsity Press is committed to ecological stewardship and to the conservation of natural resources in all our operations. This book was printed using sustainably sourced paper.

Library of Congress Cataloging-in-Publication Data

Names: Seibert, Eric A., 1969- author.
Title: Enjoying the Old Testament : a creative guide to encountering
* scripture / Eric A. Seibert.*
Description: Downers Grove, IL : IVP Academic , 2021. | Includes
* bibliographical references and index.*
Identifiers: LCCN 2021030784 (print) | LCCN 2021030785 (ebook) | ISBN
* 9781514001202 (print) | ISBN 9781514001219 (digital)*
Subjects: LCSH: Bible. Old Testament—Appreciation. | Bible. Old
* Testament—Miscellanea.*
Classification: LCC BS538.5 .S45 2021 (print) | LCC BS538.5 (ebook) | DDC
* 221—dc23*
LC record available at https://lccn.loc.gov/2021030784
LC ebook record available at https://lccn.loc.gov/2021030785

P   26   25   24   23   22   21   20   19   18   17   16   15   14   13   12   11   10   9   8   7   6   5   4   3   2   1

Y   43   42   41   40   39   38   37   36   35   34   33   32   31   30   29   28   27   26   25   24   23   22   21

For

TERRY L. BRENSINGER

Professor,

Mentor,

Pastor,

Friend,

whose enjoyment of the Old Testament

captivated my imagination

and inspired me to follow in his footsteps

....

And in loving memory

of my father

LAVERNE SEIBERT (1942–2020)

whose presence among us is sorely missed

For whatever was written in former days
was written for our instruction,
so that by steadfastness
and by the encouragement of the scriptures
we might have hope.

ROMANS 15:4

CONTENTS

x

ACKNOWLEDGMENTS

A NUMBER OF YEARS AGO, I was meeting with a student on campus. As we talked, he shared something that stuck with me. He said that many of his friends had little interest in reading the Bible. It wasn't just that some people had a hard time understanding the Bible (though many certainly do) or that the Bible contains unfamiliar customs and practices (though it certainly does). Rather, the issue was deeper than that. They were just not interested. This got me thinking. How can we help people *want* to open the Bible? What can be done to increase their desire to read Scripture and get more involved with it? I am thankful to this student, whose name I have forgotten (sorry!), for setting me on this path.

Every book has a long list of people to thank, and this one is no different. Let me begin with a word of thanks to all the students I have had the privilege of teaching over the years in classes like Encountering the Bible, Old Testament Literature, and Selected Old Testament Books. You have taught me so much and have given me opportunities to "test-drive" some of the ideas contained in this book.

I owe an incalculable debt of gratitude to three Old Testament professors for instilling in me a deep and abiding love for this part of the Bible. My passion for the Old Testament was kindled under the wise and skillful teaching of Terry Brensinger, to whom this book is dedicated. Were it not for him, it is difficult to say what direction my life and vocational path would have taken. John Oswalt was also instrumental in cultivating my deepening interest in this part of the Bible. Though our scholarship moves in some very different directions, I remain grateful for the privilege of sitting under his excellent instruction during my time in seminary. Herbert Huffmon introduced me to the power of persuasion in the prophets and opened the treasures of the ancient world to me. I benefited greatly from the time and energy he invested in my life during my doctoral studies.

To each of you, I offer my heartfelt thanks for the crucial role you have played in my journey. Your love for the Old Testament has encouraged mine in countless ways. As you will see, I have incorporated a number of things into this book that I first learned from the three of you. I have tried to give appropriate credit where things seemed most derivative. Beyond that, I am hopeful this general word of acknowledgment will suffice as an adequate substitute for what would otherwise require many, many more footnotes.

A number of people read a draft of this manuscript and provided valuable comments and feedback, making it much better than anything I could have produced on my own. I owe each of them my thanks and gratitude: Terry Brensinger, John Byron, Emily Cowser, Michelle Curtis, Jay McDermond, Elisa Joy Seibert, Hannah Sledge, Brian Smith, Chris Wenger, and Mitch Wirth. I deeply appreciate you taking time away for a hundred other things you could have been doing to read and comment on this book. Your insights and questions enhanced my work in so many ways, and I have freely incorporated many of your suggestions into the final version. Of course, all remaining shortcomings and errors are my own.

Jay McDermond takes the prize for being the first person to read through the entire manuscript and return it marked with many—often humorous—comments (though I confess to some disappointment for feedback written in blue rather than purple ink). Your early enthusiasm for this book was a great encouragement to me.

Michelle, your comments were immensely helpful to me at many points. Thank you for reading this manuscript so carefully and for offering such excellent feedback. My "happy Old Testament book," as you liked to call it, is now finished and is quite a bit "happier" thanks to you.

As always, a very special word of thanks is due to Elisa, my beloved wife of thirty years. Your consistent mantra of "you have good things to offer" has worked its way deep into my soul. It gives me courage to write and speak with the hope that it actually makes some difference. Thank you for reading and commenting on yet another book, and for believing in me and supporting me. Life with you is a gift of grace that brings me great joy and keeps my work in perspective. You are a blessing beyond compare.

Writing while parenting is no easy task, and I am grateful to Nathan, Rebecca, and Hannah for putting up with a "book writing" Daddy. I owe each of you an ice cream cone and a friendly wrestling session (no, you are *not* getting unlimited screen time).

I also owe my parents a great debt of gratitude for regularly watching "the kids" so I could have time to write. Thank you for sacrificing so much and giving so freely of your time so I could write and tend to other things that needed to be done. I hope you feel some pride and satisfaction knowing what an important role you played in making this book possible. Dad, I hope you can now rest in peace knowing this book is finally finished. I only wish you were still here so I could give you a copy in person. I love you, Dad and Mom, always and forever!

Finally, I want to say a word of thanks to the good folks at IVP, particularly Dan Reid and Anna Gissing. Dan, I appreciated meeting with you in Baltimore to discuss this book proposal many years ago. Thank you for your interest in this book and your advocacy on my behalf. Although I didn't get this manuscript completed before you retired, I hope you feel the final product has been worth the wait! Anna, it has been a pleasure getting to know you and working with you on this project. Thank you for your gracious help with numerous details. I am grateful for all you did to move this book through various stages of production to publication. I also wish to thank the anonymous reader who worked through a draft of the manuscript and offered a number of good suggestions for improvement. Thanks as well to Emily Varner for doing such an excellent job copyediting and to David Fassett for the beautiful eye-catching book cover.

Last but not least, thanks to my student assistant Lily Montgomery for preparing the author index so carefully and efficiently.

To all who read this book, I hope you find new ways to engage the Old Testament that help you enjoy it and that keep you coming back for more.

PART ONE

PREPARING *to* READ *the* NEGLECTED TESTAMENT

1

WHY DO WE NEED
THIS BOOK?

*When inspired, I pick up the Bible for a few minutes at the
beginning or end of the day. But often I am tired, and I do not
get very far. I enjoy the feel of the pages; I glance over the chapter
headings. Yet, over the course of days or weeks, I rarely make it
through an entire book of the Bible, despite my best intentions. I
have often found it more interesting to pick up a book about the
Bible than to read the Bible itself.*

JOHN P. BURGESS, *WHY SCRIPTURE MATTERS*

OVER THIRTY YEARS AGO, in the spring of 1989, something unexpected happened: I *fell in love* with the Old Testament. I was a first-year student at Messiah University (then College) and was enrolled in Old Testament Literature, a required course for my major. In that course, in an otherwise unremarkable classroom in the Sollenberger Sports Center, the Old Testament came alive for me in ways I never dreamed possible.

To be honest, I had never really paid much attention to the Old Testament while I was growing up. My knowledge of this part of the Bible mainly came through what I was taught in church—and I attended a lot of church: Sunday school, Sunday morning worship, Vacation Bible School, Sunday evening services and, for a time, even Wednesday evening prayer meetings. Still, for all that, I did not spend much time with the Old Testament on my own. I certainly had not read most of it, and my knowledge of what it contained was quite limited. Though I had heard many of the most popular Old Testament stories, I had little real knowledge of how they fit together into Israel's larger story. Had someone pressed me to put twenty different Old Testament events in order, I am sure I would have done quite poorly.

True, I had once spent hours listening to sermons by Chuck Swindoll on the life of Moses. I can still picture myself sitting at home in my room in rural Pennsylvania, listening to Pastor Swindoll while I worked on an art project for school. It was a latch-hook rug I had designed that contained the symbol of a popular Christian rock band surrounded by lots of black yarn. As I was latch-hooking, I passed the hours listening to this mesmerizing preacher draw out lessons from the life of Moses. It was fascinating. Still, for all that, it did not propel me to dive into the Old Testament on my own. Instead, I spent most of my time focusing on that "other" part of the Bible, the New Testament.

Armed with a beautiful, burgundy-bound, one-volume *Wycliffe Bible Commentary*, I spent countless hours working through individual study guides on various New Testament books. The New Testament intrigued me. It contained so much wisdom and practical advice for Christian living that was easy to extract and export.

But that college class in 1989 really turned things upside down for me and charted a new course for my future. The professor, Dr. Terry Brensinger, brought the Old Testament to life in ways I had not previously experienced. Time and again he demonstrated how relevant the Old Testament was for people of faith like me. I was amazed that these ancient texts contained such profound insights about God, the world, and the way human beings were to relate to God and others. I was captivated.

Since I had neglected the Old Testament for so long, I had to make up for lost time. There was so much new terrain to cover, and I thoroughly enjoyed taking many Old Testament classes over the next three years of my college career. It was a blast! I loved those courses and the world they opened up to me.

Ultimately, this led me to seminary and graduate school where I earned a PhD in the area of Old Testament. Now, I have the good fortune of teaching the Old Testament to undergraduate students at my alma mater. Not many people get to talk about the Bible for a living, and I consider myself very fortunate in that regard.

A VERY REAL DILEMMA

Teaching the Bible for many years has made it abundantly clear that not everyone shares the same level of enthusiasm for the Old Testament that I have described here.[1] Truth be told, many Christians really struggle with this part of Scripture, especially with its archaic laws, tedious genealogies, strange customs, and prophetic tirades. They know they are *supposed* to read the Old Testament but feel little desire to do so. While some stalwart churchgoers continue reading out of sheer duty, others give up on the Old Testament altogether, opening it only occasionally to revisit a few familiar psalms, stories, or well-known verses. And though many feel guilty about their lack of love for the Old Testament and may sincerely wish they could get more out of it, they have no idea how to make that happen.

Perhaps this describes you. Maybe you tried to read through the Old Testament in the past but got discouraged when you ran into material that failed to capture your interest. Or maybe you feel confused by what you have read and are unsure how to make sense of it all. Perhaps you find some parts morally offensive or theologically troubling. Or maybe you have been personally harmed by the Old Testament and have felt the sting of verses used to judge or condemn you. Or maybe you just find this whole part of the Bible largely irrelevant to your life today. Whatever the case may be, if you don't really like the Old Testament and want that to change, you have come to the right place!

---

[1]Though Protestants, Catholics, and Orthodox Christians differ over exactly which books constitute the Old Testament, I am using the term to refer to the thirty-nine books Protestants recognize as the complete Old Testament. Catholics and Orthodox Christians include these thirty-nine books along with others. For an orientation to the other books, see David A. deSilva, *Introducing the Apocrypha: Message, Context, and Significance* (Grand Rapids, MI: Baker Academic, 2002).

READING THE OLD TESTAMENT: BLESSING OR BURDEN?

The purpose of this book is to offer some suggestions that can help you take joy in reading the Old Testament. I want the Old Testament to become something you are eager to return to time and again, not because you feel obligated to do so, but because you genuinely *want* to engage it. My hope is that you come to regard reading the Old Testament as a blessing rather than a burden, something to anticipate, not dread.

This is precisely what happened to Philip Yancey many years ago. In his book *The Bible Jesus Read*, Yancey talks about how he "came to stop avoiding and start reading—ultimately loving—the Old Testament."

> From initial resistance, I moved to a reluctant sense that I *ought* to read the neglected three-quarters of the Bible. As I worked past some of the barriers . . . I came to feel a *need* to read, because of what it was teaching me. Eventually I found myself *wanting* to read those thirty-nine books, which were satisfying in me some hunger that nothing else had—not even, I must say, the New Testament. They taught me about Life with God: not how it is supposed to work, but how it actually does work.[2]

Yancey's journey from resisting the Old Testament to relishing it represents the kind of movement I hope this book inspires. Even if you don't currently enjoy the Old Testament, I hope you feel more enthusiastic about it after reading this book.

But be warned. Some people start having so much fun with the Old Testament that they devote their lives to it. Take my friend David Lamb, for example. David is professor of Old Testament at Missio Seminary in Hatfield, Pennsylvania. Early in his academic career, he needed to decide which part of the Bible would be his focus. Although drawn to the New Testament, he opted to study the Old Testament instead. He was especially intrigued by the rich and multifaceted portrait of God he found there. As Lamb describes it:

> The most compelling factor drawing me toward studying the Old Testament was God himself. . . . God in the Old Testament was complex.

---

[2]Philip Yancey, *The Bible Jesus Read* (Grand Rapids, MI: Zondervan, 1999), 20-21, emphasis original.

There was so much about God in the Old Testament that I didn't understand. I thought I could study the Old Testament for the rest of my life and never feel bored.[3]

His feelings have not changed. "I still can't imagine getting tired of studying the Old Testament," says Lamb. "I love the Old Testament, and in particular examining the God who is revealed there."[4]

One of my primary goals as a college professor is to get people excited about reading Scripture. While I may not be able to persuade everybody to *love* the Old Testament the way David Lamb does, I can at least help them learn how to like it a whole lot more. When I teach a Bible class, I want people to leave that class with a *greater* desire to read the Bible than when they began. If this does not happen and students leave the class *less* interested in reading the Bible than when they began, I have surely failed. After all, what good is it to produce students who know lots of facts about the Old Testament but leave class vowing never to read it again? This book, like my classes, is designed to leave you wanting *more* of the Old Testament.

The benefits of reading the Old Testament are enormous, and we will have an opportunity to explore some of these in chapter three. For now, suffice it to say that reading the Old Testament can strengthen your faith, deepen your relationship with God, and show you how to live faithfully with hope, conviction, and joy. These texts have nurtured and sustained communities of faith for centuries, and they continue to be vital for the spiritual health and well-being of the church. Treasures await those who open its pages.

WHAT TO EXPECT FROM THIS BOOK

Before we get too far along, it might be helpful to say a few words about what to expect in the pages that follow. We'll begin with what the book is not. This book is *not* intended to be a general introduction to the Old Testament, and it makes no attempt to offer any kind of systematic

---

[3]David T. Lamb, *God Behaving Badly: Is the God of the Old Testament Angry, Sexist, and Racist?* (Downers Grove, IL: InterVarsity Press, 2011), 10.
[4]Lamb, *God Behaving Badly*, 10-11.

summary of the basic content and themes of various Old Testament books. This book also does not concentrate on the context, background, and historical setting of Old Testament literature, or on historical-critical questions related to the study of this part of Scripture. While all these things are important, there are already many books on the market that cover them quite well.[5]

Instead, this book is designed to increase your interest in the Old Testament by demonstrating how reading it can be both pleasurable and rewarding. You will find an assortment of creative approaches to the Old Testament that are interactive, engaging, and enjoyable. This practical, "hands-on" approach will encourage you to return to this oft-neglected part of the Bible time and again with renewed interest and enthusiasm.

Along the way, numerous examples are included that illustrate the Old Testament's contemporary relevance and applicability. Hopefully, this too will persuade you to open the Old Testament more frequently and discover for yourself its profound value and worth for spiritual growth and theological reflection.

WHY THIS APPROACH?

The approach taken in this book is rooted in the conviction that having a variety of ways to encounter the Old Testament is what keeps people engaged with it over the long haul. Although some people do the same thing with the Bible year in and year out—and seem to enjoy it—most of us cannot sustain such a routine. We need different ways to connect with the text. Otherwise, we get bored and lose interest. As the saying goes, "Variety is the spice of life." If you want to enjoy reading the Bible, find various ways to engage it. That keeps things interesting.

I also believe people are most inclined to do what they love. That is why our family goes to the beach each year. It is why I have spent too much time playing Minecraft and Clash Royale over the years. And it's why I consume so much sugar! It is easy to do what gives us pleasure.

---

[5]See "Old Testament Introductions" in the appendix.

That is why this book is so intentional about demonstrating various ways to enjoy reading the Old Testament. Admittedly, it will likely take more effort to have fun with the Old Testament than it does to go to the beach, play a video game, or eat a chocolate bar, but it is possible. You *can* discover ways of reading and engaging the Old Testament that are quite pleasurable and deeply satisfying.

Just to be clear, my goal in emphasizing the fun you can have reading the Old Testament is not simply so you can add "Bible reading" to a list of hobbies you relish doing from time to time, like hiking, boogie boarding, woodworking, or crocheting. Rather, I want you to have meaningful and edifying encounters with the Old Testament on a *regular* basis because I believe this is one of the key ways Christians grow and mature. Bible reading is an essential spiritual practice for Christians because of what the church claims these texts to be: authoritative Scripture. As the writer of 2 Timothy 3:16 puts it, "All scripture is inspired by God and is useful for teaching, for reproof, for correction, and for training in righteousness, so that everyone who belongs to God may be proficient, equipped for every good work." The Old Testament shapes our behaviors and beliefs and is therefore crucially important to the life of faith.

For the past two thousand years, the Old Testament has been an indispensable resource for the church. The church preaches and teaches from it, writes about it, reflects on it, and is sustained by it. It has played a vital role in bringing people to faith, freeing people from oppression, and inspiring people to live holy lives. The Old Testament is a crucial part of the Christian tradition, and we must continue to find new ways to engage it and be engaged by it. Having fun with it is one way to ensure this happens.

As you will discover in the pages that follow, many of the practical suggestions offered in this book require nothing more than a Bible, a comfortable chair, and perhaps paper and pencil close at hand. I have tried to suggest activities that do not require the use of other books such as commentaries, Bible dictionaries, and the like. While these are valuable reference tools, having firsthand experience with the biblical text itself is *most* essential. While it is valuable to read books *about* the Old Testament (like this one), there is no substitute for your own direct encounter with the Bible itself. Ultimately, this is what gets you hooked.

The other reason for offering practical suggestions that can be implemented with just a Bible in hand is because I assume some of you may not have easy access to a theological library. I do not want you to feel that enjoying the Old Testament depends on being surrounded by scholarly books and articles. It does not. While I will recommend several books and websites that can enhance your appreciation of the Old Testament, there are lots of ways to have deeply satisfying encounters with this part of the Bible that do not require any additional resources.

A BRIEF OVERVIEW OF COMING ATTRACTIONS

This book is divided into three parts. The first section, "Preparing to Read the Neglected Testament," begins by explaining why so many people don't seem to like the Old Testament very much. Chapter two briefly describes the declining use of the Old Testament among Christians and then discusses some of the reasons people commonly give for their lack of interest in this part of the Bible (e.g., it's boring, morally problematic, irrelevant, confusing, and so forth). People sometimes wonder whether the Old Testament is even worth the effort. If there are so many "problems," why bother with it? Chapter three addresses this question by highlighting seven of the Old Testament's most attractive features in an effort to provide a compelling rationale for reading it. The following two chapters lay the necessary groundwork for having a positive encounter with the Old Testament. Chapter four discusses the importance of developing realistic expectations when reading this part of the Bible by exploring what you should and should not expect of the Old Testament. Chapter five extends this conversation by describing the kind of attitude you should have when approaching the Old Testament. I emphasize being observant, expectant, respectful, and honest with the text.

The next section of the book, "Having Fun with the Old Testament," considers a number of concrete ways to enhance your enjoyment of this part of the Bible. Chapter six focuses exclusively on Old Testament narratives. It discusses how observing important literary features such as repetition, naming, and the use of personal details is both pleasurable and profitable. Chapter seven explores prophetic literature, exposing common misperceptions about the prophets while emphasizing their importance as persuasive speakers who cared deeply about the communities they served. The remaining two chapters provide guidance for dealing with some of the most disagreeable parts of the Old Testament. Chapter eight offers advice for how to benefit from the "boring" parts of the Old Testament, such as the law codes, while chapter nine suggests ways to overcome some of the most formidable obstacles to enjoying the Old Testament, namely, passages you find morally or theologically problematic. Each chapter includes specific practices you can "try at home" to help you get more out of these intriguing stories, prophetic speeches, ancient laws, and troubling texts.

The final section of the book, "Encountering the Old Testament in New Ways," provides a wide array of creative options for engaging the Old Testament. Chapters ten and eleven lay out some very practical ways to interact with the Old Testament. The ideas in chapter ten range from very basic suggestions (memorize Old Testament verses) to more targeted approaches (read a familiar Old Testament story from a different perspective). The suggestions in chapter eleven fall into one of three categories: those which are topically motivated (use the Old Testament to explore a topic of interest), artistically oriented (create a work of art related to a person, passage, event, or theme in the Old Testament), or personally reflective (connect your story with others in the Old Testament). Most of these suggestions are designed to help you move beyond just reading the Old Testament; all are offered with the hope they will help you find more ways to savor this part of the Bible. Chapter twelve focuses exclusively on one particular way to encounter the Old Testament, namely, doing a book survey. This easy-to-use method will enable you to get an overview of the basic content and structure of individual books of the Old Testament and can be used with the New Testament as well.

The final chapter, chapter thirteen, is especially important. It talks about the nuts and bolts of implementing the ideas presented in this book. I encourage readers to develop a plan for interacting with the Old Testament, experiment with different approaches along the way, and take practical steps to make their experience with the Old Testament more pleasurable, among other things.

The book concludes with an appendix containing a brief list of resources that can enrich your reading and enjoyment of the Old Testament immensely. While many of these are referenced throughout the book, they are brought together here for convenience's sake.

Conclusion

Though many books are published each year that promise to help people understand the Old Testament better, they often fail to address a prior issue: Why bother reading it in the first place? This book is different. It is intentionally designed to help you see that reading the Old Testament is not only worth the effort but is actually quite rewarding.

Throughout this book, you will gain many tools that will help you find creative ways to enjoy the Old Testament as you engage it in all its beauty and complexity. But before we offer these practical suggestions, it is necessary to consider what makes the Old Testament so challenging to read in the first place.

2

WHY DON'T PEOPLE ENJOY the OLD TESTAMENT?

*For the most part, Christians do not reject the
Old Testament; they simply ignore it.*

Henry O. Thompson, "Why Christians Should
Bother with the Old Testament"

There is an intriguing story in the Old Testament about a
very important book found while the temple is undergoing repairs.[1] The
book is discovered by the high priest Hilkiah and is brought to the attention of King Josiah of Judah.

> The high priest Hilkiah said to Shaphan the secretary, "I have found the
> book of the law in the house of the Lord." . . . Shaphan the secretary in-
> formed the king, "The priest Hilkiah has given me a book." Shaphan then
> read it aloud to the king.
>
> When the king heard the words of the book of the law, he tore his clothes.
> Then the king commanded the priest Hilkiah, Ahikam son of Shaphan,
> Achbor son of Micaiah, Shaphan the secretary, and the king's servant
> Asaiah, saying, "Go, inquire of the Lord for me, for the people, and for all
> Judah, concerning the words of this book that has been found; for great
> is the wrath of the Lord that is kindled against us, because our ancestors
> did not obey the words of this book, to do according to all that is written
> concerning us." (2 Kings 22:8, 10-13)

---

[1]Though the passage never specifies the name of this book, it is generally thought to refer to the
book of Deuteronomy, or a portion of it.

This inquiry results in the unhappy confirmation that Jerusalem will indeed be destroyed, though mercifully not in the days of Josiah (2 Kings 22:16-20). King Josiah then arranges for a public reading of the book to all inhabitants of the land, and the people enter into a covenant with the Lord (2 Kings 23:1-3). After this, the king undertakes a series of sweeping reforms to bring the practices of the people into line with the ways of the Lord (2 Kings 23:4-24). For Josiah's zeal and obedience, the writer reserves his highest praise:

> Before him there was no king like him, who turned to the LORD with all his heart, with all his soul, and with all his might, according to all the law of Moses; nor did any like him arise after him. (2 Kings 23:25)

Josiah was hands down the best king Judah ever had.

On the face of it, this story raises a number of very intriguing questions. How could a book of such importance ever get "lost" in the first place? How could something that ostensibly held the key to Judah's very survival be neglected and forgotten for so many years?

While such a loss may seem astonishing or even unfathomable to us, we should consider one simple fact before we rush to judge. Many of us have also lost some very important books, the ones that make up the Old Testament. Although we have not literally misplaced them—we know where they are, in the Bibles that adorn our bookshelves and travel with us to church each Sunday—we have virtually lost all knowledge of them because we don't read them very much. Most of the Old Testament, which comprises over three-fourths of the Bible, is largely unfamiliar to many Christians. It has become a stranger.

LOSING THE OLD TESTAMENT

This loss has not gone unnoticed. Numerous scholars have commented on the declining use of the Old Testament in recent years. They recognize it no longer plays a very significant role in the lives of individual Christians or the church at large. In her poignantly titled essay, "Losing a

Friend: The Loss of the Old Testament to the Church," Ellen Davis assesses the situation with these sobering words:

> Many Christians, both ordained and lay, view the Old Testament as a historical document that is impenetrably complex and morally problematic. Even in evangelical traditions, few pastors, teachers, or preachers feel confident in drawing upon it for theological insight and guidance for their lives. In a word, *the Old Testament is ceasing to function as Scripture* in the European-American mainstream church.[2]

Similarly, Elizabeth Achtemeier believes, "the Old Testament is largely a lost book in many parts of the U.S. church."[3] She continues:

> The people in our congregations have only the most limited knowledge of its contents. Many preachers rarely, if ever, preach from the Old Testament. . . . Our people may know or recognize a few lines from some psalms; they hear a number of prophetic promises at Christmastime; they can recognize the creation story when someone reads it to them. But beyond that, the Old Testament is unknown and unimportant to them, an unopened antique book from the distant past that can safely be left with the other antiques on the curio shelf.[4]

This neglect of the Old Testament is even *more* acute today than when these words were written decades ago.

The most extensive analysis of this undesirable situation is found in Brent Strawn's recent book provocatively titled *The Old Testament is Dying.* "For many contemporary Christians, at least in North America," writes Strawn, "the Old Testament has ceased to function in healthy ways in their lives as sacred, authoritative, canonical literature."[5] As Strawn sees it, many Christians "would prefer to do without the Old Testament,

---

[2]Ellen F. Davis, "Losing a Friend: The Loss of the Old Testament to the Church," in *Jews, Christians, and the Theology of the Hebrew Scriptures*, ed. Alice Ogden Bellis and Joel S. Kaminsky, SBL Symposium Series 8 (Atlanta: Society of Biblical Literature, 2000), 83, emphasis mine.

[3]Elizabeth Achtemeier, *Preaching from the Old Testament* (Louisville, KY: Westminster John Knox, 1989), 21.

[4]Achtemeier, *Preaching from the Old Testament*, 21.

[5]Brent A. Strawn, *The Old Testament Is Dying: A Diagnosis and Recommended Treatment* (Grand Rapids, MI: Baker Academic, 2017), 4-5.

and for all practical purposes do exactly that by means of their neglect and ignorance of it, whether in private devotion or public worship or both."[6] He convincingly supports these claims by an impressive array of empirical data.[7]

It is a sad but indisputable fact that large numbers of Christians don't know much about the Old Testament and have very little interest in reading it. My concern here is not to belabor this point. Rather, my interest is to understand why. Why do so many Christians, who hold the Bible in such high regard, neglect reading vast portions of it? What accounts for this strange state of affairs, especially given their claim that the Bible—both Old and New Testament—is the inspired, authoritative word of God?

WHY DON'T PEOPLE ENJOY READING THE OLD TESTAMENT?

Christians who struggle to enjoy the Old Testament often cite a handful of reasons for their lack of love for this part of the Bible, and it is helpful to identify these. Doing so enables us to understand what hinders people from appreciating the Old Testament, and this lays the groundwork for addressing some of their concerns.

It's boring. One of the most frequent complaints leveled against the Old Testament is that it is boring. And who wants to read something boring? To be sure, there are portions of the Old Testament that do not make for very scintillating reading: genealogies, census lists, purity laws, and the like. Most people I know do not get very excited about reading long lists of hard-to-pronounce names, pages of instructions about how to build a tabernacle, or judgment oracles against people they have never met in countries that no longer exist. Most modern readers understandably have little appetite for such things.

Of course, the critical question is *why* people find the Old Testament boring. Sometimes when we claim to be bored with something, we are simply saying it's just not interesting to us. Yet boredom is often symptomatic

---

[6]Strawn, *Old Testament Is Dying*, 5.
[7]See Strawn, *Old Testament Is Dying*, 19-58.

of a deeper dissatisfaction. When people claim the Old Testament is boring, is it because they find it too difficult to understand? Too outdated? Too offensive? Determining the cause of our boredom—as some of the reasons below may help us to do—gets us closer to the heart of the problem.

It's irrelevant. Many people avoid the Old Testament, or at least large portions of it, because they believe it is irrelevant. They just don't see how it applies to their everyday lives. This is often keenly felt when reading parts of the Old Testament that deal with matters of ritual purity and sacrificial offerings. For example, there are two *very* long chapters in the book of Leviticus that deal with the diagnosis and treatment of various skin diseases. These two chapters, Leviticus 13–14, go into *great* detail about what must be done if someone contracts such a disease. It includes multiple visits to the priest, cleansing rituals, and ceremonial offerings. This seems completely irrelevant to modern life. Today, if we notice something funky going on with our skin, we pick up the phone and call the dermatologist. Most readers see little value in reading about laws that no longer directly apply to us, laws about what kind of food Israelites could eat (Lev 11), what kind of garments they could wear (Lev 19:19), and what kind of sacrifices they could make (Lev 1–7).

But it is not just the legal and ritual portions of the Old Testament that create barriers for many readers. People also struggle to find relevance in many other parts of the Old Testament, including narratives and prophetic oracles. Why does it matter what Omri, Ahab, or any other Israelite king did over 2,500 years ago? How does that knowledge help us live more faithfully today? Or what am I to "take away" from a prophetic book like Nahum that contains nothing but harrowing judgment oracles against Assyria, an ancient empire no longer on the map? What relevance is there in texts like these? Finding little or none, some people give up on the Old Testament.

It's hard to understand. The sheer difficulty of understanding certain parts of the Old Testament also contributes to its relative neglect among many Christian readers. Lots of people struggle to make sense of what they read in this part of the Bible. They are unfamiliar with the historical context, cultural practices, and theological worldview described in the Old Testament, and this limits their comprehension of it.

Unfortunately, people who find the Old Testament confusing and hard to understand often stop reading it. Why bother expending so much effort to make sense of the Old Testament when there is an abundance of great Christian literature at our fingertips that is so much easier to read and understand?

This carries over to Sunday morning and also partly explains the limited use that is made of the Old Testament in some churches. Listen to what Matthew Schlimm says about churches that do little or nothing with the Old Testament on Sunday mornings:

> People in these congregations are painfully aware of all the difficult issues the Old Testament raises. They recognize that these issues are too complex to address in the middle of a worship service. They realize that people often feel stupid when the Bible doesn't make sense—as though there's something wrong with them for not knowing what's going on. And so, it simply becomes easier to lay the Old Testament aside, to treat it as a stranger, rather than fix our attention on it.[8]

The level of difficulty associated with reading and understanding the Old Testament, or at least parts of it, discourages some from even trying.

It's foreign and peculiar. Part of what people find so difficult about the Old Testament is its foreignness. It comes from a time and place long ago. Or, better said, it comes from *many different* times and places from long ago. We encounter many customs, practices, and ideas that are completely unfamiliar to us. Most of us don't make a habit of casting lots, wearing sackcloth, sacrificing animals, building temples, or besieging cities, to name just a few of the ways the world of the Old Testament differs from our own. Schlimm believes "the Old Testament is *so* strange that Christians have a much easier time ignoring it than wrestling with all the issues it presents."[9]

---

[8]Matthew Richard Schlimm, *This Strange and Sacred Scripture: Wrestling with the Old Testament and Its Oddities* (Grand Rapids, MI: Baker Academic, 2015), 5.
[9]Schlimm, *Strange and Sacred Scripture*, 4, emphasis original.

Some of this "strangeness" comes from the miraculous elements we encounter in the Old Testament: the creation of the world in six days, the Red Sea parting, water from a rock, a staff that turns into a snake, a fish that swallows a man (who survives)—the list goes on. These unusual occurrences contribute to the perception that the Old Testament is strange and unfamiliar, making it difficult for many modern readers to connect with it.

It's filled with problematic portrayals of God. Some of the most substantial barriers to reading the Old Testament have to do with the way God is portrayed there. Many readers are particularly troubled by stories of God's violent behavior and by all the killing God reportedly sanctions.

Throughout the Old Testament, God frequently engages in acts of violence that result in countless deaths.[10] God floods the earth (Gen 6–8), destroys entire cities (Gen 19), and commands Israel to mercilessly kill Canaanites and to "utterly destroy" Amalekites. All this leaves many readers bewildered and confused. These extremely violent portrayals of God do not correspond well with their beliefs about God's goodness, mercy, and love. Sometimes, this precipitates a faith crisis. The following story told by C. S. Cowles dramatically illustrates this point:

> A former student shared with me the sad story of his father, a dedicated lay leader of an evangelical church, who in mid-life set out to read the Bible through for the first time. He was first surprised, then shocked, and finally outraged by the frequency and ferocity of divinely initiated and sanctioned violence in the Old Testament. About halfway through the book of Job, he shut his Bible never to open it again and has not set foot inside a church since.[11]

---

[10]Using numbers reported in the Old Testament, Steve Wells puts the total at approximately 2.5 million. Wells proposes a number about ten times higher when you add estimated casualties from texts which provide no specific figures. Steve Wells, *Drunk with Blood: God's Killings in the Bible* (USA: Giordano Press, 2010), 3-5.

[11]C. S. Cowles, "A Response to Eugene H. Merrill," in *Show Them No Mercy: Four Views on God and Canaanite Genocide*, by C. S. Cowles et al. (Grand Rapids, MI: Zondervan, 2003), 97.

While that reaction may seem extreme, the presence of so much divine violence in the Old Testament makes it very difficult for many people to like the Old Testament.[12]

It's morally offensive. Relatedly, the inclusion of morally offensive passages dampens the enthusiasm some readers might otherwise have for this part of the Bible. In the Old Testament, a Levite's "concubine" is gang raped and dismembered (Judg 19). The women of Jabesh-gilead are kidnapped, relocated, and forced to marry (Judg 21). A Moabite king sacrifices his son, and would-be successor, during a battle that is going badly for him (2 Kings 3:27). An Israelite woman resorts to cannibalism during the siege of Samaria (2 Kings 6:28-29).[13] This is just a brief sampling of stories that do not make for easy reading. In the words of Thomas Long:

> Anyone who has taken a serious trip through the Old Testament knows that there are some rough neighborhoods to be found there. One does not have to go very far before running up on some brutal war being waged, some blood being spilt, or even some children being gobbled up by bears, often in the name of God.[14]

These "rough neighborhoods" are difficult to traverse because they offend our moral sensibilities, raising questions about their spiritual value and worth.

It's oppressive. The Old Testament's troubling legacy is another reason why some people find it challenging to like this part of the Bible.[15] Throughout history, Christians have repeatedly used various verses from the Old Testament to justify an enormous amount of violence toward

---

[12]See chapter nine for suggestions about how to mitigate some of the challenges these passages raise. For an extensive treatment of problematic portrayals of God in the Old Testament, see Eric A. Seibert, *Disturbing Divine Behavior: Troubling Old Testament Images of God* (Minneapolis: Fortress, 2009).

[13]In this particularly gruesome story, an unnamed woman makes a desperate pact with another woman. She agrees to kill her own son and share the "meal" with the other woman on the condition that she will do the same with her son the next day. But when the next day comes, the other woman reneges and hides her child.

[14]Thomas G. Long, "The Fall of the House of Uzzah . . . and Other Difficult Preaching Texts," *Journal for Preachers* 7.1 (1983): 16-17.

[15]For a brief discussion of the Old Testament's troubling legacy, see Eric A. Seibert, *The Violence of Scripture: Overcoming the Old Testament's Troubling Legacy* (Minneapolis: Fortress, 2012), 15-26.

others. This has led to harm, suffering, and death for countless individuals. People who are routinely marginalized have often borne the brunt of these oppressive readings of biblical texts.

For example, over the years, women have suffered greatly from the Old Testament's patriarchal ethos and sexism, making it difficult for many of them to value this part of the Bible.[16] While some have still found ways to use these texts constructively, others have given up on the Old Testament altogether. From their perspective, the only appropriate thing to do with a text as problematic as the Bible is to reject any claims of authority that might be ascribed to it.

Likewise, members of the LGBTQ community often have a difficult time with the Old (and New) Testament because of the way it has been used to condemn them. As Terence Fretheim observes:

> Christians have often alienated people from the Bible by the way in which they have used it. . . . Christians who disagree about a whole host of matters, from homosexuality to the place of women in the church, often use the Bible in highly polemical ways, more as a bludgeon or an Uzi than as a source of life. The not uncommon reaction is: "If the bible causes such division, violence, and vituperative behavior, I don't need it."[17]

Other groups, like Native Americans, also have a complicated relationship with the Old Testament. For them, Israel's exodus-conquest narrative is highly problematic, especially given the fact that European settlers viewed themselves as the "New Israel" and regarded Native Americans as the people of the land who needed to be destroyed. Likewise, Palestinians find it difficult to be enthusiastic about the Old Testament, given the way some of these same texts have often been used to justify

---

[16]For an excellent introduction to the range of concerns the Old Testament raises for women and for some of the ways women have responded to these, see Kathleen M. O'Connor, "The Feminist Movement Meets the Old Testament: One Woman's Perspective," in *Engaging the Bible in a Gendered World: An Introduction to Feminist Biblical Interpretation in Honor of Katharine Doob Sakenfeld*, ed. Linda Day and Carolyn Pressler (Louisville, KY: Westminster John Knox, 2006), 3-24.

[17]Terence E. Fretheim and Karlfried Froehlich, *The Bible as Word of God: In a Postmodern Age* (Minneapolis: Fortress, 1998), 85.

their forcible removal from the land. As Palestinian Christian Naim Stifan Ateek has written:

> Before the creation of the State [of Israel], the Old Testament was con- sidered to be an essential part of Christian Scripture, pointing and wit- nessing to Jesus. Since the creation of the State, some Jewish and Christian interpreters have read the Old Testament largely as a Zionist text to such an extent that is has become almost repugnant to Palestinian Christians. As a result, *the Old Testament has generally fallen into disuse* among both clergy and laity.[18]

Those who have been harmed by oppressive interpretations of the Old Testament understandably experience difficulties appreciating this part of the Bible.

While all seven of these reasons explain why people have difficulty happily engaging with the Old Testament, the last three are especially potent. Problematic portrayals of God, morally offensive texts, and op- pressive readings make it exceedingly difficult for some people to see much value in the Old Testament. Because of this, I have devoted an entire chapter of the book to these issues. If this is a real sticking point for you, feel free to skip ahead and read chapter nine now. This may help you be more receptive to what is shared in the intervening chapters since little mention of these passages is made elsewhere in the book. In any case, I want to assure you that I am keenly aware of how troublesome these texts are and am not simplistically bypassing them in pursuit of some sort of "feel good" reading of the Old Testament.

ADDITIONAL BARRIERS TO READING THE OLD TESTAMENT

So far, all the reasons we have considered for why people find it difficult to read the Old Testament have had to do with its *content*.[19] But this is

---

[18]Naim Stifan Ateek, *Justice and Only Justice: A Palestinian Theology of Liberation* (Maryknoll, NY: Orbis, 1989), 77, emphasis mine.

[19]For more reasons why people avoid the Old Testament, see William L. Holladay, *Long Ago God Spoke: How Christians May Hear the Old Testament Today* (Minneapolis: Fortress, 1995), 10-16. He discusses ten "factors," or "barriers," he believes have contributed to the Old Testament's relative neglect.

only part of the story. There are many other reasons why people don't read this part of the Bible that have nothing to do with what is actually in the Old Testament.

Consider our cultural context, for example. We live in an age of distraction. In our hyper-connected, plugged-in world, we have lost the art of sustained and serious reading. It is so much easier to turn to a favorite video game, or to check your email or Facebook feed, than it is to open the Bible, Old *or* New Testament. In fact, if we're honest, I suspect many would admit they find listening to a favorite podcast or watching a good movie more pleasurable than reading Scripture. How can ancient texts even begin to compete with the recreational technology we have at our fingertips?

In addition to these challenges, many of us live very busy lives. There are so many things vying for our attention that many of us find it difficult to set aside time to read the Bible. We have jobs to perform, classes to take, children to watch, chores to complete, houses to maintain, orders to place, meetings to attend, lawns to mow, appointments to keep, laundry to fold, dishes to do, and so on and so forth. Tending to all these things sometimes leaves little time for reading and studying the Bible. On those rare occasions when we do manage to find a little spare time, we turn to hobbies and pleasurable pursuits we are sure will be fun before turning to the Old Testament.

Another factor in all this is what might be described as a declining emphasis on the devotional life among Christians. Though it is difficult to say with certainty, I suspect fewer Christians today are "doing devotions" or having "quiet time" than in past generations.[20] Without a spiritual practice like this in place, Bible reading often becomes rather sporadic, much more hit-or-miss.

I say all this not to render judgment or to increase our collective guilt. Rather, my point in noting these challenges is to help us better understand *why* we often find it so difficult to spend time with Scripture.

---

[20]My thanks to Jay McDermond for highlighting this idea.

Openly naming the things that hinder our efforts to read the Old Testament puts us in a much better position to address them.

CONCLUSION

The formidable challenges to enjoying the Old Testament raised in this chapter might cause some to wonder if reading the Old Testament is really worth the effort. Should we bother with it? Does the church still need it? Or would we be better off focusing on the New Testament and other books from trusted Christian writers?

In light of all the problems the Old Testament raises and the very limited attention most Christians actually give to it, these are fair questions to raise. But abandoning the Old Testament is not the answer. It would be a clear case of throwing out the proverbial baby with the bathwater. We would lose far too much in the process.

In the next chapter, we'll consider what's at stake here. To counter some of the objections that have been raised, we will highlight some of the Old Testament's most attractive features—and there are many! Hopefully, this will begin to persuade you that reading the Old Testament *is* worth the effort and can be quite rewarding.

3

WHY BOTHER *with* *the* OLD TESTAMENT?

The problem with ignoring the Old Testament is that we make ourselves deaf to all the incredible things that God has to say to us through it.

Matthew Richard Schlimm,
Strange and Sacred Scripture

In the Star Wars universe, Jedi knights have many extraordinary abilities. They use "the force" to guide them and are particularly adept with a lightsaber. The Jedi also have the ability to exert a simple form of mind control over others. With just the slightest wave of a hand, Jedi can make drones, human beings, and other forms of sentient life do their bidding. Such powers protect them from harm and enable them to escape dangerous situations.

In the movie *Star Wars: The Force Awakens* (Episode VII), there is a scene in which the protagonist, Rey, is being held captive by Kylo Ren, grandson of the infamous Darth Vader. Rey has been confined to an interrogation chair, with arm and leg restraints that make it impossible for her to move, let alone get away. Though Rey has not trained as a Jedi, the force is strong in her. Still, she has only recently begun to experiment with her newfound power.

Given the desperateness of her situation, and lacking other options, Rey attempts to use the force to persuade the stormtrooper standing guard to set her free. She says, "You will remove these restraints and leave this cell with the door open." It takes a few tries, but eventually the storm-trooper dutifully replies, "I will remove these restraints and leave this cell with the door open." And that is exactly what he does.

As the stormtrooper exits the room, Rey hastily adds one further in-struction: "And you will drop your weapon." His obsequious reply: "And I will drop my weapon." (Thud.) It works like a charm. Rey is free.

YOU WILL OPEN YOUR BIBLE AND ENJOY THE OLD TESTAMENT!

If merely saying "You will open your Bible and enjoy the Old Testament" would make it so, I suspect many ministers, church leaders, professors, and religious educators would speak these words without hesitation. But truth be told, most people do not enjoy the Old Testament just because someone says they should, even if that person is a trusted pastor or close friend. Alas, the force is just not that strong in us! People need to be convinced. They need reasons to believe, deep down, that reading the Old Testament really *is* worth the effort. This is especially true for indi-viduals who express the kind of concerns raised in the previous chapter.

I am convinced that it is absolutely vital for Christians to read, study, and discuss the Old Testament. I think the church should regularly preach and teach from it, and I think Christian colleges and seminaries should devote far more attention to it than they often do.[1] There is much to be gained from the Old Testament, and we are impoverished when we ignore it or relegate it to the margins.

Again, I realize that just hearing me say these things probably won't convince you to value the Old Testament, especially if you harbor serious reservations about its worth and contemporary relevance. But maybe you would think differently if someone took the time to explain just how beneficial and applicable it actually is. Perhaps you would see the Old Testament in a better light if you caught a glimpse of what it has to offer

---

[1] For various ideas about making the Old Testament more prominent and engaging in the class-room, see Richard S. Hess and Gordon J. Wenham, eds., *Make the Old Testament Live: From Curriculum to Classroom* (Grand Rapids, MI: Eerdmans, 1998).

Christians living in the twenty-first century. And maybe, just maybe, you would be persuaded to give it another try if you were aware of the treasures that await your discovery.

The purpose of this chapter is to demonstrate that reading the Old Testament is well worth the effort. But before I make that case, it is helpful to say a few words about the most common answer people give to the question, Why bother with the Old Testament?

THE STANDARD ANSWER: THE OLD TESTAMENT IS NECESSARY TO UNDERSTAND THE NEW TESTAMENT

Many Christians believe the primary value of the Old Testament lies in its ability to help us better understand the New Testament. People say you can't really understand the New Testament without the Old Testament. Obviously, there is a lot of truth in this. The Old Testament provides the necessary background, worldview, and foundation for making sense of many of the stories and ideas presented in the New Testament. And New Testament writers frequently allude to, and quote from, the Old Testament. If you have any doubts, look at the *Commentary on the New Testament's Use of the Old Testament* which contains over 1,150 pages exploring example after example of this.[2] Clearly, these ancient writers knew the Hebrew Scriptures very well. That fact alone should encourage us to develop a greater familiarity with this part of the Bible.

But for many Christians, what is most important about the Old Testament is that it points to Jesus and helps us interpret his life and ministry. In other words, the Old Testament not only helps us understand the New Testament generally, it helps us make sense of Jesus specifically. People often point to Jesus' teaching on the road to Emmaus to support this way of reading the Old Testament. The two travelers on the road do not initially recognize Jesus. Jesus listens to them speak about what has just transpired in Jerusalem and "then beginning with Moses and all the prophets" reveals "the things about himself in all the scriptures"

---

[2]G. K. Beale and D. A. Carson, *Commentary on the New Testament's Use of the Old Testament* (Grand Rapids, MI: Baker Academic, 2007).

(Lk 24:27). Later that same day Jesus appears to the disciples gathered in Jerusalem and says, "These are my words that I spoke to you while I was still with you—that everything written about me in the law of Moses, the prophets, and the psalms must be fulfilled" (Lk 24:44). Jesus is part of a long tradition. Understanding that tradition is essential for understanding Jesus.

These ideas, that the Old Testament is foundational for the New Testament, and that it is necessary for understanding the life of Jesus (and by extension the Christian faith), represent the thesis of a book written by Paul and Elizabeth Achtemeier over twenty-five years ago. In their book, tellingly titled *The Old Testament Roots of Our Faith*, the Achtemeiers write:

> If, then, we are to understand this faith of ours, if we are to know Jesus Christ as the New Testament knows him, . . . we, too, must start with their beginning. We must start with the Old Testament story, seeing not only God's final act in Jesus Christ, but also all of his acts before that. The action in Jesus Christ is the summation, the completion, the fulfillment of many events before it. And unless we comprehend that which has gone before, we cannot grasp the full significance and meaning of the end.[3]

In other words, the story of Jesus cannot be fully understood without understanding the story of Israel. The two are inextricably linked.

That said, I would like to raise a caveat. I have concerns about making this approach the *primary* reason we value the Old Testament. Emphasizing the Old Testament's foundational role in making sense of Jesus and the New Testament tends to consign this part of the Bible to secondary status. It seems to imply that the Old Testament is *only* (or at least mainly) useful as a prologue to the New Testament, an informational preamble to the main attraction. Although I assume this is *not* the intention of those who make this argument, it is the message many people take from it.

---

[3]Paul J. Achtemeier and Elizabeth Achtemeier, *The Old Testament Roots of Our Faith*, rev. ed. (Peabody, MA: Hendrickson, 1994), 5.

I worry that this way of thinking may *dampen* enthusiasm for the Old Testament rather than create it. If the Old Testament exists to serve the New Testament, why do more than what is minimally necessary with this part of the Bible?[4] Yet the Old Testament has integrity in and of itself. Its worth is not contingent on its ability to help us comprehend the New Testament or to make the life of Jesus more understandable. There are lessons to be learned, applications to be made, and truths to be gleaned from the Old Testament that are not dependent on the New. And while it is always good to bring these two testaments into conversation with each another, subordinating the Old Testament to the New or suggesting that its real value lies in its ability to illuminate the New Testament is misguided. The importance of the Old Testament, *even for Christian readers*, is not dependent on its serviceability to the New.

For that reason, I have chosen to focus exclusively on the Old Testament itself in what follows. We will look at the Old Testament on its own terms, as a collection of sacred texts with its own inherent worth. As we do, we will quickly discover that it is brimming with theological insight and wisdom, offering limitless opportunities for application and reflection.

Why We Need the Old Testament

While many wonderful things could be said about the Old Testament at this juncture, I will limit my discussion to seven of the Old Testament's most attractive features. Since my goal is to be persuasive rather than comprehensive, I trust these will sufficiently demonstrate why we can look forward to reading this part of the Bible.

Given the limitations of space, what follows is necessarily brief. Each of these seven items could have easily occupied a chapter all its own. The discussion given for each one is more like a short movie trailer than a full-length film. But hopefully this will be enough to whet your appetite

---

[4]As Brent Strawn argues, "The Old Testament cannot be saved by any strategy that focuses exclusively or even overmuch on the New Testament." Strawn, *The Old Testament Is Dying: A Diagnosis and Recommended Treatment* (Grand Rapids, MI: Baker Academic, 2017), 225.

for more as you discover some of the things that make the Old Testament so very enjoyable.

The Old Testament has fascinating stories that are profoundly relevant. The Old Testament's narratives are among its greatest treasures. For many readers, these stories are some of the most beloved and well-known parts of the entire Bible. They are compelling, powerful, and often quite memorable. They yield many fruitful insights and are very useful for reflecting on our life with God and others. Their ongoing relevance and applicability is part of what makes them so significant for the church today.

Later, we will devote an entire chapter to reading and enjoying Old Testament narratives. For now, I will highlight two stories from the book of Exodus to demonstrate how beneficial they can be to Christian readers.

A burning bush (Ex 3). According to Exodus, after years of oppression and pain, God calls Moses to lead the Hebrew people out of Egyptian bondage and slavery. The divine call comes in dramatic fashion while Moses is in a remote part of the wilderness caring for his father-in-law's sheep (Ex 3:1-10). A bush spontaneously begins to burn but is not consumed. Understandably curious, Moses turns aside and hears the voice of God. God tells him to return to Egypt, the place he fled forty years ago after murdering an Egyptian taskmaster. He is to speak to Pharaoh about releasing the Hebrew people.

This divine call is the catalyst for a fascinating dialogue between Moses and God (Ex 3:11–4:17). Moses asks a series of questions and God graciously responds to each one. It is only at the end of the conversation, when Moses tells God to select someone else, that God becomes angry. Ultimately, God still sends Moses, along with his brother, Aaron, as a spokesperson.

There are many different ways to reflect on Exodus 3–4. One that I have found especially useful is to consider what this passage contributes to our understanding of a divine call. How does God call people? What does that look like? And what is involved in responding to such a call? Here are some ways to answer these questions based on this narrative and the preceding chapter in Exodus (a point of connection to the biblical text is provided after each statement).

1. Past failure does not disqualify you from future service. (Moses murdered an Egyptian yet God still called him—Ex 2:11-12; 3:7-10.)

2. God's call often comes in the mundane. (Moses is watching sheep in the wilderness when God calls him—Ex 3:1-6.)

3. God's call may involve vocational and locational change. (Moses was required to leave Midian for Egypt and would now shepherd people, not sheep—Ex 4:18-20.)

4. Feelings of inadequacy do not excuse us from God's call. (Moses questions his significance and complains of his inability to speak well, but God's call persists—Ex 3:11-12; 4:10-12.)

5. God equips us for the task to which we are called. (God promises to be with Moses—and his mouth—and also sends Aaron to help—Ex 4:10-17.)

6. God sometimes makes the call very clear. (The burning bush gets Moses' attention, and Moses clearly understands what God wants him to do—Ex 3:1-10.)

7. When God calls, God allows for real dialogue. (Moses is free to ask questions, and God graciously responds with additional information—Ex 3:11–4:12.)

8. Obedience to God's call is voluntary, but not optional. (Moses could refuse to obey this call [making it voluntary], but this would be disobedient [meaning it is not optional]—Ex 4:13-17.)

9. God's call matches the desires of our heart. (Moses is a man with a passion for justice, as evidenced by his behavior in Egypt prior to this call—Ex 2:11-13.)

When I teach a course on the book of Exodus, I like to elaborate on these "Nine Notes about God's Call." I have found them helpful in generating conversation about the nature of God's call in our lives. This helps students realize how rich and relevant the Old Testament is and models a responsible way to use and apply this part of the Bible.

A manna miracle. The manna miracle is another story that has much to offer Christian readers. This story comes a bit later in the book of Exodus, after the Hebrew people have been delivered from Egypt. As they are en route to Mount Sinai, they face a series of difficulties along the way, one being a lack of food (Ex 16). In response to their complaints, God miraculously provides manna for them. The people are instructed to gather as much as they need each day. They are not to take any extra because God sends more each morning, except on the Sabbath day. Therefore, on the day before the Sabbath, the Israelites could gather twice as much as they needed for that day so they would have some on the Sabbath. If manna was kept overnight any other day of the week, it would spoil and be full of worms the next morning (Ex 16:19-20).

This narrative invites us to reflect on what it means to trust God and how that trust is developed. It suggests that trust is not learned in one fell swoop. Despite all the Israelites had seen and experienced as they exited Egypt (the ten plagues, the dramatic Red Sea crossing, etc.), when they faced another crisis, they still had difficulty trusting God. Trust is not something gained all at once but is cultivated over time as people experience God's constant daily faithfulness. The manna miracle was designed to encourage trust. The people had to depend on God to send them manna each morning. And sure enough, day after day, week after week, month after month, year after year, God consistently supplied them with bread. Imagine the effect that would have! By experiencing God's daily faithfulness, the people learned to trust God more and more.

This story also contains an implicit warning: "Trust in God and self-sufficiency are mutually exclusive."[5] If the Israelites had been able to find a way to collect, preserve, and store enough manna to last until they reached the Promised Land, it would have been unnecessary to rely on God for this provision. But hoarding was not possible—unless you

---

[5]I am indebted to Dr. Terry Brensinger for this idea, which he introduced in class when discussing Genesis 3. I believe this is a direct quote, or nearly so.

wanted worm-infested manna in the morning. That's why the text repeatedly emphasizes that people should collect only as much as they *need* for that day (Ex 16:4, 16, 18, 21). No more, no less. It's a way of saying, "Don't gather tomorrow's manna today!"[6] That is why we who pray the Lord's Prayer say, "Give us *this* day our *daily* bread" (Mt 6:11, emphasis mine). Not tomorrow's bread. Not next week's bread. Today's bread. That is all we need. The manna miracle was designed in such a way to discourage all attempts at self-sufficiency apart from God. If you want to learn to trust God, you can't stockpile manna!

Stories like the burning bush and the manna miracle have great relevance and applicability to our lives. The more we realize this, the more likely we are to enjoy reading and exploring Old Testament stories like these.

The Old Testament models a gutsy kind of faith. While biblical characters don't always get it right—and sometimes get it really, really wrong—there are numerous places in the Old Testament where people exhibit a gutsy, courageous kind of faith, the kind of faith that is at once both inspiring and instructive. Abraham's response to God in Genesis 12 is one such example.[7] Abraham is called by God to abandon all that is comfortable and familiar in order to travel to a place he has never been. "Now the LORD said to Abram, 'Go from your country and your kindred and your father's house to the land that I will show you.' . . . So Abram went, as the LORD had told him" (Gen 12:1, 4).

In a day and age when many of us are hesitant to move out of our comfort zone—let alone travel to a distant place at the call of God—Abraham's obedience is convicting. His sojourn to a new land reminds us that *faithful* living should never be equated with *easy* living. If we are fully committed to following God, there's no telling where that might take us or what might be required.

---

[6]I am indebted to Joe Dongell for this quote, for the connection to the Lord's Prayer that follows, and for helping me view this narrative through the lens of trusting God.

[7]For a more negative evaluation of Abraham and his motives, see David M. Gunn and Danna Nolan Fewell, *Narrative in the Hebrew Bible* (Oxford: Oxford University Press, 1993), 90-100.

Daniel's three friends—Shadrach, Meshach, and Abednego—also exemplify a gutsy kind of faith. As the story goes, the narcissistic and megalomaniacal Babylonian king Nebuchadnezzar erected an enormous statue (possibly of himself), and whenever people heard a particular "musical ensemble" they were supposed to immediately bow down and worship it (Dan 3:1-5). Failure to comply would result in a one-way trip to the fiery furnace (Dan 3:6).

Since obedience to the king's command would be an act of idolatry and an offense against God, Daniel's three friends refuse to participate. Shadrach, Meshach, and Abednego are brought before the enraged King Nebuchadnezzar who gives them a final ultimatum "to fall down and worship the statue I have made" or else (Dan 3:15)! Daniel's three friends are unfazed. Unwilling to violate their conscience or compromise their convictions, they boldly declare:

> O Nebuchadnezzar, we have no need to present a defense to you in this matter. If our God whom we serve is able to deliver us from the furnace of blazing fire and out of your hand, O king, let him deliver us. But if not, be it known to you, O king, that we will not serve your gods and we will not worship the golden statue that you have set up. (Dan 3:16-18)

Shadrach, Meshach, and Abednego exhibit a gutsy kind of faith. By refusing to bow down, they stand up for what is right. They are prepared to follow God faithfully even if it costs them everything. Their actions remind us of the importance of staying true to our convictions in the face of enormous pressure to compromise and capitulate.[8] Would that more Christians lived with such resolve!

Of course, these are only *two* examples of people in the Old Testament who model a gutsy kind of faith. There are many more. There are faithful prophets—perhaps most notably Jeremiah—who delivered oracles under very unfavorable circumstances, sometimes at great personal cost. And there are individuals like Moses, Habakkuk, and certain psalmists who

---

[8] See Terry L. Brensinger, "Compliance, Dissonance, and Amazement in Daniel 3," *Evangelical Journal* 20 (2002): 7-19.

go head-to-head with God over questions of divine justice. The Old Testament also bears witness to a number of women who lived with great courage and conviction and who took risky actions to save lives. Two Hebrew midwives, Shiphrah and Puah, directly disobey Pharaoh's execution orders to save Hebrew baby boys (Ex 1:15-21), Jehosheba rescues Joash from certain death at the hands of Queen Athaliah by hiding him for six years (2 Kings 11:1-3), and Esther approaches a king unbidden, thereby risking her own life to save the lives of her people (Esther 5:1-2).

Old Testament stories of women and men who lived out their faith with grit and determination remind us of what faithfulness to God sometimes requires. Their actions challenge us to live more boldly and to take risks for God. And they remind us not to be ruled by a spirit of fear, especially one that would keep us from doing what is good and right. We desperately need these stories, perhaps today more than ever.

The Old Testament contains invaluable resources for worship and prayer. Every religion has sacred texts they use to guide their spiritual practices, especially core practices like worship and prayer. The Bible functions this way for Christians. Within the Old Testament, the book of Psalms is particularly valuable in this regard. In ancient Israel, psalms were used individually and corporately to express a wide range of thoughts and feelings. They helped the community praise God and give thanks. They also helped the people celebrate the law, confess their sins, and request help from God. Like sacrifices, psalms were central to Israel's worship.

Today, the book of Psalms continues to be one of the most beloved portions of the entire Bible. This is evident by the simple fact that you can purchase "Bibles" that contain *only* the New Testament and Psalms. The fact that some publishers choose this particular book of the Old Testament—and only this book—to include with the New Testament speaks volumes about its enduring value and significance.

One of the reasons the book of Psalms (the Psalter) is so beneficial for Christian life and practice is because it invites us to worship and pray. Rolf and Karl Jacobson remind us of this in their book *Invitation to the Psalms.*

They write, "The prayers of the Psalter are meant to be prayed. The songs of the Psalter are meant to be sung. The lessons of the Psalter are meant to be lived."[9] And this is precisely how many in the church have used them. For years, Christians have prayed the psalms, finding the language of the Psalter helpful in expressing their deepest longings, hopes, and fears to God.[10] "Reading and chanting the psalms aloud, individually and in community," writes Richard Foster, "has been a practice across centuries of Christian history, taking the People of God through the entire Psalter in cycles of worship and prayer tied to seasons of the liturgical year."[11]

Singing the psalms has a long and venerable history, and the writer of Colossians 3:16 commands believers to "sing psalms, hymns, and spiritual songs to God." Quite a few contemporary praise songs take their lyrics from the book of Psalms, and worship leaders routinely use portions of the Psalms liturgically, as a call to worship or a responsive reading. Given its usage in these ways, there can be little doubt about the significance of the Psalter for Christian faith and practice. Indeed, it is difficult to imagine what the church's worship would look like without it.

Obviously, there are many other parts of the Old Testament that can inform our spiritual practices beyond the Psalter, and we will have an opportunity to discuss some of these later. My point here is simply to emphasize that that the Old Testament is a rich resource for worship and prayer, a resource that not only points us toward God but equips us to live lives of heartfelt praise and grateful obedience.

The Old Testament tackles life's biggest questions. The Old Testament is especially useful for wrestling with some of life's biggest questions, questions relating to things such as the meaning of existence and the problem of evil. Exploring questions like these is one of the primary functions of wisdom literature, a common literary genre in the ancient

---

[9]Rolf A. Jacobson and Karl N. Jacobson, *Invitation to the Psalms: A Reader's Guide for Discovery and Engagement* (Grand Rapid, MI: Baker Academic, 2013), 2.

[10]See Eugene H. Peterson, *Eat This Book: A Conversation in the Art of Spiritual Reading* (Grand Rapids, MI: Eerdmans, 2006), 104-6.

[11]Richard J. Foster, *Life with God: Reading the Bible for Spiritual Transformation*, with Kathryn A. Helmers (New York: HarperOne, 2008), 92.

world. In the Old Testament, the books of Job, Proverbs, and Ecclesiastes are all examples of wisdom literature.

The book of Job, for example, raises a number of challenging questions: Why do people suffer? Is suffering always the result of sinning? How is God involved in human suffering? How should we respond to human suffering? Although the book of Job does not fully or finally answer these questions, it begins important conversations around these issues. For instance, it contests the notion that *all* human suffering results from someone's sinful behavior, a point we will revisit later. Decoupling the link between sinning and suffering challenges crude notions of divine quid pro quo and enhances our view of God.

One of the most penetrating questions raised in Job emerges at the beginning of the book in the dialogue between God and the adversary ("Satan"). The adversary boldly claims that the only reason Job worships God is because of all the good things God has given him.

> Then Satan answered the LORD, "Does Job fear God for nothing? Have you not put a fence around him and his house and all that he has, on every side? You have blessed the work of his hands, and his possessions have increased in the land. But stretch out your hand now, and touch all that he has, and he will curse you to your face." (Job 1:9-11)

As readers discover over time, this charge is baseless. Still, it invites *us* to ask, What motivates *my* worship? Do I worship God only because of the blessings I have received? Would I worship God just as enthusiastically if I fell on hard times and found myself unemployed, seriously ill, and financially ruined, or would I turn my back on God? These are very important questions to consider, and the book of Job provides a great starting point for doing so.

In the book of Ecclesiastes, the "big question" the writer explores is one of ultimate significance: What is the meaning of life? The answer comes in the second verse: "'Meaningless! Meaningless!' says the Teacher. 'Utterly meaningless! Everything is meaningless'" (Eccles 1:2 NIV). Many Christians will not find this answer particularly satisfying since most do not think life is meaningless. This suggests that what makes some books valuable is not the answers they give but the questions they raise. Ecclesiastes is one of those books. It focuses our attention on a question that really matters and encourages us to join the conversation. We need opportunities like these to consider big questions and to consider various responses. Old Testament books like Job and Ecclesiastes are especially helpful in this regard. We are very fortunate to have them as part of the Old Testament.

The Old Testament reveals a relational God who loves lavishly. Some of the most beautiful images of God in the Bible are found in the pages of the Old Testament. Many Christians seem unaware of this. It is not uncommon for people to draw a sharp distinction between what they perceive to be the harsh, wrathful "Old Testament God" and the gracious, loving "New Testament God." But despite the fact this view stretches all the way back to the second century, it represents an unfair caricature of God. Yes, there are many passages in the Old Testament that speak of God's anger, wrath, and vengeance. Of that there is no doubt.[12] Yet these violent images are not the only way God is portrayed in the Old Testament. On the contrary, some of the most tender and compassionate images of God reside in this part of the Bible.

For example, some passages speak of God's magnanimous love and care for Israel from the beginning.

When Israel was a child, I loved him,
and out of Egypt I called my son.
The more I called them,
the more they went from me;
they kept sacrificing to the Baals,
and offering incense to idols.

Yet it was I who taught Ephraim to walk,
I took them up in my arms;

---

[12]We will address these difficult passages in chapter nine since they are frequently cited as one of the reasons people have a hard time enjoying the Old Testament.

but they did not know that I healed them.
I led them with cords of human kindness,
with bands of love.
I was to them like those
who lift infants to their cheeks.
I bent down to them and fed them. (Hos 11:1-4)

Other passages speak words of hope and promise to the people of Israel after they had experienced the devastating tragedy of exile:

I will take you from the nations, and gather you from all the countries, and bring you into your own land. I will sprinkle clean water upon you, and you shall be clean from all your uncleannesses, and from all your idols I will cleanse you. A new heart I will give you, and a new spirit I will put within you; and I will remove from your body the heart of stone and give you a heart of flesh. I will put my spirit within you, and make you follow my statutes and be careful to observe my ordinances. Then you shall live in the land that I gave to your ancestors; and you shall be my people, and I will be your God. (Ezek 36:24-28)

These words of divine mercy, redemption, and renewal demonstrate the strength and depth of God's commitment to Israel.

The Old Testament bears witness to a God who desires to be in relationship with the people of Israel, and it reveals the great lengths to which God will go to remain connected to Israel *even when* the people repeatedly sabotage that relationship. This kind of commitment is described by the Hebrew word *khesed*, a word typically translated as "steadfast love" or "lovingkindness" though it is very difficult to capture its full meaning in English. It has strong connotations of love and loyalty and describes the way God sticks with the Israelites even when they repeatedly walk away. This attribute of God is part of Israel's "core confession," as it is sometimes called, a brief declaration of God's character that appears numerous times in the Old Testament.

For example, when God's glory is revealed to Moses after the golden calf debacle, God passes by and proclaims:

The LORD, the LORD, a God merciful and gracious, slow to anger,
and abounding in steadfast love (*khesed*) and faithfulness,
keeping steadfast love (*khesed*) for the thousandth generation,
forgiving iniquity and transgression and sin,
yet by no means clearing the guilty,
but visiting the iniquity of the parents
upon the children and the children's children,
to the third and the fourth generation. (Ex 34:6-7)

Part of this is also found in Psalm 103:8-13 in one of the most beautiful and moving passages in the entire Bible:

The LORD is merciful and gracious,
slow to anger and abounding in steadfast love.
He will not always accuse,
nor will he keep his anger forever.
He does not deal with us according to our sins,
nor repay us according to our iniquities.
For as the heavens are high above the earth,
so great is his steadfast love toward those who fear him;
as far as the east is from the west,
so far he removes our transgressions from us.
As a father has compassion for his children,
so the LORD has compassion for those who fear him.

What constantly amazed the people of Israel was not that God would punish them for their sins—everyone in the ancient world believed the gods did that. What they found astonishing was the simple fact that God stuck with them and continued to love them even *after* they screwed up.

Passages that reveal God's enormous capacity to love, deliver, guide, protect, and sustain are not difficult to find in the Old Testament, and one could easily devote an entire book to nothing but these positive and inspiring images. The Old Testament is an invaluable resource in this regard, helping us understand and appreciate various aspects of God's good character. Our view of God would be greatly diminished without it.

The Old Testament prioritizes social justice. Another attractive feature of the Old Testament is the emphasis it places on doing justice. Numerous passages indicate that doing justice is regarded as one of the key responsibilities of the people of God. In a frequently cited passage from the book of Micah, we observe the increasing desperation of an unnamed Israelite wondering what God wants from him. After suggesting increasingly extravagant sacrifices—to the point of offering his firstborn son—this anxious Israelite receives a simple and straightforward answer.

He has told you, O mortal, what is good;
and what does the LORD require of you
but to do justice, and to love kindness,
and to walk humbly with your God? (Mic 6:8)

Want to please God? Then do justice.

Today, many people think of justice in very punitive terms. When we speak of "seeing justice done" or "bringing people to justice" we often think of wrongdoers being punished. While this idea is not absent from the concept of justice in the Old Testament, it is too restrictive. Doing justice involves setting things right.[13] Whenever people are oppressed or in need, or wherever things are out of whack, the people of God are expected to help. They are to come alongside the most vulnerable members of society and assist them. Sometimes this means providing material resources—food, clothing, lodging. Other times it involves delivering people from oppressive situations.

This call to do justice is predicated on the nature and character of God. Israel is to set things right because that is what God does. In Deuteronomy, God is described as one "who is not partial and takes no bribe, who executes justice for the orphan and the widow, and who loves the strangers, providing them food and clothing" (Deut 10:17-18). The psalmist describes God as a "lover of justice" (Ps 99:4), and the prophet

---

[13]See Christopher J. H. Wright, *Old Testament Ethics for the People of God* (Downers Grove, IL: InterVarsity Press, 2004), 256-57.

Jeremiah speaks of the pleasure God takes in doing justice: "I act with steadfast love, justice, and righteousness in the earth, for in these things I delight" (Jer 9:24). When God commands the people of Israel to do justice, they are being asked to behave exactly as God does.

The prophet Amos was especially outspoken about the need to do justice. Amos prophesied in the mid-eighth century, about twenty-five years before the fall of the northern kingdom of Israel. It was a time of great economic prosperity—at least for some. Yet much of this wealth was ill-gotten: judges took bribes, merchants cheated customers, lenders sold people into slavery, and so forth. Amos castigates the Israelites for their oppressive behavior and declares, in no uncertain terms, that their failure to do justice has rendered their worship unacceptable to God.

> I hate, I despise your festivals,
>   and I take no delight in your solemn assemblies.
> Even though you offer me your burnt offerings and grain offerings,
>   I will not accept them;
> and the offerings of well-being of your fatted animals
>   I will not look upon.
> Take away from me the noise of your songs;
>   I will not listen to the melody of your harps.
> But let justice roll down like waters,
>   and righteousness like an ever-flowing stream. (Amos 5:21-24)

Although the sacrificial system was central to Israel's worship, it was worthless without a commitment to do justice. "If you're not doing justice," God says, "then don't bother offering sacrifices." It's that important!

The overwhelming emphasis on doing justice in the Old Testament is at once both inspiring and convicting. If you are already committed to social justice, the Old Testament will be a welcome resource to sustain you on that journey. If you are *not* committed to doing justice, the Old Testament will challenge you to reorder some of your priorities. Either way, we need the Old Testament to remind us of how important this is to God and to encourage us to be diligent about setting things right whenever we can.

The Old Testament offers creative alternatives to violence. The final feature of the Old Testament to be highlighted in this chapter is arguably one of the best kept secrets of the Bible. Unbeknownst to most readers, the Old Testament contains numerous stories that contain creative alternatives to violence. Many people associate the Old Testament with warfare, violence, and bloodshed. This is hardly surprising given how often Old Testament texts directly, or indirectly, deal with these topics. Yet this routinely obscures other texts that offer peaceful alternatives to violence. As John Wood observes, "While moderns are quick to take offense at the violence and warmaking in the Old Testament, they are prone to overlook the surprising number of instances in the text where the Israelites handled conflict in non-violent ways."[14]

One especially intriguing example is tucked away in 1 Samuel 25. It is the story of a woman who prevents a massacre. Abigail, said to be both "clever and beautiful," is married to Nabal, described as being "surly and mean" (1 Sam 25:3). At this point in the book of Samuel, David has not yet ascended the throne. Instead, he is a fugitive, desperately trying to elude the grasp of King Saul, who is hell-bent on killing him. David has managed to attract a sizable number of men who are loyal to him and ready to do his bidding. As a fugitive on the run, David is dependent on others for provisions, and this need precipitates the ensuing conflict.

David sends a delegation of ten men to Nabal who, in addition to being surly and mean, is very, very rich. We are told that Nabal is shearing his sheep. This would have been a festive occasion when there would have been plenty of food and drink available. David sends his delegation with words of peace and a request: "Please give whatever you have at hand to your servants and to your son David" (1 Sam 25:8). But instead of receiving food, David's men receive insults. Nabal gives them absolutely nothing.[15] When they return to David and report what has

---

[14]John A. Wood, *Perspectives on War in the Bible* (Macon, GA: Mercer University Press, 1998), 104.
[15]While Nabal is portrayed in the worst possible light, this may be due to an effort to defend David from charges of wrongdoing in Nabal's death and subsequent marriage to Nabal's wife. Also, 1 Sam 25:7 may suggest the reason David made this request to Nabal was because he and his men had been offering "protection," albeit unsolicited, to Nabal's shepherds. Apparently, Nabal had

happened, David's response is swift and vengeful: "Every man strap on his sword!" (1 Sam 25:13). He means to slaughter Nabal and his men.

Meanwhile, one of Nabal's workers tells Abigail what has happened and urges her to take action: "Know this and consider what you should do; for evil has been decided against our master and against all his house" (1 Sam 25:17). With that, Abigail swings into action. The moment she becomes aware of the threat of violence, she takes bold and decisive steps to stop it—and she does so *non*violently.

> Then Abigail hurried and took two hundred loaves, two skins of wine, five sheep ready dressed, five measures of parched grain, one hundred clusters of raisins, and two hundred cakes of figs. She loaded them on donkeys and said to her young men, "Go on ahead of me; I am coming after you." (1 Sam 25:18-19)

Obviously, Abigail could have responded quite differently. She could have chosen to do nothing, or she could have organized some of Nabal's servants to ambush David and his men. Likely, there would have been many casualties.

But rather than resorting to weapons, Abigail uses words. Rather than relying on force, she brings food—lots of it. With gifts of food and gracious words, Abigail meets David, speaks with him, and is able to avert disaster (1 Sam 25:23-35). And lest we have any doubt about David's intentions, we need only consider his ominous words to Abigail: "For as surely as the LORD the God of Israel lives, who has restrained me from hurting you, unless you had hurried and come to meet me, truly by morning there would not have been left to Nabal so much as one male" (1 Sam 25:34). Abigail's quick thinking and actions prevent a massacre.

The story of Abigail is just one of many stories in the Old Testament about women and men who find creative, nonviolent ways to resolve

---

no interest in paying for services he did not request, prompting David to take action. As Joel Baden observes, "To run a protection racket, one must be willing to do the dirty work if the victim refuses to pay up." Whatever the reason behind Nabal's refusal to provide provisions, and the insulting manner in which he did so, it proved disastrous for him. Baden, *The Historical David: The Real Life of an Invented Hero* (New York: HarperCollins, 2013), 96.

conflict and confront injustice. For some others, consider the story of Joseph, the man who forgave his brothers (Gen 45 and 50), and the story of Elisha, the prophet who fed his enemies (2 Kings 6). Oh, and don't miss the story tucked away in Joshua 22 of the conversation that prevented a war. Stories like these should excite our imagination and encourage us to consider alternative ways to reduce violence and make peace. In a world riddled by religiously motivated violence, alternatives such as these are desperately needed. They remind us of the value and ongoing relevance of the Old Testament.

CONCLUSION

I hope this chapter has convinced you that reading the Old Testament really *is* worth the effort and has encouraged you to pick up your Bible and try again. There is so much to be discovered and explored—and we have only uncovered the tip of the iceberg.

So what are you waiting for? Go ahead. Dive in![16]

---

[16] A logical place to begin would be the book of Genesis. If you want something shorter, try a book like Ruth, Esther, or Jonah. Whatever book you choose, I would suggest starting at the beginning and reading through the entire book rather than jumping around from book to book. See chapter twelve along with the other suggestions and strategies for reading the Old Testament that are offered throughout this book.

4

DEVELOPING REALISTIC EXPECTATIONS

The problem isn't the Bible.
The problem is coming to the Bible with
expectations it's not set up to bear.

PETER ENNS, *THE BIBLE TELLS ME SO: WHY DEFENDING SCRIPTURE HAS MADE US UNABLE TO READ IT*

TO A LARGE DEGREE, our enjoyment of the Old Testament is connected to the expectations we bring to it. Even if we have never consciously articulated those expectations, we all have them. Their fulfillment—or lack thereof—governs how we feel about what we read. When our expectations of the Old Testament are unmet, it is not uncommon to feel discouraged and disappointed. Over time, this may cause us to lose the desire to read and study this part of the Bible altogether.[1]

Quite often, expecting the Bible to be something it is not results in intense frustration. Professor Timothy Beal has witnessed this firsthand in multiple settings. He writes,

> Nearly two decades of teaching the Bible in college classrooms and church Sunday school classes (all ages) have shown me that *the most common source of frustration stems not from the Bible itself but from the expectations that come with it.* The Bible does not deliver what readers have come to believe it's supposed to deliver.[2]

---

[1]Obviously, the same could be said about the New Testament, or anything we read for that matter.
[2]Timothy Beal, *The Rise and Fall of the Bible: The Unexpected History of an Accidental Book* (Boston: Houghton Mifflin Harcourt, 2011), 36, emphasis mine.

So what is it that many readers think the Bible is supposed to deliver—and doesn't? And what can we realistically expect from the Bible, particularly the Old Testament?

This chapter is designed to answer these questions. Developing appropriate expectations for engaging the Old Testament will greatly increase your chances of enjoying what you read. We will first expose some *un*realistic expectations many readers have of the Old Testament and then discuss what readers can expect from this part of the Bible.

Before proceeding, I would encourage you to take a few minutes to jot down some expectations you have of the Old Testament. What do you expect from the Old Testament and how do you envision it functioning in your life? Once you have identified your own expectations, step back and evaluate them. Are they all realistic? Might some be in need of modification? Keep these questions in mind as you read through this chapter.

Unrealistic Expectations of the Old Testament

Obviously, people come to the Old Testament with a broad range of different expectations. What follows is a brief sampling of some of the expectations commonly held by many Christians. I will argue that all of these expectations, in one way or another, are ill-founded and ultimately unrealistic. As such, they should be rejected.

The Old Testament is easily understandable (especially to those reading it through eyes of faith). One of the most common misperceptions about reading the Bible is that it should be easy to understand. Christian Smith uses the phrase "democratic perspicuity" to describe the expectation that "any reasonably intelligent person can read the Bible in his or how own language and correctly understand the plain meaning of the text."[3] Smith includes democratic perspicuity in a list of ten assumptions inherent in "biblicism," a way of viewing the Bible he believes is "misguided" and should be "abandoned."[4]

---

[3]Christian Smith, *The Bible Made Impossible: Why Biblicism Is Not a Truly Evangelical Reading of Scripture* (Grand Rapids, MI: Brazos, 2011), 4.
[4]Smith, *Bible Made Impossible*, 3.

Where do many Christians get the idea that the Bible is an easy read? I suspect the church is responsible for much of this kind of thinking. In fact, some churches seem to encourage this view by certain things they say and do. For instance, when a church (like mine) gives a Bible to each child in the congregation after they complete first grade, it seems to imply that reading and understanding the Bible is so easy that even a first grader can do it. And when pastors encourage people to "spend time in the Word," the assumption seems to be that anyone—or at least any *Christian*—should be able to pick up a Bible, read what it says, and understand it. After all, don't we believe that God's Spirit will lead us "into all the truth" (Jn 16:13)?

Yet the reality is that some parts of the Old Testament are extremely difficult to understand, even for well-trained biblical scholars and religious specialists. Those who assume that understanding the Old Testament should be easy, or take little effort, are bound to be disappointed.

Let me be clear. I am *not* suggesting that churches should withhold Bibles from children or that pastors should discourage congregants from committing themselves to regular Bible study and prayer. These are certainly good things. But we should be careful not to give the impression that reading and understanding the Old Testament is a cakewalk.

As I have emphasized and will continue to emphasize throughout this book, people *can* get a great deal out of the Old Testament without using secondary sources or getting assistance from biblical scholars. You don't have to have specialized training or all the right books to understand a great deal of the Old Testament. You can read and enjoy this part of the Bible whatever age you are, and your understanding can grow over time. I want that to come through loud and clear.

Still, there *are* parts of the Old Testament that are really hard to understand without some help. This is unsurprising since we are dealing with ancient texts written in a foreign language from an unfamiliar culture that existed over two thousand years ago. We should anticipate some challenges and should not burden people with the unrealistic expectation that reading and understanding this part of the Bible will always be easy. It will not.

All parts of the Old Testament are equally enjoyable. Another unrealistic expectation some have of the Bible is that all parts of it are equally rewarding. This is reinforced by the way people sometimes talk about the Bible. For example, if we talk about the Bible as "God's love letter," what's not to enjoy? Who doesn't look forward to reading a love letter? Yet, as we have seen, this expectation to relish reading the Bible—especially the Old Testament—is frequently unmet. As a result, many churchgoers assume there must be something wrong with *them*. They become convinced that their lack of desire to read the Old Testament is symptomatic of a deeper spiritual problem. While this *could* be the case, it is not necessarily so. Is it really a sign of spiritual weakness if I do not feel great enthusiasm for reading nine chapters primarily describing Israel's territorial allotments (see Josh 13–21)? Or is there something spiritually wrong with me if I don't get all that excited about reading eight chapters of genealogical material in a row (see 1 Chron 1–8)? No, I don't think so.

Some parts of the Bible are sure to interest us more than others. Our personal preferences will, to some extent, dictate which parts of the Old Testament we naturally like most. For example, someone who is already predisposed to enjoy poetry may find those portions of the Old Testament especially delightful. Others, who seem to have an allergic reaction to poetry and actively avoid it, are likely to experience these same texts quite differently. While there are ways to increase our enjoyment of portions of the Old Testament we are not naturally inclined to like (that is part of what this book is all about), we should not feel guilty about the fact that some parts of the Old Testament interest us more than others. That's normal. Nobody finds every part of the Old Testament equally enjoyable.

Everything we read in the Old Testament should be immediately applicable to our lives. One of the most deeply held expectations many Christians bring to the Bible is the notion that everything they read should be immediately applicable to their lives. This is especially pronounced among evangelical Christians, though certainly not limited to them. Yet this expectation also leads to great frustration. As Peter Enns puts it, "If we come to the Bible expecting something like a spiritual owner's manual complete with handy index, a step-by-step field guide to the life of faith, an absolutely sure answer-book to unlock the mystery of God and the meaning of life, then conflict and stress follow right behind."[5]

To be sure, there are *many* ways to read and apply the Old Testament to our lives. That's part of what makes it so fascinating to read. Demonstrating how to use the Old Testament in this way is one of the key aims of this book. Still, we need to have realistic expectations. We will be disappointed if we expect every single passage to have such immediate relevance.

This expectation becomes particularly problematic—and even dangerous—when it is tethered to the practice of using the Bible for instant divine guidance. Some people are convinced that God will use specific verses of Scripture to guide and direct them when they face significant life decisions, such as whom (or if) to marry, what job to choose, or where to live. This can have far-reaching consequences, as the following story illustrates:

> One of us . . . knew a young man who had to decide whether to enlist in the armed forces or go to college. Opening his Bible at random, he saw the passage in Ezekiel that speaks of people coming from Tarshish to Tyre in ships (Ezek 27:25). Although this passage contains no command for anyone to go anywhere in a ship and has nothing to do with becoming part of the armed forces, this young man interpreted the text as a call to join the Navy. Chances are good that he deprived himself of a college education by making a decision he thought was God's will but probably was not. More seriously, though, he completely misunderstood what role the Bible should have in the Christian decision-making process.[6]

Using the Bible randomly, as this young man did, to ascertain "God's will for your life" expects too much of the Bible. While God leads and guides in many ways—through the church, our circumstances, the words of

---

[5]Peter Enns, *The Bible Tells Me So: Why Defending Scripture Has Made Us Unable to Read It* (New York: HarperOne, 2014), 8.

[6]William W. Klein, Craig L. Blomberg, and Robert L. Hubbard, Jr. *Introduction to Biblical Interpretation* (Dallas: Word, 1993), 404.

others, internal promptings of the Spirit, *and* the Bible—it would be presumptuous to expect God to direct us to a specific verse (or passage) each time we have a major life decision to make.

MORE REALISTIC EXPECTATIONS OF THE OLD TESTAMENT

So then what can we expect from the Old Testament? What will we find there, and what kinds of *realistic* expectations can we bring to this part of the Bible?

A broad range of literary genres. One thing we can expect to encounter in the Old Testament is a broad range of literary genres: law, narrative, poetry, psalms, prophetic literature, wisdom literature, apocalyptic literature, and so forth. This is part of the beauty of the Old Testament. If one particular literary genre doesn't interest you, chances are another will. And while we should not ignore genres we find less interesting, we can be thankful the Old Testament is more than *just* a set of laws or *only* a collection of judgment oracles. The Old Testament's rich literary diversity encourages us to press on, reminding us that even if this or that particular genre is not our favorite, there are many others waiting to be explored.

Recognizing the Old Testament's literary diversity helps us develop more realistic expectations of what we are reading. It reminds us that we cannot read all parts of the Old Testament the same way. Each genre has its own distinct interpretive guidelines. For example, you don't handle an Old Testament law the same way you deal with a prophetic oracle. Nor do you interpret a psalm the same way you might read an Old Testament narrative. Each genre is unique and has its own special form and function. This prompts us to look for different things as we read. When reading an Old Testament narrative, for instance, it is very important to pay attention to the use of repetition (who would have thought!). And when reading prophetic oracles, it's instructive to pay attention to the use of persuasion. We will have much more to say about both of these genres in the next part of the book. Knowing what to look for when encountering different genres—and knowing how to interpret what we see—is part of what increases our enjoyment of the Old Testament.[7]

A great deal of theological diversity. In addition to all the literary diversity in the Old Testament, there is also a considerable amount of *theological* diversity. Many different views about the nature of God and how God operates in the world are found throughout the Old Testament. The "theology of retribution," as it is sometimes called, was one of the most popular ways to explain this divine activity. According to this view, those who obeyed God could expect to be healthy and wealthy and to live a very long life, while those who did not could expect exactly the opposite: to be sickly and poor and to die prematurely. This perspective is spelled out in great detail in Deuteronomy 28 and is evident throughout much of the Old Testament.

To give just one example, consider how the theology of retribution is used to explain why Israel was conquered by the Assyrians:

> This [Israel's downfall to the Assyrians] occurred because the people of Israel had sinned against the LORD their God, who had brought them up out of the land of Egypt from under the hand of Pharaoh king of Egypt. They had worshiped other gods and walked in the customs of the nations whom the LORD drove out before the people of Israel, and in the customs that the kings of Israel had introduced. (2 Kings 17:7-8)

Explanations like this are common throughout the Old Testament.

But this way of understanding the connection between sin and suffering was not embraced by everyone in Israel. As previously noted, the book of Job directly challenges this way of seeing things.[8] It pushes back against a mechanistic view of divine-human affairs by recognizing that human suffering and tragedy are not always the result of sinning. Although Job's three friends were committed to viewing the world this way, Job was not. People in ancient Israel had different opinions about this

---

[7]See, e.g., Michael R. Cosby, *Interpreting Biblical Literature: An Introduction to Biblical Studies* (Grantham, PA: Stony Run Publishing, 2009); Gordon D. Fee and Douglas Stuart, *How to Read the Bible for All Its Worth*, 4th ed. (Grand Rapids, MI: Zondervan, 2014).
[8]See chapter three.

issue—and many others—and these differences are reflected on the pages of the Old Testament.[9]

That dissonant voices coexist on the pages of the Old Testament should come as no great surprise given the fact that the Old Testament was formed over a period of about eight hundred years (950–150 BCE) by many different writers. As Professor Beal observes, "It [the Bible] holds together a tense diversity of perspectives and voices, difference and argument—even and especially . . . when it comes to the profoundest questions of faith."[10]

While those who expect the Bible to speak with one voice may consider theological diversity in the Old Testament a problem to be solved, it is better seen as an opportunity to be seized. It reminds us that people of faith do not always view things the same way, and it gives us the opportunity to explore a range of different possibilities as we reflect on our own beliefs and behaviors. By presenting a diverse array of perspectives about God, faith, and life, we are invited to join in the conversation as we grapple with questions of ultimate significance in our journey with God. The theological diversity of the Old Testament provides wonderful resources for engaging constructively in these important conversations, which can also help us enjoy this part of the Bible.

Worldview assumptions that differ considerably from our own. As we read the Old Testament, we can expect to be transported to a time and place radically different from our own. It is a crosscultural experience, one that takes us to a distant world filled with many unfamiliar customs, practices, and beliefs. While the people of Israel permitted polygamy, approved of slavery, and sacrificed animals, Christians today would object to all these practices. And while there are certainly points of continuity between their world and ours, the differences are significant and should not be minimized. In fact, our ability to understand the

---

[9]There are a host of other theological differences that could be noted as well including whether God knows the future, whether God punishes children for the sins of their parents, whether God is merciful, whether God is approachable, etc.

[10]Beal, *Rise and Fall of the Bible*, 173.

Old Testament well depends, to no small degree, on our ability to get inside the minds of those who wrote it. How did *they* view the world? What did *they* believe about right and wrong, good and evil? How did *they* understand the divine-human relationship? Paying attention to questions like these reminds us to be careful about imposing twenty-first-century assumptions on these very ancient texts.

Even a cursory reading of the Old Testament reveals that people in antiquity held quite different assumptions about the nature of reality than most of us do. Israelites believed the world was flat and thought all people went to Sheol when they died. We would take issue with both of these ideas. In addition, the Israelites believed God was actively involved in world affairs: controlling weather, initiating warfare, opening and closing wombs. This directly influenced their interpretation of events in ways that can be seen throughout the Old Testament. In the worldview of an ancient Israelite, for example, a famine is not just an unfortunate consequence of the lack of rain. It is divine judgment. Likewise, victory in battle is not due to superior firepower or elite troops. It is the result of divine blessing. *God* was on your side. Their outlook on the world and the explanations they give for certain events are markedly different from the way many people see and understand the world today. Thus, when you read the Old Testament, you should expect to encounter these alternate worldview assumptions from the ancient world.[11]

Ancient texts written for many different reasons. You should also expect to encounter a diverse array of texts produced for many different reasons. Some writers created beautiful poems for individual and corporate worship (Psalms). Others tried to make sense of national tragedies, like the fall of Jerusalem (see 1 and 2 Kings).[12] Some wrote political propaganda, crafting narratives to support the legitimacy of kings like David and Solomon and to defend them against charges of

---

[11]For more on Israel's theological worldview, see Eric A. Seibert, *Disturbing Divine Behavior: Troubling Old Testament Images of God* (Minneapolis: Fortress, 2009), 145-66.
[12]More broadly, the so-called Deuteronomistic History (Josh–2 Kings).

misconduct and wrongdoing.[13] Still others, like the writer of Ecclesiastes and the writer of Job, produced texts that explored some of life's biggest questions, as discussed earlier. Texts were also written to express the beauty of romantic love (Song of Songs), to give hope to people in exile (Is 40–55), and to urge faithfulness to God while living under foreign domination (Daniel).

Although it is by no means always clear why a certain biblical text was written or how it was intended to function, it is still useful to ask the question. At the very least, it reminds us that these texts were not originally written to us. They had another audience. It is important to take that into consideration as we read and interpret the Old Testament and try to figure out how these passages might apply to us today.

Violent verses and troubling passages. Sometimes, reading parts of the Old Testament can be very difficult, not because we *don't* understand what we are reading, but because we *do*. This is especially true of verses that describe people being harmed in some way: kidnapped, imprisoned, raped, beheaded, impaled, mutilated, slain in battle—the list goes on. The Old Testament does not shy away from telling these stories, and reading them can be very disconcerting.

It becomes even more challenging when certain acts of violence are said to have been sanctioned by God. Many readers are bothered by this and struggle to understand how such behavior is consistent with notions of divine goodness and mercy. This is a real problem, and we'll have more to say about it later.[14] My purpose in raising it now is to ensure you have realistic expectations going into the Old Testament.

Sometimes, people who are unfamiliar with the Old Testament and start reading it are surprised and bewildered to find examples of violence—sometimes *extreme* violence—strewn across its pages. This reaction is

---

[13]On David, see conveniently Steven L. McKenzie, *King David: A Biography* (New York: Oxford University Press, 2000), 25-46, esp. 32-34. For Solomon, and an argument that the ostensibly propagandistic account of Solomon's acquisition of the throne and consolidation of power in 1 Kings 1–2 is riddled with subversive elements, see Eric A. Seibert, *Subversive Scribes and the Solomonic Narrative: A Rereading of 1 Kings 1–11*, LHBOTS 436 (New York: T&T Clark, 2006), 111-57.

[14]See chapter nine.

especially common among those who have been raised in a Christian environment that has always spoken positively about the Bible and never really grappled with its more challenging elements. They feel completely unprepared to deal with these troubling texts. For some, this precipitates a faith crisis. For others, it results in a lack of desire to read further.

I don't want that to happen to you. I don't want you to be caught off guard by what you find in the Old Testament. As I've said, you will encounter some violent verses and problematic passages. But knowing to expect them should begin to prepare you for them. You may still be troubled by these texts and uncertain what to do with them, but at least you will be going into the Old Testament with your eyes open. Hopefully, this will help you keep your balance and will give you the space you need to wrestle with these passages without losing your footing.

Passages containing wisdom about life with God and others. Finally, as noted in the previous chapter, when you read the Old Testament you can expect to find texts that contain invaluable insights, greatly needed perspectives, and meaningful points of application. The Old Testament has considerable wisdom to offer us about life with God and others if we are patient enough to discover it.

As I said at the beginning of the book, my passion for the Old Testament developed during my first year of college while enrolled in Old Testament Literature with Terry Brensinger. This class and many others I took over the next several years helped me realize just how relevant the Old Testament is for people of faith like me. As I've written elsewhere:

> During those eight years in college and seminary, the Old Testament came alive for me and profoundly shaped my understanding of God, the world, and humanity in more ways than I can recall. I came to appreciate how central trusting God is to Christian faith. I learned how dangerous it is for people to create their own solutions apart from God. I witnessed God's deep and abiding desire to be in relationship with people and observed how time and again God tenaciously stuck with the Israelites even *after* they repeatedly messed up. In short, I realized the Old Testament was teeming with theological insight and wisdom.[15]

---

[15]Seibert, *Disturbing Divine Behavior*, 3-4, emphasis original.

Today I am more convinced of this than ever. The Old Testament contains a great deal of wisdom for living life and for loving God and others. We should expect to find this as we read these texts with open hearts and minds.

MEETING GOD IN THE OLD TESTAMENT: A DISTINCTLY CHRISTIAN EXPECTATION

Before concluding this chapter, it's helpful to identify one additional expectation Christians often bring to the Old Testament, that of meeting God. For many Christians, the possibility of encountering God in the pages of Scripture is what prompts them to open their Bible in the first place. They read the Bible because they believe doing so will deepen their faith and strengthen their relationship with God. They read for transformation, not just information, as the saying goes.

Christians who read this way expect God to "speak" to them through the pages of the Old Testament. While most do not anticipate hearing God speak audibly, they do expect God to communicate with them. This can happen in a number of ways. As they read the Old Testament, they may sense God reminding them of a personal sin that needs to be confessed or a relationship that needs to be mended. Or they may sense God prompting them to undertake an act of service for a needy neighbor or to volunteer for a leadership role at church. Then again, reading the Old Testament may convince them of God's love for them, or it might reassure them of God's peace and presence in their lives during a difficult time. It might also fill them with hope that God will heal them, help them, or otherwise do good in their lives, or the lives of others around them. In these and many other ways, Christians experience a real connection with God through reading the Bible. This strengthens their relationship with God and keeps them coming back time and again.

For Christian readers of all stripes, expecting to "hear" from God in some of these ways strikes me as a *generally* realistic expectation. God can—and does—speak to us through these ancient laws, stories, poems, and prophecies. But as most Christians would testify, this doesn't happen every time we read the Bible, and it doesn't look the same for everybody.

Thus we need not feel we have failed if we finish our reading without having "heard" from God in some particular way. God communicates as the Spirit wills and as we are ready and willing to receive. The simple fact that sometimes God *does* speak through Scripture should encourage us to open the Bible with a sense of hopeful expectancy, prepared to experience God and ready to hear and receive whatever God might wish to say.

Conclusion

Throughout this chapter we have emphasized the importance of developing appropriate expectations for engaging the Old Testament. This is crucial because our ability to enjoy the Old Testament is, to a large extent, correlated to what we expect from it. If we have unrealistic expectations about the Old Testament, we will likely be frustrated and unsatisfied when we read it, and we may even decide to stop reading it at all. On the other hand, if we approach the Old Testament with eyes wide open, and have reasonable expectations, we are much more likely to have many pleasant encounters with it.

5

CULTIVATING *the* RIGHT MINDSET

*Movies and television, even modern novels have taught us to
expect dramatic scene painting, psychological probing, explosive
exchanges. But the Bible tells a story like Rembrandt etches one.
You have to slow down and look closely to see much of anything at
all, and then let your heart dwell on what you see.*

ELLEN DAVIS, *GETTING INVOLVED WITH GOD*

BEACH GLASS HUNTING AND THE OLD TESTAMENT

For three years, my wife and I lived in Erie, Pennsylvania. We moved
there in 1998 so Elisa could begin her doctoral work in counseling psychology at Gannon University. One of the perks of living in Erie is
Presque Isle State Park, a beautiful stretch of land that juts out into Lake
Erie for many miles. It's a great place for rollerblading, canoeing, bird
watching, and . . . beach glass hunting.

I had never heard about beach glass prior to our three-year stint in
Erie, but during our time there, finding these beautiful pieces of tumbled
glass became a new passion for me. I spent many happy hours walking
up and down the shoreline looking for pieces of smooth glass in a wide
array of shapes, sizes, and colors. Beach glass, or sea glass as some call it,
is formed when broken glass is tumbled in large bodies of water like the
Great Lakes or oceans. Eventually, this glass makes its way to the shore
where beachcombers eagerly search for it. Some of the most common

colors are white, brown, and green. But you can also find teal, cobalt blue, yellow, and orange. On a *really* good day, you might even find red, the "holy grail" of beach glass hunting.

People do lots of interesting things with the beach glass they find. Some make jewelry with it. Others use it for crafts. I like to display mine in jars. I have a triangular-shaped jar in my office that stands about 8½ inches high, filled with white, brown, and green glass. It serves as a memory of happy hunting days, and it beckons me to return to find more.

Of course, glass is not the only thing you can collect on the beach at Presque Isle State Park. Seashells, fossils, rocks, and pieces of tile, some with patterns still visible, can also be found there. For me, part of the allure of beachcombing is not knowing what you will find next: the bottom of a Heinz ketchup bottle, a beautiful piece of jewelry grade cobalt blue beach glass, an interesting piece of tile, or even just run-of-the-mill pieces of white, green, and brown. The beautiful setting and the thrill of the hunt make the whole experience lots of fun.

As any seasoned beach glass enthusiast will tell you, not every day is a good day for finding beach glass. Winter complicates these efforts tremendously—especially when parts of the lake freeze! But even during spring and summer, there are days when the waves are so rough, and the water so high, that all the best places to find glass have been covered. Some days yield great treasure; some do not. Still, one of the wonderful things about beach glass hunting is the simple knowledge that there is *always* more glass to be found. Lake Erie alone seems to have an endless supply. You can traverse the same small section of the shoreline for hours and find beach glass even in places you have just looked because the waves are constantly churning up more. Beach glass will exist as long as people continue to make and use glass.

But what, you may be asking, does hunting for beach glass have to do with reading the Old Testament?

For me, it serves as an apt analogy of how we should approach the Old Testament. Finding beach glass takes time, patience, and careful observation. If you walk too fast, you will pass right by it. You need to slow down, pay attention, and really look. The same is true with the Old Testament. In addition, like beach glass, the riches of the Old Testament are inexhaustible. We can read the same passage again and again and still find new insights and perspectives previously unconsidered.

When I search for beach glass, I do so with a real sense of expectancy. I anticipate finding treasures. That is what compels me to search in the first place, and it is what keeps me going when the pickings are slim. Even a bad day of beach glass hunting does not discourage me from returning and trying again. Why? Because I know there will be better days ahead. I know I will go to the beach again and return with pockets bulging, filled with treasures from the sea. In much the same way, even when I have unsatisfying encounters with the Old Testament, I do not give up on it. I keep coming back for more because I know better days will come. I know there are treasures waiting to be discovered. Even if they did not appear this time, tomorrow is a brand-new day.

WHAT SHOULD YOUR ATTITUDE BE TOWARD THE OLD TESTAMENT?

This chapter is about developing the right mindset for reading the Old Testament. If we can learn to approach the Old Testament with the same kind of attitude we bring to our favorite hobbies and pastimes, chances are good we will have a more enjoyable encounter with it. But if we are convinced the Old Testament is boring and irrelevant, that is likely how we will experience it. Negative expectations often become self-fulfilling prophecies.

So then how should we approach this part of the Bible? What kind of attitude should we have toward the Old Testament? This question will guide our discussion in the following pages.

Careful observation. Learning to observe carefully what is actually in the Old Testament is one of the most important things we can do to enhance our enjoyment of what we are reading. Allow me to explain in a somewhat roundabout way.

Growing up, I was never much of the "summer camp" type, especially if that required staying overnight. The boys my age were too rowdy for

my taste, and I didn't really like being away from the comfort and familiarity of home. Still, for a couple years I did spend a week at Kenbrook
Bible Camp, a summer camp run by my church. Located in the beautiful
countryside of Lebanon, Pennsylvania, the camp had a swimming pool,
hiking trails, and targets for archery. Each day there was time set aside
to be alone with God, to join in group activities, and to participate in
corporate worship.

One of the activities we did at camp that made a lasting impression on
me involved a simple act of observation. As I recall, we were outside and
were told to sit down and look closely at a small square section of ground
in front of us to see what we could observe. If you have never done this
before, try it sometime. Find a spot of grass. Sit down on the ground.
And mark off a small area to investigate. Then spend ten minutes or so
and see what's there. Even in a relatively small area you will likely be
amazed by the amount of diversity you find: pebbles, weeds, worms,
flowers, bird droppings, grass, insects, a candy wrapper, dirt—the list
goes on. Most of these things are imperceptible to passersby who walk
right over it unawares. But it's there just the same.

Though I cannot remember the intended purpose of this activity—
perhaps it was to marvel at the incredible beauty and diversity of God's
great creation—what stuck with me all these years later is the value of
careful observation. *It's amazing how much you see when you slow down
and take the time to look.* This is equally true whether you are looking at
a patch of grass or a biblical text.

The importance of careful observation cannot be overestimated
when it comes to reading and enjoying the Old Testament. The reason
for this is simple and self-evident: *you cannot interpret or apply what
you do not see.* We miss a great deal because we read too quickly. We
skim over large swaths of text without stopping to investigate carefully
or reflect deeply and then wonder why we haven't gotten much out of
it. Yet, as Ellen Davis wisely recognizes, "The Bible discourages us from
making mileage a measure of success. In many cases, its riches are
perceptible only to those who move slowly, like mushroom hunters,

peering closely where at first there appears to be nothing at all to see."[1] Sometimes, less *is* more.

If we hope to enjoy the Old Testament, we need to slow down and observe the text with care and diligence. This will take some practice and some patience. It will require us to linger over texts, to ruminate upon them, to read them repeatedly, and to view them from a variety of different perspectives. When we do, new insights will emerge, and we will experience the joy of discovery.

Just to be clear, I am *not* suggesting it is wrong to "read-and-run." It is okay to dip into the Old Testament for only a few minutes, especially if that's all the time you have. In the same way that five minutes of practicing the piano is better than no practice at all, doing *some* Bible reading is better than none. My point here is simply this: if you *only* have brief encounters with the Old Testament, that will limit how much you get out of it and how much fun you can have with it. The more you can slow down and pay close attention to what you are reading, the more you will be able to see. And the more you see, the greater your chances will be of liking the Old Testament.

Hopeful expectancy. It is also helpful to read the Old Testament with a sense of hopeful expectancy, convinced there are treasures waiting to be found (like beach glass hunting). This is what helps us persist and keeps us coming back to the Old Testament time and time again. If we *lose* hope and don't expect to find much that is worthwhile there, our desire to read this part of the Bible will certainly diminish. But if we expect to discover valuable insights and ideas, and if we are hopeful we might even encounter God in the process, we will be encouraged to keep trying. Seeing the Old Testament as a resource for spiritual growth, as something that can draw us closer to God and help us "hear" from God, encourages us stay engaged with this part of the Bible.

Admittedly, developing this kind of attitude toward the Old Testament can be difficult, especially if your past experiences with this part of the

---

[1]Ellen F. Davis, *Getting Involved with God: Rediscovering the Old Testament* (Cambridge, MA: Cowley, 2001), 3.

Bible have been largely negative and unsatisfying. While there is no magic formula that will ensure you think positively about the Old Testament, there *are* some things you can do to cultivate an attitude of hopeful expectancy.

First, regardless of how challenging it might be for you to enjoy the Old Testament at present, it is worth remembering that it can be done. How do I know this? Because it *has* been done. For nearly two thousand years, millions of Christians around the world have found enormous value and worth in the Old Testament. Books could be written to tell the stories of women and men who have found this part of the Bible to be transformative and life-giving. The simple fact that so many Christians have derived such great benefit from the Old Testament for centuries demonstrates that it is possible to enjoy this part of the Bible. This simple fact should encourage us all to redouble our efforts and dig in.

Second, if you are serious about cultivating a sense of hopeful expectancy, surround yourself with others who are enthusiastic about the Old Testament. Find pastors, friends, and fellow church members who are passionate about this part of the Bible. Ask them why they love the Old Testament and what helps them enjoy reading it. Allow their enthusiasm to rub off on you. You could also read books or listen to podcasts that exude a deep and abiding love for the Old Testament.[2] Since we are shaped by the company we keep, hanging out with those who love the Old Testament can form your own attitudes toward it in positive ways.

Third, keep in mind that there are many, many ways to read the Old Testament. People lose hope when the limited options they have for reading this part of the Bible all seem to fail. But maybe that's the problem. Maybe our lack of enjoyment has more to do with *how* we have been reading the Old Testament rather than with the Old Testament itself. If so, the good news is there are *lots* of creative ways to engage the Old Testament. We will

---

[2]For books, you might try Davis, *Getting Involved with God* or Matthew Richard Schlimm, *This Strange and Sacred Scripture: Wrestling with the Old Testament and Its Oddities* (Grand Rapids, MI: Baker Academic, 2015), 5. A down-to-earth podcast that deals responsibly with the Old Testament (and much more) is *The Bible for Normal People* hosted by Peter Enns and Jared Byers, https://thebiblefornormalpeople.podbean.com/.

discuss many of these in the chapters to follow. The more options you have for reading the Old Testament, the more likely it is you will find some that work well for you. Knowing there is a broad range of options at your disposal can encourage you to try again, even if past encounters with the Old Testament have been disappointing. The more able you are to approach the Old Testament with a sense of hopeful expectancy, believing there truly are ways to read and relish it, the more likely you will be to have positive and rewarding encounters with this part of the Bible.

Humility and respect. If we are to enjoy the Old Testament, we will need to read it with humility and respect.[3] This is true *even if* we find significant portions boring, irrelevant, or morally offensive. Reading with humility and respect means learning to appreciate the Old Testament as it is, not as we might wish it was. It means trying to understand the Old Testament on its own terms, by reading it in light of its historical and cultural context.

Reading the Old Testament with humility and respect also means coming to the text with a teachable spirit. If we have already judged the Old Testament to be primitive and barbaric, without contemporary value or moral significance, it is doubtful we will learn anything from it. But if we approach these texts with genuine openness and receptivity, we are likely to discover they have a great deal to teach us.

In many ways, our disposition toward the Old Testament should be similar to the one we should have when traveling to a foreign country. When you are a guest in another culture, it is important to be respectful of their customs and practices. You should be grateful for the hospitality you receive and the beauty you discover. And you should always be humble in your interactions with others, ready and eager to learn. If you constantly look down on the people you meet and regard their practices and beliefs as inferior to your own, chances are you will not have a very

---

[3]As John Calvin once prayed, "O Lord, heavenly Father, in whom is the fullness of light and wisdom, enlighten our minds by your Holy Spirit, and *give us grace to receive your Word with reverence and humility*, without which no one can understand your truth. For Christ's sake. Amen." Cited in Dorothy M. Stewart, comp., *The Westminster Collection of Christian Prayers* (Louisville, KY: Westminster John Knox, 2002), 15-16, emphasis mine.

pleasant trip. But if you enter another country as a gracious guest, one who is genuinely open to a diverse range of customs and perspectives, you are much more likely to have a positive experience.

Approaching the Old Testament this way will involve abandoning some assumptions we may hold—consciously or unconsciously—about our cultural, intellectual, and moral superiority to people in the ancient world. We need to be willing to learn from them and from the texts they produced. We need to recognize the wisdom they offer and should be open to changing our mind when that is warranted. This means that when we encounter unusual practices and unfamiliar beliefs, rather than rushing to judgment, we should seek to understand them. Why did the Israelites hold these beliefs? What led them to behave in these ways? We should also ask what we can learn from them. How might their unique perspectives help us understand life with God? What positive values in these texts are worth revisiting and perhaps reclaiming? Asking questions like these demonstrates a healthy respect for the text and signals our intention to read them as charitably as possible.

Of course, reading with humility and respect does *not* mean agreeing with everything we read (a point we will take up momentarily). Nor does it mean uncritically adopting the values and viewpoints of the text as our own. Rather, we need to engage in a process of careful discernment and evaluation to determine what we can embrace and what we cannot. For example, people of faith today should reject the Old Testament's patriarchal perspectives and practices since they oppress and degrade women. But the Old Testament's summons to care for the most vulnerable members of the community, a call consistent with the teachings of Jesus, should be embraced and enacted. Choices like these must be made, but even these choices can be made respectfully. Ridiculing and disparaging the Old Testament serves nobody well and hinders our efforts to appreciate this part of the Bible.

Honest engagement. Finally, to truly enjoy the Old Testament, we need to have the freedom to be completely honest with it, particularly with the difficulties we encounter in it. As Thomas Merton contends:

The point is . . . that becoming involved in the Bible does not mean simply taking everything it says without the slightest murmur of difficulty. It means at once being willing to argue and fight back, provided that if we are clearly wrong we will finally admit it. The Bible prefers honest disagreement to a dishonest submission.[4]

When you read the Old Testament carefully, you will surely discover things that offend you: beliefs that run contrary to your own, values you don't endorse, and behaviors you cannot condone. What should you do when this happens? Minimally, you should be honest about the difficulties you have with these texts. Being able to articulate what you find problematic about these texts is an important first step. It opens the door for conversation and creates space for further exploration.

Yet many Christians are hesitant to be honest about the problems they have with the Old Testament. They have been taught the Bible is above reproach, a repository of ultimate and absolute truth. How can they question it, let alone critique it? Isn't that tantamount to blasphemy since the Bible is, after all, *God's* word? These pious convictions make it very difficult for some Christians to be honest about what bothers them in this part of the Bible. As a result, many say nothing and struggle alone with their questions, doubts, and frustration.

Since the troublesome parts of the Old Testament seriously hinder some people's enjoyment of it, we will address this topic more fully later.[5] For now, I simply want to emphasize our need to be completely honest with the problems these texts raise for us. As we'll see later, the biblical witness contains a long line of individuals—people like Abraham, Moses, and Habakkuk—who saw this kind of honest engagement (albeit directed toward God), as an act of profound faithfulness.

Rather than being a sign of disrespect, wrestling honestly with the biblical text demonstrates our commitment to it. Merton recognized this and suggested that a struggle-free reading of Scripture may reflect a lack of genuine engagement.

---

[4]Thomas Merton, *Opening the Bible* (Collegeville, MN: Liturgical, 1986), 44. My thanks to Jay McDermond for directing me to this quote.
[5]See chapter nine.

Let us not be too sure we know the Bible just because we have learned not to be astonished at it, just because we have learned not to have problems with it. Have we perhaps learned at the same time not to really pay attention to it? Have we ceased to question the book and be questioned by it? Have we ceased to fight it? Then perhaps our reading is no longer serious.[6]

If we are going to stay involved with the Old Testament, we need to have the freedom to register our concerns about portions of the Old Testament that promote values which may conflict with some of our core Christian convictions (e.g., the acceptability of owning slaves, the permissibility of having multiple sexual partners, the appropriateness of using violence, and the inferior view of women it promotes). It is very difficult to have a healthy relationship with the Old Testament otherwise.

Conclusion

Hopefully, this chapter has helped you recognize the kind of attitude you need to have in order to get the most out of the Old Testament. When we approach the Old Testament through careful observation, hopeful expectancy, humility, respect, and honest engagement, we position ourselves well for many positive encounters with this part of the Bible. Developing the right attitude toward the Old Testament goes a long way toward having positive experiences with it.

Having considered what we might expect *from* the Old Testament (chapter four), and what kind of attitude we should bring *to* the Old Testament (chapter five), we are finally ready to start having some real fun *with* the Old Testament. In the next section of the book, we will discuss how to read and enjoy the Old Testament's two predominant literary genres, narrative and prophecy,[7] and will then consider what to do with the "boring parts" of the Old Testament so many people struggle to appreciate. Let the fun begin!

---

[6]Merton, *Opening the Bible*, 37.
[7]Together, these two genres account for well over half of the Old Testament. While narrative and prophecy will be the primary focus here, some attention will also be given to law and to imprecatory psalms.

PART TWO

HAVING FUN

with the

OLD TESTAMENT

6

FINDING NEW MEANING
in OLD STORIES

*It seems to me . . . that reading a biblical story is like observing
a polished gem, and the more you examine it from various angles,
the more you are captivated by the many facets of its brilliance.*

YAIRAH AMIT, *READING BIBLICAL NARRATIVES*

APART FROM BELOVED PSALMS, like Psalm 23, or foundational
laws, like the Ten Commandments, the best-known parts of the Old
Testament are the narratives, or stories, it contains: Noah's ark; Abraham
and (the near-sacrifice of) Isaac; Joshua and the Battle of Jericho;
Samson and Delilah; David and Goliath; Elijah and the prophets of
Baal; Ruth and Naomi; and the story of Queen Esther—to name just a
few. Stories like these are what many young children are taught in
Sunday school, Vacation Bible School, and summer church camps. Many
of these stories have been immortalized in Veggie Tales videos such as
King George and the Ducky, a retelling of the David-and-Bathsheba
debacle (2 Sam 11), and *Rack, Shack, and Benny*, a version of the story
about Daniel's three friends and the fiery furnace (Dan 3). The popu-
larity of Old Testament narratives is also evident in children's Bibles,
which selectively retell very small portions of the Old Testament and
include more stories than anything else. Why? Because stories are engaging and captivating. They are dramatic, memorable, and instructive.
Everyone loves a good story.

The Israelites clearly prized crafting and telling stories. The sheer number of stories that have survived in the Old Testament bear ample testimony to this. According to one estimate, over 40 percent of the Old Testament consists of narrative.[1] Considering the enormous size of the Old Testament, that's a lot of story!

Personally, I'm glad there are so many stories in the Old Testament. I love Old Testament narratives and maybe you do too. Whatever your current attitude may be, I hope this chapter enhances your enjoyment of these time-honored tales. I also hope it leaves you feeling better equipped to investigate them from different angles and perspectives. Doing so will enable you to get more out of these stories as you explore them with renewed energy and enthusiasm.

A FEW BASIC SUGGESTIONS TO GET YOU STARTED

While many Christians are familiar with the most popular stories in the Old Testament, the majority of them remain virtually unknown. How often do we hear a Sunday school lesson or sermon about the tragic sacrifice of Jephthah's daughter (Judg 11:34-40) or the moral courage of Saul's concubine Rizpah (2 Sam 21:1-14)? Who tells the story of King Jehu's treacherous treatment of Baal worshipers in Samaria (2 Kings 10:18-31) or David's gracious treatment of Jonathan's son Mephibosheth in Jerusalem (2 Sam 9:1-13)? These stories and many others have been lost to us. They are typically not taught in the church, are not a part of the Revised Common Lectionary, and are not the stuff of children's books or Bibles.

Even stories that are familiar to us often aren't as well-known as we might think. Take the story of Jonah, for example. If you were to ask someone for the basic storyline, you might get something like this: "The book of Jonah is about a disobedient prophet who tries to avoid God's call, ends up inside the belly of a 'whale' for a few days, and eventually does what God commands by preaching to the Ninevites whose remarkable repentance causes God to spare the city." End of story, right?

---

[1] Gordon D. Fee and Douglas Stuart, *How to Read the Bible for All Its Worth*, 4th ed. (Grand Rapids, MI: Zondervan, 2014), 93.

Wrong. There is still another chapter to go! But many readers are unfamiliar with Jonah 4, the final chapter of the book in which Jonah wants to die because he is so angry that God showed mercy on his enemies. Children's books that retell the story of Jonah routinely omit this chapter, and many churchgoers are completely unaware of it.

In light of our basic unfamiliarity with many of these Old Testament narratives, it seems that getting acquainted with them would be a good place to start. This would be time and energy well spent, especially given the historically low rates of biblical literacy in the church today.[2] What follows are some brief and very basic guidelines for how you can get to know these stories better.

Select a story you want to explore. The first thing you need to do is figure out what story you want to read. As we've said, there are lots to choose from. If you would find it helpful to have a list of options, a simple internet search of "popular Bible stories" will yield this. Stories about individual characters in the Old Testament come in many shapes and sizes and are of varying lengths. Some individuals have multiple chapters devoted to them (e.g., Abraham, Gen 12–25) while others merely get a single verse (e.g., Shamgar, Judg 3:31). For starters, I would suggest selecting a story that interests you and is not too long.[3] Over time, you can examine longer stories and choose those you know little or nothing about. But to begin, start small and find something that piques your interest. If you are really unfamiliar with the Bible or want to work at this more systematically, you could look at the stories listed in the table of contents of Timothy Beal's book, *Biblical Literacy: The Essential Bible Stories Everyone Needs to Know.*[4]

---

[2]See Ed Stetzer, "The Epidemic of Biblical Illiteracy in Our Churches," *The Exchange* (blog), *Christianity Today*, July 6, 2015, www.christianitytoday.com/edstetzer/2015/july/epidemic-of -bible-illiteracy-in-our-churches.html.

[3]If you want to find a Bible story about a particular topic, such as jealousy or forgiveness, you could use a topical Bible to locate one. See chapter eleven for a discussion of topical Bibles and how to use them. For some topical Bibles online, go to www.openbible.info/topics/ or www .biblestudytools.com/concordances/naves-topical-bible/.

[4]Timothy Beal, *Biblical Literacy: The Essential Bible Stories Everyone Needs to Know* (New York: HarperCollins, 2009).

Determine the boundaries of the story. Next, determine where the story begins and ends. Sometimes, this is made easy because the story begins with the main character's birth and ends with the person's death. The story of Abraham, for example, runs from Genesis 11:27–25:11, and the story of Samson is found exclusively in Judges 13–16. Other times you may be introduced to a person at a certain age: we meet Joseph when he is seventeen (Gen 37:2)[5] and Josiah at age eight (2 Kings 22:1). This marks the beginning of their accounts in the Old Testament. One easy way to get a quick sense of where someone's story begins and ends is to type the person's name into a searchable Bible, see what comes up, and then go to the earliest and latest references to see if you can determine the parameters of the story.

Once you have identified the boundaries of a particular story, keep in mind that it might also be part of a larger story. The story of Abraham (Gen 11:27–25:11), for example, is part of the patriarchal narrative which runs from Genesis 12–50. And the story of Samson (Judg 13–16) is part of the story of Israel's judges told in Judges 3–16. It is always helpful to read smaller stories in their larger literary context, especially when they are part of longer narratives.

Read the story in its entirety. After you have identified the story you want to explore and have determined where it begins and ends, read through the story in its entirety to get a general overview. You may want to have paper and pencil in hand so you can make some initial observations about things you find interesting or puzzling.

Create a basic outline of the story. When you are finished reading through the story, I would then suggest creating a basic outline of it.[6] If it is a long story, you might want to work on this over several days. Stories about people like Abraham and Samson that occupy several chapters are comprised of several smaller stories embedded within the larger narrative. You can identify these and use a standard outline to

---

[5]His birth is mentioned briefly in Gen 30:22-24.

[6]In chapter twelve, we'll discuss how to divide an entire book of the Bible into major units and sub-units. You can use the same general principles discussed there to create the outlines described here.

map out the story. Alternatively, you might consider drawing a series of pictures that "outline" the major components of the story you are investigating. Either way, the goal is to produce a roadmap through the story. This will keep you from getting lost and will divide the story into more manageable portions.

You can repeat this process for as many Old Testament stories as you like. It is good way to become more familiar with these fascinating narratives.

WHAT SHOULD I LOOK FOR IN AN OLD TESTAMENT NARRATIVE?

There are all sorts of interesting things to look for when reading Old Testament narratives. This is one of the reasons they are so much fun to explore. Many of us have been taught to look for the moral of the story or *the* lesson we should learn from it. But the truth is these stories cannot be reduced to a single lesson or moral. We can learn *many* things from them. There are intriguing questions to be explored and various perspectives to be considered. These stories are brimming with interpretive possibilities that offer seemingly endless opportunities for reading and reflection. They can be approached from a variety of different angles and vantage points, yielding new insights along the way.

In light of this, my goal here is rather modest. After discussing some common literary features of Old Testament narratives, I will suggest several creative ways to interact with these stories. While this is just a starting point, I hope it will whet your appetite for more.

COMMON LITERARY FEATURES OF OLD TESTAMENT NARRATIVES

As with any ancient literary genre, Old Testament narratives were written in very specific ways. They used a form and style that distinguished them from other types of literature. Observing some of the common literary conventions used to construct these stories gives us greater insight into them.

In what follows, we will consider three common literary features of Old Testament narratives: repetition, naming, and the functional significance of personal details. While these are not hard to spot, most readers don't pay much attention to them, if they notice them at all. Yet once you begin looking for these, you soon start seeing them everywhere. The same sort of thing happens after buying a car. Purchase a silver Honda Civic, and next thing you know, silver Honda Civics are everywhere! That's not because there are more of this particular make and model of car on the road today than there were yesterday (well, maybe one more). Rather, it's simply because you are now paying attention to what has always been there. The same thing happens when we know what to look for in Old Testament narratives.

Pay attention to the use of repetition. As modern readers, we have little appreciation for the use of repetition in formal writing.[7] In fact, we are told to avoid it since it generally is considered a sign of poor writing. Not so in antiquity. In the ancient world, repetition was a powerful literary tool that was skillfully deployed in many different ways. We will consider three examples.

Example 1: The birth announcement of Samson. The story of Samson, Israel's strongman, begins with an announcement of his birth as follows:

> There was a certain man of Zorah, of the tribe of the Danites, whose name was Manoah. His wife was barren, having borne no children. And the angel of the LORD appeared to the woman and said to her, "Although you are barren, having borne no children, you shall conceive and bear a son. Now be careful not to drink wine or strong drink, or to eat anything unclean, for you shall conceive and bear a son. No razor is to come on his head, for the boy shall be a nazirite to God from birth. It is he who shall begin to deliver Israel from the hand of the Philistines." (Judg 13:2-5)

Given the way Old Testament narratives work, we might expect the next verse to read, "Then the woman came and told her husband what the angel had told her." Instead, the writer has chosen to have Samson's (unnamed) mother repeat the message to her husband Manoah.

---

[7]According to Robert Alter, "One of the most imposing barriers that stands between the modern reader and the imaginative subtlety of biblical narrative is the extraordinary prominence of verbatim repetition in the Bible." Alter, *The Art of Biblical Narrative* (New York: Basic, 1981), 88.

> Then the woman came and told her husband, "A man of God came to me, and his appearance was like that of an angel of God, most awe-inspiring; I did not ask him where he came from, and he did not tell me his name; but he said to me, 'You shall conceive and bear a son. So then drink no wine or strong drink, and eat nothing unclean, for the boy shall be a nazirite to God from birth to the day of his death.'" (Judg 13:6-7)

While modern readers might be annoyed at the apparent redundancy, or at least view it as unnecessary, ancient writers used repetition like this purposefully. Therefore, you need to slow down and look very closely. Sometimes things are repeated verbatim. Other times the words are altered by adding something to them or subtracting something from them.

In this particular instance, Samson's birth announcement is *not* reproduced verbatim by Manoah's wife. It is altered in at least two significant ways. First, she omits one of the key instructions she received about the care of her promised son. If you did not catch it the first time, take a moment and go back and look again. Do you see it? Nothing is said about the prohibition of a razor coming to his head. Is that particular detail important in the Samson narrative? Absolutely! It is the key to Samson's strength and the cause of his downfall (see Judg 16:4-22).

But there is more. Notice how the original message from the angel of the Lord ends on a positive note by referring to Samson as the one "who shall begin to deliver Israel from the hand of the Philistines" (Judg 13:5). Yet when Manoah's wife repeats the message, her retelling ends with a much more ominous description of her yet-to-be-born son: "The boy shall be a nazirite to God from birth to the day of his *death*" (Judg 13:7, emphasis mine). Samson has not even been born yet and already there is mention of his death. This suggests Samson will be something of a tragic figure.[8]

By repeating the birth announcement with these variations, the writer is foreshadowing things to come.[9] The absence of the razor in the retelling of the birth announcement alerts the reader to look for its appearance elsewhere in the story. And the altered ending reveals that

---

[8]This particular example of "varied repetition" is from Alter, *Art of Biblical Narrative*, 101.

[9]Foreshadowing is a literary device used to provide hints or clues about something yet to come.

despite Samson's auspicious birth, he is not going to be a perfect deliverer. By using repetition in this way, the writer provides important clues about where this story is heading, making it easier to read more intelligently from the start.

Example 2: Samuel's warning about the nature of kings (1 Sam 8:10-18). In today's world of desktop publishing and digital technology, there are many easy ways to emphasize words and ideas. We can put them in bold or italics, enlarge the size, or use fonts with attention-getting colors. Though options were more limited in the ancient world, repetition was one way ancient writers emphasized a key point or idea.

A classic example of this is evident in Samuel's dire warning about the nature of kingship in 1 Samuel 8. When the elders of Israel approach Samuel and request a king for the first time, Samuel tries to dissuade them by describing the stark reality of life under a king. In making his case, Samuel repeatedly uses one particular word to indicate what a king would do to them. See if you can spot it.

> He [Samuel] said, "These will be the ways of the king who will reign over you: he will take your sons and appoint them to his chariots and to be his horsemen, and to run before his chariots; and he will appoint for himself commanders of thousands and commanders of fifties, and some to plow his ground and to reap his harvest, and to make his implements of war and the equipment of his chariots. He will take your daughters to be perfumers and cooks and bakers. He will take the best of your fields and vineyards and olive orchards and give them to his courtiers. He will take one-tenth of your grain and of your vineyards and give it to his officers and his courtiers. He will take your male and female slaves, and the best of your cattle and donkeys, and put them to his work. He will take one-tenth of your flocks, and you shall be his slaves. And in that day you will cry out because of your king, whom you have chosen for yourselves; but the Lord will not answer you in that day." (1 Sam 8:11-18)

Did you find it? No less than six times Samuel talks about the king *taking* something away from them. The king will conscript their sons for military service (v. 11) and will take their daughters to prepare food (v. 13).

The king will take their *best* fields, vineyards, and orchards and give them to people in his service (v. 14). He will also take their male and female slaves and some of their best animals (v. 16). In addition, the king will take a tenth of their produce and their flocks (vv. 15, 17). *Kings take things.* The point is hard to miss.

By repeatedly using two Hebrew terms for taking, the writer emphasizes the serious drawbacks of having a king.[10] While you might think this would give Israel pause, they are undeterred. The people are determined to have a king, come what may.[11]

Example 3: Tabernacle details twice told (Ex 30 and 37). To get the full effect of this next example, grab a couple Bibles and see if you can find someone to help you for a few minutes. Ready? Now turn to Exodus 30:1. Tell your friend to turn to Exodus 37:25. For this to work best, you should both use the same translation of the Bible. Once you've both found your place, read Exodus 30:1-2 aloud. Then ask your friend to read Exodus 37:25 aloud. Continue reading aloud, one verse at a time, alternating back and forth. Do this for a few more verses and then stop. What's going on here?

If you don't have any friends nearby, read through the verses in figure 6.1, and you'll get the same effect.

As you can see, these two passages are virtually identical. The first passage includes *instructions* for building a tabernacle, the second contains a *description* of the people actually doing it. Why would the writer repeat these details twice? To demonstrate that the people did exactly what they were told.[12] In this instance, repetition is used to emphasize Israel's obedience. This is not insignificant at this point in the book of Exodus, especially when you realize the golden calf debacle, an extremely serious act of Israelite *dis*obedience, happens between these two passages.

---

[10]The common Hebrew word for taking, *laqakh*, is used four times (1 Sam 8:11, 13, 14, 16). The word *asar* is used the other two (1 Sam 8:15, 17).

[11]For another example of repetition used for emphasis, note the seraphim's proclamation of God to be "holy, holy, holy" (Is 6:3).

[12]In this particular case, the verses emphasize that Bezalel, an Israelite craftsman, is doing exactly what had been commanded (Ex 37:1).

As these examples illustrate, whenever you encounter repetition in Old Testament narratives (and elsewhere), slow down and take a closer look to see if you can determine what purpose it might serve. If you want to try a couple examples on your own before reading further, look at the instruction God gave Adam in the Garden of Eden (Gen 2:16-17), and notice how Eve relays this to the serpent (Gen 3:2-3). Does she change anything, or does she repeat it verbatim? What is significant about this? Or take a look at the repetition in 1 Samuel 15 surrounding the divine directive given to King Saul. What is King Saul commanded to do (1 Sam 15:3)? Is Saul fully obedient (1 Sam 15:7-9)? Is he honest with Samuel about what he has done (1 Sam 15:13-15, 18-21, 24)? Why do you think the

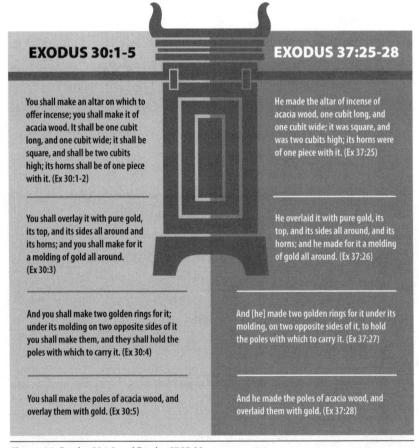

EXODUS 30:1-5

You shall make an altar on which to offer incense; you shall make it of acacia wood. It shall be one cubit long, and one cubit wide; it shall be square, and shall be two cubits high; its horns shall be of one piece with it. (Ex 30:1-2)

You shall overlay it with pure gold, its top, and its sides all around and its horns; and you shall make for it a molding of gold all around. (Ex 30:3)

And you shall make two golden rings for it; under its molding on two opposite sides of it you shall make them, and they shall hold the poles with which to carry it. (Ex 30:4)

You shall make the poles of acacia wood, and overlay them with gold. (Ex 30:5)

EXODUS 37:25-28

He made the altar of incense of acacia wood, one cubit long, and one cubit wide; it was square, and was two cubits high; its horns were of one piece with it. (Ex 37:25)

He overlaid it with pure gold, its top, and its sides all around, and its horns; and he made for it a molding of gold all around. (Ex 37:26)

And [he] made two golden rings for it under its molding, on two opposite sides of it, to hold the poles with which to carry it. (Ex 37:27)

And he made the poles of acacia wood, and overlaid them with gold. (Ex 37:28)

Figure 6.1. Exodus 30:1-5 and Exodus 37:25-28

divine command to annihilate Amalekites is repeatedly referenced in this narrative?[13]

Notice how people are "named." The use of naming is another interesting literary technique found in Old Testament narratives. Sometimes people are identified by their proper name; other times various designations are used. This happens in contemporary speech and writing as well. People can be referred to by familial designations (the son of Kathy, the brother of Vicky), by status or profession (teacher, lawyer, custodian), by nationality (German, Swiss, American), or in a variety of other ways. This is significant because different designations evoke different connotations.

To illustrate, consider the following scenario. Imagine you are married and have one child, a twelve-year-old boy named John. One day, you receive a phone call from the principal's office. The principal informs you that John was caught stealing in school and wants to meet with you to discuss the situation. After you hang up the phone, you decide to call your spouse to convey this unwelcome news. But instead of simply saying, "John got caught stealing in school today," you say, "*Your son* got caught stealing in school today." Hear the difference? The statement using John's proper name merely reports what happened, while the one using the designation "your son" implies some measure of blame.

When designations like these are used in the Old Testament, they often have special significance and help you view things from a certain perspective. To see how this works, let's look at a couple examples. First, take a moment to read the infamous story of David and Bathsheba in 2 Samuel 11:1–12:25. As you do, notice how Bathsheba is most commonly referred to throughout the narrative. What did you discover? No less than six times in these two chapters, Bathsheba is referred to as the *wife* of Uriah:

---

[13]For more on repetition in biblical narrative, see Patricia Dutcher-Walls, *Reading the Historical Books: A Student's Guide to Engaging the Biblical Text* (Grand Rapids, MI: Baker Academic, 2014), 77-81; Alter, *Art of Biblical Narrative*, 88-113; and Jerome T. Walsh, *Old Testament Narrative: A Guide to Interpretation* (Louisville, KY: Westminster John Knox, 2009), 81-95, esp. 93-95 which include several examples to try on your own.

11:3 "Bathsheba daughter of Eliam, the wife of Uriah the Hittite"

11:11 "my wife" (Uriah is speaking)

11:26 "the wife of Uriah"

12:9 "his [Uriah the Hittite's] wife"

12:10 "the wife of Uriah the Hittite"

12:15 "Uriah's wife"

Clearly, the writer does not want us to lose sight of this fact. By emphasizing her marital status, the writer reminds us that Bathsheba is not an unattached, single woman living in Jerusalem. She is married and, therefore, off limits. While kingship had many perks, sleeping with another man's wife was not one of them. David commits adultery, plain and simple. The recurring reference to Bathsheba as the wife of Uriah drives this point home.

To look at another example, let's consider the tragic story of Cain and Abel in Genesis 4. As the story goes, these two brothers bring an offering before God. Abel's offering is accepted by God; Cain's is not. Cain becomes so angry that he murders Abel. What's especially interesting here is the way Abel is named in this part of the story. The writer had numerous options to choose from: Abel, the son of Adam, the son of Eve, the brother of Seth, the brother of Cain, or the keeper of sheep. Notice which of these appears repeatedly in the following three verses.

> Cain said to his brother Abel, "Let us go out to the field." And when they were in the field, Cain rose up against his brother Abel, and killed him. Then the LORD said to Cain, "Where is your brother Abel?" He said, "I do not know; am I my brother's keeper?" And the LORD said, "What have you done? Listen; your brother's blood is crying out to me from the ground!" (Gen 4:8-10)

Five times Abel is referred to as the *brother* of Cain. This emphasis is important. What makes Cain's sin so horrific is not just the fact that he killed another human being, but that he killed *his own brother*. In a culture where family loyalty was especially important, this is very grave indeed.

For some examples to try on your own, observe how Sarai is named in Genesis 12:10-20. What is going on here? Or take a look at how both Amnon and Tamar are referred to in 2 Samuel 13. What designations are used, and why do you think the writer chose them? How does this enhance your understanding of the narrative?

Recognize the functional significance of physical details. When reading the Old Testament, it is rare to find specific information about a person's physical appearance. Most stories in the Bible typically say very little about what people looked like. Joseph is described as "handsome and good-looking" (Gen 39:6), though we have no idea what made him so. Likewise, Bathsheba is said to be "very beautiful" (2 Sam 11:2), but no details are given. Nothing is said about her eye color, the way she did her hair, or anything else that would give a hint of her appearance. If you want to know what "handsome" Joseph or "beautiful" Bathsheba looked like, you're on your own.

Given the Old Testament's reticence to supply details like these, when they are included, they are there for a reason. "When we are given some detail about a character's appearance or dress," says Adele Berlin, "it is usually because this information is needed for the plot."[14] This is clearly the case in the well-known story of David and Goliath (1 Sam 17).[15]

The opening verses of this story devote a significant amount of attention to Goliath. We quickly learn he is over six feet, which is extremely tall by ancient standards.[16] Not only is Goliath tall, he is also very, very strong. This is never said in so many words, but it is implied by his armor and weaponry. These items are described in unusual detail. We are told Goliath wore a bronze helmet, bronze shin guards, and "a coat of mail" weighing

---

[14] Adele Berlin, *Poetics and Interpretation of Biblical Literature* (Winona Lake, IN: Eisenbrauns, 1994), 34.

[15] My thanks to Terry Brensinger for introducing me to the concept of "functional details" by way of Goliath.

[16] While this might not seem all that tall by today's standards, people in antiquity were generally shorter than people today, so this would have been quite impressive. Goliath is even taller according to the Masoretic Text, where he is described as being over nine feet tall.

approximately 125 pounds (1 Sam 17:5-6). In addition, his weaponry included a bronze javelin, a sword, and a spear with an iron head weighing about fifteen pounds (1 Sam 17:6-7, 45). Goliath is portrayed as being so big and so powerful that he could defeat Captain American, Iron Man, and the Hulk *simultaneously* without even working up a sweat. The details about his height and strength create the image of an unstoppable warrior. He appears to be an undefeatable, insurmountable foe.

His opponent, on the other hand, is a young, inexperienced shepherd boy whose entire arsenal consists of nothing more than a homemade sling and some common stones. David doesn't stand a chance. But who emerges victorious? David! Why? Because he is skilled with a sling? No. Because God is on his side. At least that's what the writer wants you to believe. How else could such a victory be explained? All those details about Goliath help make this point forcefully.

Since we don't have space to discuss additional stories at length, let me briefly suggest two other examples you can explore on your own. Read the beginning of the story of Jacob and Esau (Gen 25:19-28). Why does the writer tell us that Esau was hairy (Gen 25:25)? Given the functional use of physical details in Old Testament narratives, we can be sure the writer is not telling us about Esau's hairiness just to give us a better mental picture of what he looked like. Instead, we are given this information because it is essential to the plot. Your job is to figure out how. If you need a hint, see Genesis 27.

For a less obvious example, take a look at the story about a Moabite king named Eglon and an Israelite judge named Ehud. We are told that Eglon, the king, "was a very fat man" (Judg 3:17) and that Ehud, his assassin, was "a left-handed man" (Judg 3:15). How are these physical details relevant to the storyline?[17]

While the use of repetition, naming, and physical details are just a few of the literary techniques used to write Old Testament narratives, paying attention to them will help you look at these old stories with new eyes.

---

[17]If you need some help with this one, see Alter, *Art of Biblical Narrative*, 38-39.

Knowing *what* to look for enhances your enjoyment of the Old Testament and enables you to understand it better.

If the thought of exploring literary features of Old Testament narratives really excites you, take a look at *Reading Biblical Narrative: An Introductory Guide* by J. P. Fokkelman or *Narrative in the Hebrew Bible* by David M. Gunn and Danna Nolan Fewell.[18] Books like these have much more to say about how Old Testament narratives were crafted, and they help you know what to look for when reading them, including things such as direct speech and characterization.[19]

SOME THINGS TO TRY AT HOME

In addition to paying attention to key literary techniques used to produce Old Testament narratives, there are many other ways to get more actively involved with these stories. A number of suggestions are offered here, with more to follow in the final section of the book.

Write character sketches of people in the Old Testament. Old Testament narratives are populated by lots of memorable characters—and some who are not so memorable. Many Christians are familiar with only a small percentage of these individuals. Often, even the most well-known characters in the Old Testament are not actually very well-known. If someone asked you what the Old Testament says about major figures like Abraham, Moses, or David, how much would you be able to tell them— *without* looking at the Bible? Or how much could you say about someone like Queen Esther or the prophet Elisha? We often know the headlines— "David kills a giant" and "Esther saves the Jews"—but many readers would be hard-pressed to fill in the details of their lives. This becomes even more difficult when talking about less prominent individuals, the kind that rarely, if ever, get mentioned in church such as Gehazi (see 2 Kings 4–5) or Baruch (see Jer 32, 36, 45).

---

[18]J. P. Fokkelman, *Reading Biblical Narrative: An Introductory Guide*, trans. Ineke Smit (Louisville, KY: Westminster John Knox, 1999); David M. Gunn and Danna Nolan Fewell, *Narrative in the Hebrew Bible* (Oxford: Oxford University Press, 1993).

[19]In addition to the aforementioned books, see Alter, *Art of Biblical Narrative*, 63-87 and 114-30, respectively, for these two features.

One way to get to know someone in the Old Testament better is by writing a character sketch, a brief synopsis of the person's life. Begin by selecting someone from the Old Testament who interests you. Then using a searchable online Bible, locate every occurrence of the person's name and make note of those passages.[20] Feel free to include any New Testament references you find as well. Depending on how this individual is named throughout the Old Testament, this search might not identify all the relevant passages, but it should help you find most of them. Read through these passages carefully to see what you can discover about the person you chose. As you read, here are some questions to keep in mind:

- What basic facts about the character's life can you discover (e.g., family connections, hometown, occupation)?

- What are this person's main accomplishments? What are the best and worst things the person does?

- How would you describe the overall portrayal of this character in the Old Testament: positive, negative, a mix of both, or something altogether different?

- Had you lived in ancient Israel, would you have wanted to be friends with this individual?

- What interesting details about this character's life do you feel are often overlooked?

- What would you like to know about this person but are not told?

As you do this, be honest about what you find. Churchgoers have a tendency to sanitize certain characters in the Bible, making them look better than they really are. But the Old Testament typically does not do this.[21] Rather, it tends to describe them warts and all. This makes them much more relatable to us. Even notable characters like Abraham, Moses, and David are not portrayed as being perfect. So feel free to

---

[20]For a collection of searchable Bibles online in many different versions, see Bible Gateway at www
.biblegateway.com/.

[21]For some exceptions, consider the way the Chronicler presents David and Solomon (discussed below).

discuss their strengths *and* their weaknesses, their successes *and* their failures.

Once you have worked through everything you can find, use what you have learned to write a short character sketch. Try limiting yourself to just a page or two that includes your most significant findings. To enhance your efforts, consider encouraging a friend or family member to do the same. Then compare notes and see what similarities and differences emerge in your respective character sketches. You might even consider drawing an artistic rendition of the person you examined if you are so inclined.[22]

If you want to go deeper, consider what others have written about the person you have sketched. A plethora of books are readily available for some characters, like David.[23] For others, like David's wife Michal, you may only find articles, chapters, or dictionary entries. Either way, after doing your own work, it is interesting to see what people have written.[24]

Look for important questions these stories raise. Old Testament narratives frequently raise profound questions that are often overlooked, especially by those who primarily regard the Bible as an "answer book." These questions should not be ignored. They open up space for thoughtful reflection and are worth pursuing.

To illustrate, consider the troubling account of the rape of Dinah in Genesis 34.[25] Dinah had gone to visit some women when Shechem rapes her and then expresses his desire to marry her (Gen 34:2-4). When Dinah's brothers learn what has happened, they are enraged and plan their revenge (Gen 34:6-7). They deceitfully lead Shechem to believe they will allow this marriage to go forward—and will themselves intermarry with his people

---

[22]For more about using art as a creative way to engage the Old Testament, see chapter eleven.

[23]See, e.g., Steven L. McKenzie, *King David: A Biography* (New York: Oxford University Press, 2000); Baden, *Historical David*; Jonathan Kirsch, *King David: The Real Life of the Man Who Ruled Israel* (New York: Ballantine, 2001).

[24]In chapter eleven, I'll discuss using creative writing to "recover" voices in the Old Testament that have been silenced or marginalized. By imaginatively telling some of these untold stories in the Old Testament, we gain a greater appreciation for these individuals.

[25]Not all scholars agree this is a rape story. For discussion and an argument that regards it as such, see Susanne Scholz, *Sacred Witness: Rape in the Hebrew Bible* (Minneapolis: Fortress, 2010), 32-38.

—on one condition: Shechem and the other men in the city must circumcise themselves (Gen 34:13-17). The Shechemites naively agree to this arrangement, and three days later, while Shechem and the other men are suffering the painful effects of this procedure, they are attacked by Simeon and Levi, Dinah's two *full* brothers. Neither Shechem nor any men in the city survive the massacre (Gen 34:25). The city is then plundered by Jacob's sons, and the women and children are taken captive (Gen 34:27-29).

When Jacob hears what his sons have done, he is *not* happy. He is worried that his sons' treacherous behavior will make him more vulnerable to attack (Gen 34:30). In response to their father's displeasure, Simeon and Levi ask, "Should our sister be treated like a whore?" (Gen 34:31). And that's where the story ends.

Rather than providing a neat set of answers, this narrative raises some very challenging questions. As Matthew Schlimm writes:

> Genesis 34 doesn't prescribe a course of action. It doesn't tell readers what they should do in response to the rape of a loved one. It doesn't end with a tidy solution. Instead, the story closes with an unanswered question. . . .
>
> Readers are left to wrestle with the human condition in all its limitations, confusion, and pain: What is the proper response to sexual violence? What should one do when a family member has been harmed and there are no good options for punishing the wrongdoer? How does one exact justice in the absence of possibilities commensurate with the offense? How can we create communities free from rape and violence?[26]

We could also add some additional questions that would help us consider Dinah's perspective. How did Dinah feel about Shechem's desire to marry her? What did she want her family to do in this situation? Did she approve of the way her brothers deceived and then massacred the men of Shechem? How is her silence in this story similar to, or different from, the silence of many women today who have been sexually assaulted? Questions like these are important and well worth exploring.

---

[26]Matthew Richard Schlimm, *This Strange and Sacred Scripture: Wrestling with the Old Testament and Its Oddities* (Grand Rapids, MI: Baker Academic, 2015), 65.

An answer to Schlimm's initial question, "What is the proper response to sexual violence?" is not found in Genesis 34. While sexual violence is absolutely unacceptable and demands a strong response, slaughtering sexual predators along with all their relatives is certainly *not* the way forward. A "proper response" needs to come from elsewhere: other parts of Scripture, conversations with survivors of sexual violence, books and articles written by experts in the field, and so forth. But the narrative provides a valuable service by raising the question in such a powerful way. This can serve as a gateway into difficult conversations, the kind we really need to have but tend to avoid. Old Testament stories like the rape of Dinah provide natural opportunities to talk about sexual violence and to confront issues of rape and sexual assault directly.

Therefore, when you read Old Testament narratives, consider what questions they might raise. Such questions are often implicit, and rarely stated directly. But they are present all the same, often hovering just below the surface of the text. Once identified, they become very useful points of departure for further reflection and discussion.

Explore parallel passages. A number of stories in the Old Testament appear more than once. For example, many of the stories about David in 1–2 Samuel, and about Solomon in 1 Kings 1–11, are also found in 1–2 Chronicles. Chronicles is thought to be written much later than Samuel and Kings, and it appears the Chronicler lifted material directly from these earlier sources.[27] Today, we would cry foul and charge the writer with plagiarism. But in the ancient world, it was acceptable to (re)use material this way. Sometimes the Chronicler essentially copied things word for word. But other times the Chronicler added to, or subtracted from, these stories for various reasons—to add an emphasis lacking elsewhere, to make a totally different point, to correct something deemed inaccurate, and so forth.

Looking for similarities and differences in parallel passages is intriguing and instructive. To illustrate, we'll consider a few examples. Take

---

[27]This is different from the way doublets in the Pentateuch (e.g., Gen 12:10-20 and 20:1-18; or Ex 17:1-7 and Num 20:1-13) were produced since these were written independently of one another.

a moment to read 1 Kings 8:6-13 and 2 Chronicles 5:7–6:2 and note what the Chronicler adds to his account. Did you find it? The Chronicler's version has lots of Levites singing and playing a wide array of instruments (2 Chron 5:12-13). It is not uncommon to find Levites in Chronicles when they are absent from parallel passages in Samuel and Kings. This emphasis on Levites, and on the temple and worship, is characteristic of the Chronicler.

Now read 1 Kings 10:28–11:8 and 2 Chronicles 9:28-29 and note what is missing from the Chronicler's account. What did you discover? The Chronicler makes no mention of Solomon's many misdeeds—like following after other gods! Written hundreds of years after the death of Solomon, this account presents us with a highly idealized and sanitized version of Israel's "wise" king.

The Chronicler does the same with David. If someone asked you to identify David's most well-known sin, what would you say? If you mentioned the Bathsheba-Uriah debacle in 2 Samuel 11, you nailed it. David lusts after Bathsheba, Uriah's *wife* (remember the importance of naming) and commands she be brought to the palace. David then commits adultery. Some time later, after Bathsheba reveals she is pregnant, David tries to cover up his reckless behavior, ultimately having Uriah, one of his most elite soldiers, killed. It's a real mess! The ramifications of David's actions are so catastrophic that the writer of 2 Samuel regards it as the turning point in the story of David's reign. So what does the Chronicler have to say about David's sexual indiscretion, abuse of power, and murder by proxy? Nary a word. The Chronicler omits this damning information in order to present David in a more favorable light. In this instance, comparing parallel passages reveals the Chronicler's intention to whitewash a revered figure from Israel's past.

In order to explore parallel passages, you have to find them first. There are several ways to do this. With respect to David and Solomon, you could flip back and forth between certain books of the Bible if you keep a few basic facts in mind: (1) the story of David in 2 Samuel finds many parallels in 1 Chronicles 11–29; (2) the story of Solomon in 1 Kings 1–11 finds many parallels in 2 Chronicles 1–9; and (3) the story of the southern kings of Judah in 1 Kings 12–2 Kings 25 finds many parallels in 2 Chronicles 10–36. Another way to locate parallel passages would be to use a searchable online Bible. Plugging in key terms and phrases can lead you to many parallel accounts. But the easiest way to do this, at least with regard to the material in Samuel, Kings, and Chronicles, is to purchase a book that lists parallel passages side by side. I would suggest a book like James Newsome's *A Synoptic Harmony of Samuel, Kings, and Chronicles.*[28] Be sure to put it on your Christmas or birthday list, and see what you can discover.

Investigate unfamiliar items. As noted earlier, reading the Old Testament is akin to traveling to a foreign country. Most people who travel abroad spend some time learning about the people and places they will be visiting before they depart. They may read about their culture or watch some YouTube videos to gain a better understanding of what to expect when they arrive. Learning what is culturally appropriate—what to wear, what to say, what kind of hand gestures to avoid—helps people successfully navigate their trip and minimizes the possibility of committing an embarrassing or potentially offensive faux pas.

This same kind of preparation is helpful for your journey through the Old Testament. When you open the Old Testament, you not only travel back in time, you travel across cultures. The pages of the Old Testament bring you face-to-face with unfamiliar customs and ideas since the people who produced these texts operated with many worldview assumptions that are radically different from our own. For example, they believed in a geocentric universe, arranged marriages, debt slavery, blood vengeance, a God who controlled conception—the list goes on. If we hope to make sense of these texts, let alone appreciate and enjoy them, we must first try to understand the world they describe. One way to do this is by learning more about the culture and practices of ancient Israel. Therefore, when you read the Old Testament and come across

---

[28]James D. Newsome, Jr., *A Synoptic Harmony of Samuel, Kings, and Chronicles: With Related Passages from Psalms, Isaiah, Jeremiah, and Ezra* (Eugene, OR: Wipf and Stock, 2006).

cultural practices or ideas that don't make sense to you, slow down and investigate them.

Let's say you are reading through the book of Ruth and notice frequent references to the practice of gleaning but don't really know much about this practice. What is gleaning? Why did people do it? Who was allowed to participate? It is worth your while to take time to explore this. Or suppose you are reading the book of Jonah and come to the part where the sailors cast lots to determine who is responsible for the storm. If you are uncertain what this practice entailed, or how people in the ancient world thought it worked, do some research and see what you learn about it.

One of the best places to find answers to questions like these is a Bible dictionary such as *Eerdmans Dictionary of the Bible* or the *HarperCollins Bible Dictionary*.[29] Books like these are an excellent place to start and are relatively inexpensive. In addition, some resources are specifically devoted to helping people navigate the ancient culture of the biblical world. Books like *Life in Biblical Israel* by Philip J. King and Lawrence Stager or *The Cultural World of the Bible* by Victor H. Matthews are very helpful in this regard.[30]

If you don't have access to these kinds of resources and prefer not to purchase them, you can visit a trusted online site such as Bible Odyssey (bibleodyssey.org). You could also consult a knowledgeable pastor or well-informed churchgoer. Individuals like these can be a wealth of information and are often happy to help. Making some effort to find answers to your questions about the unique culture and history of ancient Israel and its surroundings will enhance your understanding and appreciation of this part of the Old Testament.

Be irrepressibly curious, ask lots of questions, and answer the most important ones. One of the easiest ways of improving your enjoyment of Old Testament narratives involves fostering your own curiosity by

---

[29]See the appendix under the heading "Bible Dictionaries and Encyclopedias."
[30]See the appendix under the heading "Culture of Ancient Israel."

asking various questions of the text and then answering those you find most interesting.[31] Here is a sampling:

- What does this passage teach me about sin? About forgiveness? About God? About faithfulness? About deliverance? And so on.
- What can I learn about life in ancient Israel from this text?
- What does this story suggest about Israel's worldview? How is that similar to, or different from, my own?
- What view of women does this passage present?
- Did this story actually happen? Would my understanding of it change if I concluded it did not?
- From whose perspective is this passage written? Whose perspectives are not represented?
- How does God behave in this story? Which divine actions are most attractive and which are most disturbing?
- What are some of the main themes of this narrative? How do these correspond to other parts of the Bible?

The best questions tend to be open-ended (e.g., How are sailors characterized in Jonah 1?) rather than closed (e.g., To which city was Jonah traveling?). Open-ended questions allow space for exploration and discovery, whereas closed questions are more restrictive and limiting. Questions that focus on the significance and relevance of what happens (e.g., What does the story of the burning bush in Exodus 3 suggest about God's call?) tend to be more helpful than those which inquire after interesting, albeit secondary concerns (e.g., How was it possible that the bush kept burning without being consumed?). Questions of significance and relevance lead you deeper into Old Testament stories and can help you make new discoveries.

---

[31]For some additional guidance in how to "Ask Questions and Find Answers," see David L. Thompson, *Bible Study that Works* (Nappanee, IN: Evangel, 1994), 44-64.

Learning to ask good questions takes time and practice, but it yields great results. The better your questions, the more likely you are to have a higher degree of satisfaction exploring these fascinating stories.

Conclusion

I hope this chapter has ignited (or reignited) your passion for Old Testament narratives. As you experiment with the suggestions offered here, be prepared for new insights and fresh perspectives to emerge. There are countless ways to approach these texts, and we will consider more of them in the final section of the book. Hopefully, enough has already been said to encourage you to engage Old Testament narratives with renewed enthusiasm and excitement. These stories are worth lingering over, like a good meal with close friends. There is much to be savored. Bon appétit!

7

BEING PERSUADED
by the PROPHETS

Whether we are comfortable with the prophetic voice or not, we sense that when the prophet speaks, truth is on offer. And the richest literary source about prophets in the cultural heritage of Western civilization is the Old Testament.

Carolyn J. Sharp, *Old Testament Prophets for Today*

PROPHETIC LITERATURE IS AMONG some of the most neglected material in the entire Old Testament. In many Christian traditions, sermons are rarely preached from prophetic books, and few churchgoers would identify these books as their favorite part of the Old Testament. With the possible exception of Jonah, the vast majority of Christians would be hard-pressed to summarize any of the twelve Minor Prophets. Most would struggle to say anything at all about books like Habakkuk, Zephaniah, Haggai, or Zechariah. (This Sunday, ask some folks at church to give you a thirty second summary of one of these books and watch what happens. Be prepared for blank stares and awkward silence.) These books are largely lost to the church—even though we still carry them around in our Bible. This is unfortunate, to say the least. We deprive ourselves of significant resources for our journey with God when we neglect this section of the Old Testament.

Admittedly, prophetic literature is not always easy to comprehend. If you have ever struggled to make sense of it, you are not alone. This is not to suggest the prophets aren't worth the time and effort it takes to understand them, it just means we sometimes need to be a little more patient and do a bit more work to enjoy this part of the Bible. Despite the challenges, there are riches waiting to be discovered.

Before we can truly appreciate prophetic literature, it is important to know a little something about the prophets themselves. Yet knowing what to expect from the prophets is complicated by some deeply entrenched misconceptions surrounding them. Therefore, it is necessary to clear the air, so to speak, before proceeding. What follows is a crash course on Hebrew prophets designed to do just that.

PROPHETS AND PROPHETIC LITERATURE 101

Scholars routinely classify Hebrew prophets into one of two categories: early prophets and latter prophets. The early prophets are sometimes also known as the nonwriting prophets. This is not because they couldn't write, though many probably couldn't, but because there are no books of the Bible named after them filled with their prophetic speeches. Early prophets include individuals such as Moses (Deut 34:10), Samuel (1 Sam 3:20), the court prophet Nathan (2 Sam 12), and the ever-fascinating Elijah and Elisha (1 Kings 17–2 Kings 13). Generally speaking, with these prophets the emphasis is on what they *did* rather than what they said (Moses being a significant outlier). In a number of cases, these prophets performed various miracles. For example, in the span of just a few chapters, the prophet Elisha brings a widow's son back to life (2 Kings 4:18-37), cures a man of leprosy (2 Kings 5:1-14), makes an iron ax head float (2 Kings 6:1-7), and strikes foreign soldiers with temporary blindness (2 Kings 6:8-23).

The other category of prophets in the Old Testament, the latter prophets, are sometimes referred to as the classical or writing prophets. In contrast to the early prophets, there *are* books in the Bible named after them filled with their prophetic speeches. Though there are an unspecified number of *early* prophets, there are exactly fifteen latter prophets. Their oracles and certain details about their lives are contained in the fifteen books that bear their name, books that are referred to (unsurprisingly) as the Latter Prophets. They include the three *Major* Prophets (Isaiah, Jeremiah, and Ezekiel) plus the twelve *Minor* Prophets (Hosea–Malachi). With the latter prophets, the emphasis tends to be on what they said rather than what they did. This is not to suggest their deeds were unimportant—they certainly were. But latter prophets were not miracle workers. Their message was key. Since the Latter Prophets constitute such a significant and distinctive part of the Old Testament, they are the focus of this chapter.

THE MO OF THE LATTER PROPHETS

We don't know very much about the personal lives of these fifteen latter prophets, such as what they did when they were not prophesying (some had very short prophetic ministries), where they were from (known for only about one-third of them), or who their father was (only about half are known). For four of the latter prophets—Obadiah, Habakkuk, Haggai, and Malachi—we know absolutely nothing about them beyond the oracles attributed to them. No personal details are given about their lives and none of these four prophets appear anywhere else in the Bible.

A short prophetic profile. While this lack of biographical information may be disappointing, it is not entirely unexpected given the primary nature of the prophetic task: to proclaim God's word to the people. It was the *message* that was most important, not the messenger. Before we consider *what* they said, it is helpful to say a few words about *how* they said it and what they were trying to accomplish.

Public speakers. To begin, it is important to keep in mind that the latter prophets were public speakers who delivered prophetic speeches in public places to live audiences. This was their primary mode of operation. These prophetic speeches, or oracles, were given at different times and places. They could be addressed to the political elite, to religious leaders, or to the general population. While it is true that Israelite prophets frequently spoke *about* other nations, they spoke directly *to* the people of Israel and Judah.[1]

---

[1] Jonah's unusually brief oracle to the Ninevites is a noteworthy exception to this (Jon 3:4).

With the exception of the book of Jonah, each of the Latter Prophets contains a *collection* of oracles delivered by the namesake of the book. Sometimes it is easy to tell where one oracle stops and the next one begins. Other times it is not. Sometimes we have a fairly good idea of when the oracle was spoken and to whom. Other times, these things are very difficult to determine. What we do know is this: prophets were public speakers who proclaimed their messages in face-to-face encounters with others.

People who regarded themselves as God's messengers. Prophets were not your average run-of-the-mill public orators. Rather, they regarded themselves as God's messengers. That is why their oracles often begin with the words, "Thus says the Lord." They firmly believed they were communicating an authoritative word from God and were willing to risk punishment and even death for speaking it. You have to be very convinced of the truthfulness of your message when the stakes are so high.

Of course, not everyone who claimed to be delivering God's word was actually doing so. There were true *and* false prophets in ancient Israel, and sometimes it was rather difficult to tell one from the other. According to Deuteronomy 18:22, the surefire way to determine if someone was a true prophet was to see if their prophecy came true. If it did, you could be certain they were a true prophet. If it did not, you knew they were the other kind.

While this criterion would have been reassuring *after* the fact, it would have been less helpful before a prophetic word came to pass, especially if two prophets claiming to speak for God were giving opposite advice. This was a real dilemma facing people in the ancient world. For an especially poignant example, consider the contrasting prophetic messages given by Jeremiah and Hananiah when the people of Judah were threatened by the Babylonians (see Jer 28). Jeremiah urged the people to surrender to the Babylonians while Hananiah encouraged them to wait upon God's deliverance. Had you lived during that time, to whom would you have listened?

Historically relevant communicators. Probably the greatest misconception about the prophets concerns the nature of their prophetic oracles. Many people believe prophets were clairvoyant, able to see the future and predict forthcoming events with amazing accuracy and detail. The "prophecy" section of Christian bookstores bears eloquent witness to this. Their shelves are lined with books written by authors who assume prophetic literature is predictive of *contemporary* political and historical events. Consider, for example, John Walvoord's book *Armageddon, Oil, and the Middle East Crisis.* At one point Walvoord writes:

> The prophet Ezekiel described the time when Russia will make a military bid for power in the Middle East. The prophetic chapters of Ezekiel 38 and 39 . . . clearly describe a horde of armed might invading Israel from the north. The names given to the leader, the country, and the cities, as well as the clear description of armies out of "your place in the far north" (Ezek. 38:15), could only refer to what we know today as Russia.[2]

While such speculative interpretation is tantalizing, it is completely unwarranted. Israelite prophets were not crystal ball gazers. They did not speak of military operations that would take place thousands of years in the future by countries not yet in existence. While it *is* true that the prophets often spoke about the future, "it was usually the *immediate* future of Israel, Judah, and other nations surrounding them that they announced rather than our future."[3] Thus, it is best to think of Israelite prophets primarily as "forthtellers rather than foretellers, proclaimers, messengers, or 'preachers' rather than predictors."[4] The prophets were historically relevant communicators who had much more in common with passionate preachers today than with mystic fortunetellers.

---

[2]John F. Walvoord, *Armageddon, Oil, and the Middle East Crisis: What the Bible Says About the Future of the Middle East and the End of Western Civilization* (Grand Rapids, MI: Zondervan, 1991), 141.

[3]Gordon D. Fee and Douglas Stuart, *How to Read the Bible for All Its Worth*, 4th ed. (Grand Rapids, MI: Zondervan, 2014), 188, emphasis mine.

[4]Steven L. McKenzie, *How to Read the Bible: History, Prophecy, Literature—Why Modern Readers Need to Know the Difference and What It Means for Faith Today* (New York: Oxford University Press, 2005), 68.

Israelite prophets addressed the social and religious concerns of their day and "revealed" what God was planning to do. Of course, these plans could change depending on the people's response.

> At one moment I (God) may declare concerning a nation or a kingdom, that I will pluck up and break down and destroy it, but if that nation, concerning which I have spoken, turns from its evil, I will change my mind about the disaster that I intended to bring on it. And at another moment I may declare concerning a nation or a kingdom that I will build and plant it, but if it does evil in my sight, not listening to my voice, then I will change my mind about the good that I had intended to do to it. (Jer 18:7-10)

Prophets announced God's intentions. But those plans were alterable. Ultimately, God's actions would be conditioned by the people's response. If people changed their ways, God's plans could change as well. This is exactly what happens when Jonah preaches to the Ninevites. The people repent, God relents, and the city is spared (Jon 3:10).

Readers who are unaware of the conditional nature of prophecy often have unrealistic expectations of it. They reduce prophecy to a set of predictions that are fulfilled in the future. While some prophecy certainly functions this way, this view is far too simplistic to account for all that's going on in prophetic literature.

This is *not* to suggest the prophetic word had no relevance beyond its initial audience. It most certainly did. The New Testament's appeal to numerous prophetic texts makes this abundantly clear. But the prophetic word must first and foremost be understood in its original context. Prophesy was designed to persuade people to respond appropriately to an urgent word from God. By making people aware of God's intentions toward them, prophets created space and opportunity for them to align their ways with God's.

Passionately persuasive speakers. One of the most distinctive features of prophetic speech is the use of persuasion. Like all preachers worth their salt, the prophets desperately wanted people to hear and heed their message. Prophets were *not* mindless robots giving word-for-word recitations of scripted speeches sent down from on high. Instead, the prophets had enormous freedom deciding how to craft their oracles—and it appears they spent a considerable amount of time and energy doing so. As Terry Brensinger observes:

> The prophets did more than simply stand up on street corners and deliver emotion-packed, unrehearsed speeches. On the contrary, while they undoubtedly did precisely that at times, there are other occasions when great care and planning stand behind both the prophetic message as well as the literary forms through which it finds expression.[5]

Prophets took great pains to speak persuasively because they wanted people to respond appropriately.

Persuasive techniques. What follows is a brief sampling of some common persuasive techniques used in prophetic oracles. Learning to recognizing these, and seeing how they work, increases our understanding of the Latter Prophets and enhances our enjoyment of prophetic literature.

Rhetorical questions. Prophets sometimes used rhetorical questions in their efforts to persuade. A rhetorical question is one that expects no answer since the answer is so obvious it renders a reply unnecessary. That said, whenever rhetorical questions are used in the Old Testament, the right answer would always be "no."

Consider the following rhetorical question spoken by the prophet Jeremiah:

> Can a girl forget her ornaments, or a bride her attire?

The obvious answer is, "Of course not. That's ridiculous!" Have *you* ever seen a bride walk down the aisle in blue jeans, a T-shirt, and tennis shoes because—oops!—she forgot to bring her wedding dress that day? It's ludicrous! Yet the moment Jeremiah has everyone shaking their head at the absurdity of it all, he continues with this zinger:

> Yet my people have forgotten me, days without number. (Jer 2:32)

---

[5]Terry L. Brensinger, *Simile and Prophetic Language in the Old Testament*, Mellon Biblical Press Series 43 (Lewiston, NY: Edward Mellon, 1996), 148.

Ouch. The notion that the people of Israel could forget God was just as incomprehensible as the image of a bride forgetting her dress on her wedding day.[6] Yet this is precisely what Israel has done. By using this rhetorical question, Jeremiah delivers a powerful indictment that would hopefully get people's attention and persuade them to amend their ways.

Simile. A simile compares two essentially unlike things, often using the words "like" or "as." In his book *Simile and Prophetic Language in the Old Testament,* Terry Brensinger catalogs over five hundred similes in prophetic literature.[7] Consider this example from the prophet Hosea:

> What shall I do with you, O Ephraim?
> What shall I do with you, O Judah?
> Your love is like a morning cloud,
> like the dew that goes away early. (Hos 6:4)

Comparing Israel's love for God to "a morning cloud" and "the dew that goes away early" is clearly *un*favorable. Like dew, a morning cloud is temporary and does not stay around very long. Hosea claims there is a fickleness to Israel's love. It is there for a while and then gone.

The use of natural imagery would have certainly helped people grasp what Hosea was saying. In addition, this imagery had real staying power. It is not difficult to imagine Israelites waking up the next morning and remembering the words of the prophet when their feet hit the ground. As they stepped outside and felt the cool dew between their toes, Hosea's message would come rushing back to their minds. Ideally, it would also prompt them to correct their lackluster love for God.

Metaphor. In addition to similes, prophets used a lot of metaphors to persuade. Metaphors step things up a notch. Rather than *comparing* two essentially unlike things, metaphors *equate* them. Consider this example from the book of Isaiah:

> Israel's sentinels [watchmen] are blind,
> they are all without knowledge;

---

[6]For some other examples, see Amos 3:3-6; 6:12-13.
[7]Brensinger, *Simile and Prophetic Language,* 4.

they are all silent dogs that cannot bark;
dreaming, lying down, loving to slumber. (Is 56:10)

Many cities in the ancient world were walled for security and defense. Sentinels, or watchmen, were strategically positioned on these walls to scan the horizon and alert city dwellers if they saw danger coming. In Isaiah 56:10, the prophet refers to Israel's leaders as sentinels and disparagingly refers to them as "silent dogs that cannot bark." Obviously, a mute watchdog is not terribly effective. Israel's leaders, the very people who should be most concerned about the physical and spiritual well-being of the city's inhabitants, are portrayed as being utterly useless in this regard. They are asleep on the job. The prophet's silent dog metaphor makes this point persuasively, a stinging indictment on their failure of leadership.

Personification. Personification, the attribution of human characteristics to nonhuman objects, is another persuasive technique the prophets used at times. When using personification, the prophets speak of "something non-human . . . as if it were human."[8] Notice what the mountains, hills, and trees are doing:

For you shall go out in joy,
and be led back in peace;
the mountains and the hills before you shall burst into song,
and all the trees of the field shall clap their hands. (Is 55:12)

Obviously, mountains and hills don't possess vocal cords, and trees don't have hands to clap. The prophet personifies these aspects of the natural world to give hope to people living in Babylonian exile, hundreds of miles from home. Not only are they going to return home (something basically unheard of for people living in exile), their return trip is going to be so spectacular that all creation will join in celebration. Talk about imagination! The prophet's use of personification is designed to persuade the exilic community that God has not forgotten them. A good future lies ahead.

---

[8]William W. Klein, Craig L. Blomberg, and Robert L. Hubbard, Jr., *Introduction to Biblical Interpretation* (Dallas: Word, 1993), 246.

The persuasive techniques we have sampled here are just the tip of the iceberg. They had many others at their disposal. Sometimes they couched their oracles in the form of a covenant lawsuit to make their appeal. Other times, they put their oracles in the form of a dirge or drew on historical analogies in hopes of being persuasive. They did not hesitate to use shocking imagery and provocative rhetoric in their passionate efforts to convince people of the truth of their message.

As you read through the Latter Prophets, pay attention to the persuasive techniques they use. See if you can determine what they were attempting to persuade people to believe or do and why. As a point of application, reflect on the persuasive techniques you find most compelling and consider whether you yourself would be willing to use these to persuade someone to behave a certain way or adopt a certain belief.

JUDGMENT ORACLES AND SALVATION ORACLES

Before offering a number of creative ways to explore the prophets, it is helpful to say a few words about their two primary forms of prophetic speech, judgment oracles and salvation oracles. Some prophetic books, like Micah, appear to be structured between alternating judgment and salvation oracles. Other books, like Nahum, consist of nothing but judgment oracles. Of the two, judgment oracles appear far more frequently than salvation oracles, giving this part of the Old Testament a feeling of doom and gloom.

Judgment oracles. Judgment oracles have three basic parts: an indictment, a messenger formula, and an announcement of judgment. The *indictment*, or accusation, consists of specific charges of wrongdoing which the prophet brings against an individual or nation. When reading judgment oracles, pay close attention to the indictments being leveled against the people.

> Hear the word of the LORD, O people of Israel; for the LORD has an indictment against the inhabitants of the land. There is no faithfulness or loyalty, and no knowledge of God in the land. Swearing, lying, and murder, and stealing and adultery break out; bloodshed follows bloodshed. (Hos 4:1-2)

The prophet accuses the people of swearing, lying, murder, stealing, and adultery. Where else are these sins grouped together in the Old Testament? In Exodus 20. They are part of the Ten Commandments, the laws which serve as the foundation of the covenant God makes with Israel at Mount Sinai. Hosea claims the people have violated that covenant.

Sometimes Israel is indicted for their worship of other gods. Jeremiah indicts the people for a variety of illicit worship practices: baking cakes to the queen of heaven (Jer 7:18), loving and serving "the sun and the moon and all the hosts of heaven" (Jer 8:2), prophesying by Baal, the West-Semitic storm god (Jer 2:8; 23:13), and offering their children to Molech (Jer 32:35). Their devotion to other deities was so rampant that at one point Jeremiah cries out, "Your gods have become as many as your towns, O Judah" (Jer 11:13; cf. Jer 8:1-3; 44:1-30).

As noted earlier, other prophets, like Amos, were outraged by the injustice taking place in Israel, particularly the way people were getting rich on the backs of the poor. Impoverished Israelites who were unable to pay off small debts were sold into slavery (Amos 2:6), the legal system was rife with bribery and corruption (Amos 5:12), and merchants routinely cheated people in the marketplace (Amos 8:5).

The second part of a judgment oracle is called *the messenger formula*. This consists of the formulaic saying, "Thus says the LORD," or some version thereof. By uttering these words, the prophet claims to be speaking a word from God, one with great power and authority.

This final part of the judgment oracle, the *announcement of judgment*, could be thought of as the "sentence" for the people's sins, albeit one that might be altered depending on their response. The prophet might declare they will be handed over to their enemies or that their land will be laid waste. Jeremiah says "sword, famine, and pestilence" will befall the inhabitants of Jerusalem (Jer 24:10). Prophetic words of judgment often paint a general picture of impending doom rather than describing exactly what will happen.

Salvation oracles. Many people find salvation oracles much easier to appreciate since they are more positive and hopeful (e.g., Jer 31:31-34;

Hos 14:4-9; Amos 9:11-15; Mic 7:18-20). They promise restoration, or deliverance, from enemies and are often spoken after some great disaster has befallen Israel. They generally consist of words of assurance, healing, and restoration. These words often include a reminder of God's presence, which implies divine favor, protection, and ongoing relationship. This would have been very reassuring to people who believed they were being punished by God.

> When you pass through the waters, I will be with you;
> and through the rivers, they shall not overwhelm you;
> when you walk through fire you shall not be burned,
> and the flame shall not consume you. . . .
> Do not fear, for I am with you;
> I will bring your offspring from the east,
> and from the west I will gather you. (Is 43:2, 5)

In addition, these words of assurance sometimes include a promise of future transformation (cf. Ezek 36). God will fundamentally change people so they can live in obedience to God and avoid further divine judgment.

> A new heart I will give you, and a new spirit I will put within you. . . . I will put my spirit within you, and make you follow my statutes and be careful to observe my ordinances. Then you shall live in the land that I gave to your ancestors; and you shall be my people, and I will be your God. (Ezek 36:26-28)

A prophetic word like this would have been extremely good news to people feeling estranged from God, living in exile far from home. Such oracles would have given people great hope and encouragement.

How to Have More Fun with the Prophets

Now that we have a better sense of who prophets were and how they operated, we are ready to consider some practical things we can do to have more fun with prophetic literature.

Learn some basic information about the prophet's historical context. As I have repeatedly emphasized, there are many ways to increase your enjoyment of the Old Testament that do not require specialized training or a personal library full of scholarly tomes about the Old Testament. We'll devote a lot of attention to creative things that can be done with the text itself in the coming chapters, especially in the final section of the book.

That said, it is also true that utilizing the work of biblical scholars and other specialists is incredibly beneficial and can help you have more satisfying encounters with the Old Testament.[9] This is especially the case when it comes to reading the prophets. Since prophets were rooted in history, they spoke in particular times and places. Knowing something about their historical context goes a long way toward better understanding their message and mission. This makes reading their oracles much more meaningful.

But how can you learn more about a prophet's historical context? Many times, you can figure out when a prophet was active based on information provided by the Old Testament itself. Many prophetic books actually begin by situating the prophet historically. For example, the prophet Amos, spoke "in the days of King Uzziah of Judah and in the days of King Jeroboam son of Joash of Israel, two years before the earthquake" (Amos 1:1). With this information, you could use an online searchable Bible to find other places these kings appear. This would lead you to 2 Kings 15:1-7, where you read about the reign of Uzziah (a.k.a. Azariah), and 2 Kings 14:23-29, which describes the reign of Jeroboam II. These passages provide some context, and it is beneficial to learn all you can this way.

A fuller sense of the historical context can be found in a number of secondary sources. Most standard introductory textbooks on the Old Testament will provide this information.[10] Likewise, reputable one-volume Bible commentaries such as the *Oxford Bible Commentary* and the *HarperCollins Bible Commentary* have brief introductions that are helpful in this regard.[11] Good quality study Bibles, like *The New Oxford*

---

[9]See the appendix for selected resources.
[10]See the appendix under the heading "Old Testament Introductions."
[11]See the appendix under the heading "Commentaries (One Volume)."

Annotated Bible or *The New Interpreter's Study Bible,* also provide some historical context immediately prior to the book in question.[12]

It is worth checking out resources like these whenever you read and study the Latter Prophets. Take an hour or so and see what you can discover. Find out when the prophet was active and explore what was happening nationally and internationally at the time. What was the social, political, and economic climate like? Was it a time of safety, security, and financial prosperity for Israel? What kind of threats were looming on the horizon? Having a basic understanding of the prophet's historical context will enable you to make much more sense of what you are reading.

To illustrate, consider this familiar Old Testament passage often read in church during Advent:

> Comfort, O comfort my people, says your God.
> Speak tenderly to Jerusalem and cry to her
> that she has served her term, that her penalty is paid,
> that she has received from the LORD's hand double for all her sins.
> A voice cries out: "In the wilderness prepare the way of the LORD,
>   make straight in the desert a highway for our God.
> Every valley shall be lifted up, and every mountain and hill be made low;
> the uneven ground shall become level, and the rough places a plain.
> Then the glory of the LORD shall be revealed,
>   and all people shall see it together, for the mouth of the LORD has
>   spoken." (Is 40:1-5)

These words have been immortalized in Handel's majestic *Messiah.* People sing heartily about valleys being lifted up and mountains and hills being made low—but many have absolutely no idea what any of it means! Why? Because we are unfamiliar with the historical context.

At the beginning of the sixth century BCE, the Babylonian empire was a serious threat to the tiny southern kingdom of Judah. In 597 BCE, King Nebuchadnezzar took many people from Jerusalem into exile (2 Kings 24:1-17). A decade later, the city lay in ruins (2 Kings 25:1-21).

---

[12]See the appendix under the heading "Study Bibles."

Nebuzaradan, an official who served King Nebuchadnezzar, destroyed the city walls, burned down the temple, the royal palace, and fancy homes, and then took more people into exile (2 Kings 25:9-11).

The people of Judah knew that going to Babylon was a one-way trip. They had no expectation of ever returning to their beloved homeland. Who was this audacious prophet speaking a subversive message of hope?[13] He claimed their judgment was over and said God was going to bring them home again. It must have sounded like sheer nonsense. So in an effort to persuade his audience, the prophet paints a mental picture for them. He says, in effect, "God is going to build a superhighway through the middle of the desert. God will lower mountains and raise valleys. You will have a level path before you, making it smooth sailing all the way from Babylon to Jerusalem." These words gave people hope in the midst of their despair. Yet it's hard to grasp the meaning and significance of this prophetic oracle without having a basic understanding of the historical context of the passage.

When you read and study the prophets, be sure to take some time to situate them in real time and space. It will enhance your enjoyment of them considerably.

Keep some Bible maps close at hand. In their oracles, prophets often refer to cities and countries that are unfamiliar to us. Even if we have heard of them, many of us would be hard-pressed to find them on a map. But knowing where these places are located can help us better understand what we are reading.

In the first two chapters of Amos, the prophet utters eight short judgment oracles, each beginning with the same formulaic expression: "Thus says the LORD: For three transgressions of (place name) and for four, // I will not revoke the punishment." Each oracle is directed to a specific place: Damascus, Gaza, Tyre, Edom, Ammon, Moab, Judah, and Israel (Amos 1:3, 6, 9, 11, 13; 2:1, 4, 6). Take a moment to look at figure 7.1

---

[13]Many scholars believe the book of Isaiah contains oracles from more than one prophet. Isaiah 40–55 is often referred to as "Second Isaiah." The prophet who spoke these words is thought to have delivered them to the people of Judah living in Babylonian exile.

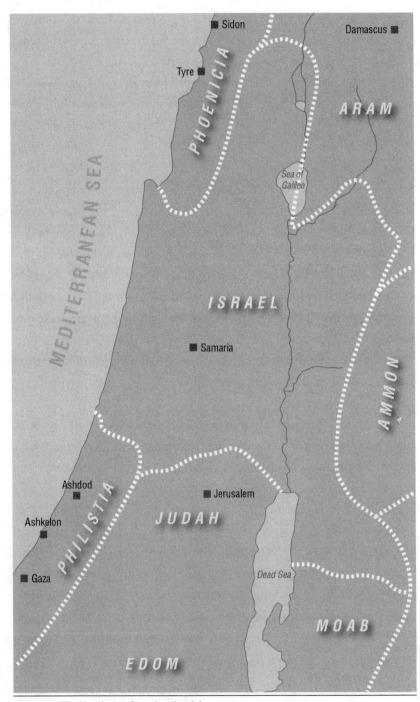

Figure 7.1. The kingdoms of Israel and Judah

and identify each of these locations, beginning with Damascus and ending with Israel.[14]

What do you notice? You should have observed that the first seven countries border Israel.[15] They are Israel's closest neighbors, and many are traditional enemies. As Amos pronounces judgment on one country after another, his listeners would have been cheering him on. "That's right, Amos. Preach it! Let those dirty rotten Damascans get what they've got coming to them." Amos is preaching to the choir, and they are absolutely loving it—until he gets to Judah.

Keep in mind that Amos is prophesying to the *northern* kingdom of Israel.[16] When Amos singles out the *southern* kingdom of Judah for judgment, the applause is not quite as loud, and the cheers are somewhat muted. There are expressions of concern and furrowed brows in the crowd. Even though there was often significant tension between Israel and Judah, collectively they were still one people. When these words of judgment are pronounced over Judah, you can almost hear the northerners in the crowd mumbling, "It's true. They *are* southerners and don't do things the right way down there. But, gee, we're still family."

But before they can resolve this cognitive dissonance, Amos fires off his eighth and final salvo: a judgment oracle against Israel itself! In doing so, Amos concludes his succession of judgment oracles in dramatic fashion, indicting the very people he is addressing. It is a brilliant rhetorical strategy. Amos has the crowd right where he wants them when he unleashes his critique. Yet the persuasive power of Amos's rhetorical strategy is difficult to appreciate fully without a basic knowledge of the location of the places he references.[17]

Knowing where places are located is also quite helpful when reading the book of Jonah. Commanded to go to Nineveh, Jonah goes to Joppa

---

[14]See the appendix under the heading "Bible Maps."

[15]Sometimes the capital city is used as a metonym for the entire country.

[16]After the death of Solomon, Israel divided into two parts: Israel in the north and Judah in the south, each with their own king. See 1 Kings 11:26–12:33.

[17]I am indebted to Herbert Huffmon for insight into the persuasive power and strategy of Amos's rhetoric in Amos 1–2 and for some of the ways I have discussed that here (e.g., the comments about Judah being family, albeit southerners who do things differently).

and boards a boat bound for Tarshish. If you look at a map, you will discover that Nineveh is about five hundred miles *east* of Jonah's location. Tarshish is as far *west* of his position as you can go before falling off the edge of the map! Knowing the location of these places helps you realize just how determined Jonah was to flee from God's presence (Jon 1:3, 10). Jonah is like a person from Pennsylvania, called to minister in Germany, who buys a one-way ticket to Hawaii! He wants to put as much distance as he can between himself and God.

Put prophetic speech in contemporary language. As we have seen, Israelite prophets talk about things from long ago and far away. They mention places we have never visited, practices we no longer observe, and people we have never met. For that reason, their words may feel foreign to us, and we sometimes struggle to read and apply these texts.

One way to address this challenge is to paraphrase their oracles using contemporary language. To illustrate, consider this celebrated passage from the book of Amos:

> I hate, I despise your festivals,
> and I take no delight in your solemn assemblies.
> Even though you offer me your burnt offerings and grain offerings,
> I will not accept them;
> and the offerings of well-being of your fatted animals
> I will not look upon.
> Take away from me the noise of your songs;
> I will not listen to the melody of your harps.
> But let justice roll down like waters,
> and righteousness like an ever-flowing stream. (Amos 5:21-24)

In dramatic fashion, Amos emphasizes the critical importance of doing justice. As Amos sees it, participating in religious rituals, while at the same time engaging in acts of injustice, is totally unacceptable to God. His sharp words decrying offerings and feast days must have struck some Israelites as scandalous. After all, weren't these things the very heart of Israel's worship? But Amos isn't pulling any punches. He insists that religiosity without righteousness is worthless.

It is difficult for most Christians to feel the full effect of these words since making sacrifices and celebrating festivals like Passover are not part of the Christian tradition. To recapture some of the original power of these prophetic words, you can "update" this prophetic speech by paraphrasing it. To illustrate, consider my *very* loose paraphrase of Amos 5:21-24:

> I don't care that you go to church every Sunday, put lots of money in the offering plate, do your devotions with religious regularity, fast, go on spiritual retreats, and sing worship songs at the top of your lungs until you are blue in the face. Stop it! It makes me nauseous. The fact that you cheat people in the marketplace on Monday, and speak falsely about your neighbor in court on Tuesday, means you have missed the whole point. What I want is simple: justice for all people, all the time.

Modernizing Amos's words underscores their gravity and enables us to hear his message more clearly and powerfully.

If putting prophetic speech into modern-day language feels like a daunting task, try reading modern paraphrases like Eugene Peterson's rendering of this passage in *The Message*:

> I can't stand your religious meetings.
> I'm fed up with your conferences and conventions.
> I want nothing to do with your religion projects,
> your pretentious slogans and goals.
> I'm sick of your fund-raising schemes,
> your public relations and image making.
> I've had all I can take of your noisy ego-music.
> When was the last time you sang to *me*?
> Do you know what I want?
> I want justice—oceans of it.
> I want fairness—rivers of it.
> That's what I want. That's *all* I want. (Amos 5:21-24, emphasis original)

Paraphrases like these help us contextualize the prophetic word in the modern world. In so doing, they enable us to find various points of connection to our own lives.

Write your own judgment or salvation oracle. One creative way to get more actively involved with the prophets is to use their oracles as a template to craft your own. Try writing a judgment oracle, for example. Begin by identifying your target audience. To whom is this directed? Are you speaking to family members, coworkers, fellow churchgoers, government officials, corporate America, or a group of friends—folks in your book club or the people you work out with at the gym? With your audience firmly in mind, carefully consider what you want to say. What indictments will you bring? What kinds of consequences do you envision? As you write, feel free to borrow and adapt persuasive techniques used by Israelite prophets or come up with some of your own. What can be said that will have the greatest potential to convince people to see things differently? What might actually cause them to change their behavior and beliefs? Once you have finished your oracle, give some thought to what you will do with it. Will you share it with others? Use it, or parts of it, to speak out on issues that are important to you?

If you are not a fan of creative writing, or don't think you would enjoy producing a prophetic oracle, consider keeping an ongoing list of things you think prophets would say to people today. Alternately, if you want to forego writing altogether, gather a group of friends and ask them what message they think prophets would have for various groups of people such as church leaders, business owners, politicians, and the like. You could then reflect on how practices like these deepen your appreciation for the work and ministry of Israelite prophets.

Provide descriptive monikers for the prophets. The last three activities suggested in this chapter are quite simple but still helpful for getting you more engaged with prophetic literature. The first one involves creating a descriptive moniker (i.e., title) for each of the prophets. This could be done for both the early and the latter prophets.

As you encounter individual prophets, pay attention to their unique characteristics and concerns. Then, associate an adjective or short descriptive phrase with each of them. For example, Jeremiah is often referred to as the "weeping" prophet because of verses like Jeremiah 9:1:

O that my head were a spring of water,
and my eyes a fountain of tears,
so that I might weep day and night
for the slain of my poor people!

Yet when I think of Jeremiah, I think of him as the "suffering" prophet because of all he has to endure (e.g., he is not allowed to marry or have children, Jer 16:1-2; he is put in stocks, Jer 20:1-2; he is beaten and imprisoned, Jer 37:15-16; and he is thrown into a muddy cistern, Jer 38:6).

Obviously, there is no right or wrong answer here. The goal is to create a descriptor that captures some essential feature of the prophet. Doing this encourages you to read prophetic texts more closely and purposefully. In addition, creating descriptive monikers for the prophets keeps them from blurring together and is a helpful way to distinguish one prophet from another.

Develop a job description for an Israelite prophet. Another creative activity you could try involves developing a job description for an Israelite prophet. What do you think was required for an individual to function well in this role? Your job description could include both a list of tasks prophets needed to perform and a list of character traits you regard as essential for faithful prophetic ministry. As you read through the prophets, keep a running list close at hand. Add to it and edit it as you go along. Include key biblical references next to items on your list so you can go back and revisit these verses in the future. As your list takes shape, consider whether your job description is a one-size-fits-all sort of document or whether you think prophetic activity was diverse enough to require different job descriptions for different kinds of prophets.

Engage in a thought experiment: imagine having a prophet move in next door. Finally, here is a simple thought experiment you can try. Imagine you are living in ancient Israel, in the capital city of Jerusalem. One day, after coming home from work, you notice a new neighbor moving in next door. Though you do not know his name, you know he is a prophet because earlier that week you heard him delivering an oracle to the ruling elite.

How would you feel about having someone like that as your next-door neighbor? Would this be a good day or a bad day for you? Would you bake some cookies and welcome him to the neighborhood? Would you invite family and friends over for a meet and greet? Or would you close the curtains and pretend not to be home? Might you even contemplate putting your house up for sale and moving out of the neighborhood? As you answer these questions, reflect on what your answers reveal about you *and* about your attitudes toward Israelite prophets.[18]

CONCLUSION

I am hopeful this chapter has inspired you to revisit the prophets. These oft-neglected books have much to offer the Christian church and the world. While it frequently takes more work to understand and apply this part of the Old Testament, it is well worth the effort.

If you are unsure where to begin reading, you might want to start with some of the Minor Prophets (Hosea–Malachi) since they are shorter. A book like Amos would be an especially good place to begin, partly because there is general agreement about the date of Amos's ministry (mid-eighth century BCE) and partly because his concern for justice may resonate with you. Alternatively, you might decide to explore a book like Isaiah, given its importance throughout the history of the church, or a book like Jonah, since it is more familiar than some of the other prophetic books. The point is to begin somewhere and see where it leads you. If you still feel you need a boost to jump-start your entry into the prophets, take a look at Carolyn J. Sharp's wonderfully rich and very accessible book *Old Testament Prophets for Today*.[19] That should be enough to get you going.

---

[18]Part of what makes this so interesting is the simple fact that the scenario is realistic, even if hypothetical. Israelite prophets would have lived next door to someone.

[19]Sharp's *Old Testament Prophets for Today* is only about one hundred pages. Carolyn J. Sharp, *Old Testament Prophets for Today* (Louisville, KY: Westminster John Knox, 2009). For a somewhat longer yet still accessible treatment, see her more recent work, *The Prophetic Literature* (Nashville: Abingdon, 2019).

In the next chapter, we turn our attention toward what many people consider to be some of the most "boring parts" of the Bible, such as Old Testament laws. How can anyone be expected to enjoy the Old Testament when significant portions of it seem so dreadfully uninteresting? We shall see.

8

ENJOYING *the* BORING PARTS

Many a pious vow to read straight through the Bible from cover to cover has foundered in the shoals of Leviticus. It is difficult to think of a book in the Bible that is less inviting.

THOMAS MANN, *THE BOOK OF THE TORAH*

LET'S BE HONEST. The dietary laws in Leviticus 11 don't make for the most scintillating reading. Slogging through forty-six verses describing what foods you can and cannot eat—prime rib but not pork chops, lamb but not lobster—does *not* qualify as "pleasure reading." Nobody recommends the dietary laws of Leviticus 11 as go-to verses for someone feeling anxious or discouraged, and I'm quite certain they never show up in any of those Bible promise boxes. Churches routinely ignore Leviticus 11—along with the rest of the book—and pastors rarely, if ever, preach from this chapter.[1] Indeed, it is difficult to even imagine a text like Leviticus 11:6-8 being used liturgically as a responsive reading:

> Leader: The hare, for even though it chews the cud, it does not have divided hoofs; it is unclean for you.

> People: The pig, for even though it has divided hoofs and is cleft-footed, it does not chew the cud; it is unclean for you.

---

[1]Leviticus is virtually absent from the Revised Common Lectionary, represented by only one reading (Lev 19:1-2, 9-18) in Year A on the seventh Sunday after Epiphany.

All: Of their flesh you shall not eat, and their carcasses you shall not touch; they are unclean for you.

Leader: This is the word of the Lord.

People: Thanks be to God!

Including something like this as part of the church service would be odd, to say the least, though not nearly as awkward as a reading from Leviticus 15, a chapter about bodily discharges.

Yet in spite of what I have just said, for one entire semester I found Leviticus 11 irresistible. I was captivated by these dietary laws—evidenced by the lengthy paper I wrote on the topic. The way these animals were classified as clean or unclean was intriguing to me. Why were some creatures edible and others not? Or to be more specific, why did Israelites regard cud-chewing, split-hoofed animals as clean, and those lacking one, or both, of these features as unclean (Lev 11:3-8)? What was it about the lack of fins and scales that rendered certain forms of aquatic life "detestable" (Lev 11:12)? And why did having jointed legs make four-footed winged insects edible when all others were off-limits (Lev 11:20-23)? Inquiring minds want to know!

Researching this topic was fascinating to me. I explored various explanations for why some foods were acceptable and others were taboo. Some argued that God gave Israel these laws for hygienic reasons (e.g., pork is forbidden since eating raw or undercooked pork might result in trichinosis). Others argued for a symbolic understanding of the classification system, suggesting it was intended to reflect, or symbolize, holiness. Some thought the animals that were excluded from Israelite consumption were forbidden because they were used for religious purposes by non-Israelites. Still others thought the laws were meant to be read allegorically by associating virtues with some animals and vices with others. These explanations, and others, represented earnest attempts to make sense of the food laws prescribed in Leviticus 11.

While my own conclusions were admittedly rather inconclusive—I think a combination of reasons best accounts for why certain foods were excluded from the dinner table—the quest to find answers to this puzzling question was both stimulating *and* enjoyable. It deepened my appreciation for this part of Leviticus and broadened my understanding of how to make sense of this challenging text.

I tell you this to make the point that a biblical text which first appears dreadfully boring may turn out to be surprisingly interesting. It *is* possible to like the "boring parts" of the Old Testament. Maybe we just haven't asked the right questions yet. Or maybe we are simply unaware of the creative possibilities at our disposal. Whatever the case may be, I am convinced we can find ways to appreciate—and perhaps even enjoy—some of the least inviting parts of the Bible. The goal of this chapter is to demonstrate how this is possible and to give you some tools to use in the process.

OLD TESTAMENT LAWS

There are numerous parts of the Old Testament people routinely classify as boring: genealogies,[2] census lists,[3] tabernacle details, and all those tedious Old Testament laws.[4] Many people skim over these sections of the Old Testament; others actively avoid them. Can we derive any value from them, let alone enjoy them? To answer that question, let's begin with Old Testament laws since most of these have little appeal to modern Christian readers.

There are a total of 613 laws in the Old Testament, all located in the Pentateuch. Their scope is very broad, and no area of Israelite life is unaffected by them. They govern Israel's relationship with God, others, and creation. Specifically, these laws deal with things such as the study of Torah, sacrifices, vows, ritual purity, dietary restrictions, the Sabbath, festivals, idolatry, war, slavery, agriculture—the list goes on.

---

[2]Many readers are bored by lists of names generally, like the list of elite soldiers in 1 Chron 11:26-47.
[3]See, e.g., the census of Levites in Num 3:14-39.
[4]Obviously, I am generalizing here. Not every reader would regard all of these parts of the Old Testament as boring. In fact, some are fascinated by judgment oracles and Old Testaments laws. Yet enthusiasm for these portions of Scripture is generally very low.

The law was central to Israel's identity and life together, and the Old Testament bears witness to Israel's appreciation and gratitude for it. Psalm 119, the longest psalm in the Psalter, emphasizes the importance and greatness of God's law. "Oh, how I love your law!" proclaims the psalmist. "It is my meditation all day long" (Ps 119:97). Most Christians today neither love Old Testament law nor spend any time meditating on it—certainly not "all day long"! Hence there is a rather large disconnect between the way churchgoers today view Old Testament law and the way Israelites did—at least on their best days.

With the notable exception of the Ten Commandments, most Christians pay little attention to Old Testament laws. Instead, they regard most of them as irrelevant, obsolete, and often just plain strange.

> You shall not boil a kid in its mother's milk. (Ex 23:19)

> You shall not give any of your offspring to sacrifice them to Molech, and so profane the name of your God: I am the LORD. (Lev 18:21)

> No one shall take a mill or an upper millstone in pledge, for that would be taking a life in pledge. (Deut 24:6)

What are Christians to do with laws like these? If they have no direct application today, why bother with them? Wouldn't it be better to skip over these archaic instructions and move on to greener pastures? I think not.

Rather than rushing ahead and assuming these laws have nothing to offer us, we should slow down and take a closer look.[5] Otherwise, we might deprive ourselves of many valuable insights. As we'll see in a moment, there is a good possibility that many of these laws still have relevance for us when we stop to look more closely. Even if the specific details of these laws no longer apply to us, they frequently embody general principles that can, and should, inform our behavior today. To illustrate this, let's look more closely at one particular law: the law of the goring ox.

---

[5]See chapter five.

The law of the goring ox. The law of the goring ox is recorded in Exodus 21:28-29 and reads as follows:

> When an ox gores a man or a woman to death, the ox shall be stoned, and its flesh shall not be eaten; but the owner of the ox shall not be liable. If the ox has been accustomed to gore in the past, and its owner has been warned but has not restrained it, and it kills a man or a woman, the ox shall be stoned, and its owner also shall be put to death.

This law envisions two possible scenarios with radically different outcomes. The first describes an Israelite who owns an ox which has no past history of goring. But one day, for reasons unknown, the ox goes berserk and gores someone to death. According to this law, the owner of that ox is *not* guilty because he had no idea his ox would behave that way.

The other scenario describes a situation in which an Israelite owns an ox that has a past history of goring.[6] Yet, despite that knowledge, the owner is careless and fails to keep this dangerous animal properly confined. Then, one day, the ox gores someone to death. In this instance, the owner *is* guilty. Both ox *and* owner must die.

I suspect most Christians who read these verses do not linger over them for very long. After all, how many Christians around the world own oxen in the first place? Yet, before we dismiss this law or declare it has nothing to contribute to Christian ethics, let's dig a little deeper. Maybe there is more here than meets the eye. Perhaps there is a general principle embedded in this law that still applies today even if the specifics do not. An analogy can help us here.[7]

Personally, I do not own any oxen. I *do*, however, own a car. (I realize jumping from cows to cars seems a big leap, but hang with me.) Let's imagine that while I am driving to work one day, a young child in pursuit of a ball darts out into the street. Thankfully, there is plenty of time for me to stop the car before hitting the child. But alas! When I slam on the

---

[6]Nonlethal goring must be assumed here. Otherwise, according to this law, the animal would have already been killed.

[7]This analogy and its use in connection with the law of the goring ox is borrowed and adapted from John N. Oswalt, one of my former professors, and is used by permission.

brakes, they fail. My car does not stop. Instead, I hear a sickening thud and watch in horror as the child is thrown many feet into the air. When I am finally able to bring the car to a complete stop, I rush back to the child, but it is too late. The injuries are severe. The child is dead.

Am I guilty? Not according to the logic that underlies the law of the goring ox. I had no idea my brakes were bad. In fact, I had just gotten the car inspected a few weeks prior. My brakes had never failed before and, through no negligence of my own, I was completely unaware of the hazard they posed.

Now let's imagine a slightly different version of the same scenario. Let's imagine I have been noticing my brakes feeling a little squishy for some time now. In fact, they seem to be getting steadily worse. I grow increasingly concerned about this and decide to take my car to Snavely and Son Automotive, a local garage just minutes from my office. I leave my car at the garage and walk from there to work. A few hours later, I get a phone call from Monte. It's bad news. The brakes are completely shot. Monte tells me the car is unsafe to drive until they are repaired.

While I have no reason to doubt Monte's diagnosis, I find myself in a bit of a dilemma. I'm short on cash, and I need the car for an out-of-town appointment later that day. So I devise a plan. I will retrieve my car, drive it *very* carefully for a few days, and then bring it back to the garage for repairs after my paycheck arrives.

But soon after I leave the garage—you know what's coming—a young child runs out into the street in front of me. Although there is plenty of time to stop before hitting the child, when I slam on the brakes, they fail. The child is dead.

In this scenario, the law of the goring ox renders me guilty. Why? Because the general principle underlying the law of the goring ox is simply this: *knowledge equals responsibility.* If you *know* something in your possession is dangerous, it is your responsibility to take appropriate precautions to ensure nobody gets hurt by it. Otherwise, you are liable for whatever harm results. In the second scenario, I knew my brakes were unsafe yet choose to drive anyway. That makes me responsible for the harm done.

This hypothetical analogy illustrates how Old Testament laws can still be relevant for Christians today. Once we discern a general principle at work—in this case, that knowledge equals responsibility—we can apply that to various areas of our lives. For instance, what do we possess that is dangerous or *potentially* dangerous? Are we taking appropriate precautions to ensure nobody gets hurt by these things? If there are guns in the house, are they locked away? Or minimally, is the trigger lock on with the ammunition securely stored in a separate location? Are your prescription medications kept out of reach of children? Have you baby-proofed your home to ensure the safety of your curious toddler? The law of the goring ox reminds us of the importance of doing what we reasonably can to ensure that people are not harmed by the things we possess.

If you want to experiment with reading Old Testament laws this way, here are two to get you started:

> When you reap the harvest of your land, you shall not reap to the very edges of your field, or gather the gleanings of your harvest. (Lev 19:9)

> When you build a new house, you shall make a parapet for your roof; otherwise you might have bloodguilt on your house, if anyone should fall from it. (Deut 22:8)

Work through the following questions with each of these laws: (1) According to this law, what were Israelites required to do or avoid? (2) What general principle or principles are embedded in this law? (3) How might these general principles apply to situations today?

Begin by being sure you understand what the law required of someone living in Israel. You might even try paraphrasing it to be certain it is clear to you. Then look for a general principle operating in the verse. There may be more than one, but to keep things simple, just focus on one at a time. Once you have identified a general principle undergirding the law, consider how you might apply it to contemporary situations and circumstances. Hopefully, this will increase your appreciation for this part of the Old Testament.

While this approach works quite nicely for many Old Testament laws, it does not work equally well for all of them. Sometimes it is not possible to identify a clearly discernible "general principle." In these instances, it is often more helpful to take a step back and reflect theologically on larger themes and broader questions. To illustrate this, let's turn our attention to Old Testament laws about sacrifices and offerings.

Laws about sacrifices and offerings. Laws pertaining to the sacrificial system in ancient Israel rank among the most difficult for modern readers to appreciate and enjoy. What are Christians to do with all those instructions about killing animals, offering grain, and splashing blood around? Traditionally, Christians have argued that these laws are important for theological reasons, to help us understand the person and work of Jesus. Specifically, many Christians believe Old Testament sacrifices prefigure, or point toward, the sacrifice of Jesus on the cross. This certainly seems to be the way the writer of Hebrews regarded them. The writer of Hebrews draws extensive analogies between the Old Testament sacrificial system and Jesus' death on the cross, attempting to use one to help readers make sense of the other.

For our purposes, I want to offer another way to reflect on these laws. Keeping in mind that sacrifices were at the heart of Israel's worship, it seems reasonable to ask what these laws, taken as a whole, might suggest about the nature of worship and how that might inform our practice today. To provide some focus to our conversation, we'll concentrate on Leviticus 1–7, seven chapters that describe various sacrifices and offerings at some length.

CASE STUDY: REFLECTIONS ON WORSHIP FROM LEVITICUS 1–7.

Worship should be structured to meet a variety of needs. Leviticus 1–7 describes a number of sacrifices that were part of ancient Israel's religious repertoire. These first seven chapters of Leviticus largely revolve around *how* these sacrifices were to be performed, and they say very little about *why* they were done in the first place. Still, given what we can discern here, and what we learn elsewhere, these sacrifices were clearly not all thought to function the same way. Some sacrifices were related to sin-removal and purification. Others were offered as a way of expressing the worshiper's total devotion to God. Still others were used to render thanks to the Lord for a blessing received or a vow completed. And some were simply offered from a glad and grateful heart.

As Christians think about structuring corporate (or personal) worship today, they would be wise to take this diversity into account. Worship can function in many different ways and can meet various needs people have. Some people need to confess sin. Others need to be reassured that they are in a right relationship with God. Still others are looking for ways to express their thanks and gratitude to God. Worship should provide space for all of this to happen. Reading Leviticus 1–7 this way raises the question, How can we structure worship in a way that will allow for a variety of needs to be met?

Worship should fully include the poor. In Leviticus 1–7, and elsewhere throughout the book, provisions are made for those who are poor (Lev 5:7-13; 12:8; 14:21-22, 30-32). For example, the purification offering described in Leviticus 5:7-13 instructs the worshiper to bring a lamb. But if the individual cannot afford a lamb, they can bring either two turtledoves or two young pigeons instead. And if this is still too much of an economic burden, they can bring a bushel of fine flour to meet the sacrificial requirements. Financial resources were never to be a limiting factor in determining who could or could not fully participate in this offering.

As we reflect on our own worship practices, it reminds us that worship should never be structured in such a way that excludes the poor. Are there ways we exclude the poor from worship today, and if so, how can we address this?

Worship should actively involve the worshiper. Another striking element in the opening chapters of Leviticus is the level of involvement the worshiper had in certain animal sacrifices. For example, if someone wanted to make a burnt offering or a peace offering, they had to handpick an animal from their flock, transport it to the priest, put their hand on its head, kill it, skin it, and cut it into pieces. This was all part of the act of worship. Gordon Wenham describes it this way:

Using a little imagination every reader of the OT soon realizes that these ancient sacrifices were very moving occasions. They make modern church services seem tame and dull by comparison. The ancient worshiper did not just listen to the minister and sing a few hymns. *He was actively involved in the worship.* He had to choose an unblemished animal from his own flock, bring it to the sanctuary, kill it and dismember it with his own hands, then watch it go up in smoke before his very eyes. He was convinced that something very significant was achieved through these acts and knew that his relationship with God was profoundly affected by this sacrifice.[8]

You could *not* worship in absentia. Instead, you needed to be physically present and actively involved.

Reflecting on these laws should prompt us to reexamine our own level of engagement in worship, especially in corporate worship. For example, when you are singing in church, do you concentrate on the words you are singing? Do you pray along with the person who is praying? Are you asking God what you might do in response to the sermon? The laws in Leviticus 1–7 cause us to question what we can do to become more engaged in worship. How can I avoid being a passive bystander and become more actively involved in worship?

Worship should be a multisensory experience. The opening chapters of Leviticus envision worship as a multisensory experience. Consider, for a moment, how many senses were involved in animal sacrifices. You were required to touch the animal, putting your hand on its head before killing it. You would have heard the animal's dying breath and the crackling of the fire. You would have seen the altar, the smoke, the blood, and much more. You would have smelled the meat being cooked and, in the case of the peace offering, you would have tasted it when it was ready. Your senses would have been fully engaged. This raises an interesting question as we reflect on our own worship practices. Which of our five senses are regularly engaged in worship, and what would it take to involve more of our senses?

---

[8]Gordon J. Wenham, *The Book of Leviticus*, NICOT (Grand Rapids, MI: Eerdmans, 1979), 55, emphasis mine.

While more could be said, these four points should suffice to demonstrate how laws about sacrifices and offerings in Leviticus 1–7 can still be useful for Christians today. A similar approach could be used with other laws and other portions of the Old Testament. For example, consider doing a search of all the laws concerning widows, orphans, and foreigners. What do these laws suggest about caring for the most vulnerable members of society? How might this apply to our current context? This approach is even useful with more beloved parts of the Old Testament, like the book of Psalms. You might consider what it has to say about prayer, using the same theologically reflective approach we used to explore worship in Leviticus 1–7. This is a helpful way to engage Old Testament texts, one that may breathe new life into your reading of Scripture.

OTHER BORING PARTS AND WHAT TO DO WITH THEM

To this point, we have focused on Old Testament laws. But what about other portions of the Old Testament that cause people's eyes to glaze over? Is it possible to find interest and value in genealogies, census lists, tabernacle details, and the like? Here are a few suggestions I think might help.

Look at the big picture. In his book *Living in the Shadow of the Second Coming*, Professor Timothy Weber refers to a story that had "recently been circulating in some premillennialist circles."[9] Here's the story:

> Some students from a theological seminary were playing basketball one night in a local gymnasium. Late in the evening the janitor arrived and prepared to lock up the building. While waiting for the game to conclude, he sat down and began reading his Bible. He was still at it when the game ended and the players began filing out. One theological student notice that the janitor was reading from the Book of Revelation and asked him, quite smugly, if he understood what he was reading. "Sure do," the man replied. Somewhat taken aback by the janitor's confidence, the student . . . asked a second question. "Oh, yeah? What does it all mean?" "Simple," replied the janitor, "Jesus wins."

---

[9]Timothy P. Weber, *Living in the Shadow of the Second Coming: American Premillennialism, 1875–1982*, rev. ed. (Chicago: University of Chicago Press, 1987), 232. Premillennialism is a Christian view of the end times that suggests Jesus will return to establish a 1,000-year reign of peace on the earth.

Whatever view you may have of the "end times," and regardless of how you interpret many of the fantastic images and mysterious numbers in the book of Revelation, most Christians agree that the big picture points to the victory of God. Whatever you do with the other parts of the book, that much is sure.

This "big picture" approach can be a useful strategy for dealing with Old Testament passages we might otherwise find boring or tedious since it enables us to appreciate some key concepts without getting lost in all the details. To illustrate this, let's look at Numbers 2. Like Leviticus, the book of Numbers receives scant attention in the church today. This is especially true of the first and last ten chapters of the book. Despite hearing thousands of sermons over roughly half a century, I can't recall ever hearing one preached from Numbers 2. Nor has any Christian I know ever committed this portion of Scripture to memory (though I wouldn't put it past Bible quizzers). This is not surprising since Numbers 2 contains lots of names and numbers, the death knell of any Old Testament text. It is one of these quintessentially "boring" chapters so many people dread. If you haven't read this chapter recently, take a moment to do so now.

As the book of Numbers opens, the Israelites are encamped at Mount Sinai. They have been there for the better part of a year and are preparing to depart for the land promised to Abraham, Isaac, and Jacob.[10] Numbers 2 is highly structured and formulaic. It describes Israelite encampments surrounding the tabernacle with three tribes each to the east, south, west, and north of the tabernacle, respectively. It also provides the tribes' order of departure when they are on the move: tribes on the east side go first, followed by those on the south side, and so on. Numbers 2 can be outlined as follows:

Introductory instructions for encamping (vv. 1-2)

> East siders (vv. 3-9)

> South siders (vv. 10-16)

---

[10]See Ex 19:1; Num 1:1.

Levites (v. 17)

West siders (vv. 18-24)

North siders (vv. 25-31)

Summary statements about Israel's obedience (vv. 32-34)

Throughout the chapter, we are told three things about each tribe: (1) their location in the camp, (2) the name of their leader, and (3) the total number of fighting men within the tribe. For example, we learn that the tribe of Judah is to camp on the east side of the tabernacle. Judah was under the leadership of Nahshon, son of Amminadab, and had a fighting force of 74,600 (Num 2:3-4). The tribe of Issachar, which was to camp next to Judah, was under the leadership of Nethanel, son of Zuar, and had 54,400 men who could fight (Num 2:5-6). This pattern repeats itself for each of the twelve tribes of Israel. Needless to say, most readers do not find this very interesting.

So what should we do with Numbers 2? Is there some deep theological significance knowing that Nahshon was the leader of the tribe of Judah (Num 2:3)? I don't think so.[11] Or should we be spiritually edified on learning there were 54,400 battle-ready soldiers in the tribe of Issachar (Num 2:6)? Doubtful. In and of themselves, these details are largely inconsequential. But perhaps this is to miss the forest for the trees. Rather than focusing too intensely on these names and numbers, maybe we are better served by looking at the larger picture.

Numbers 2 makes it clear that all the tribes were encamped *around* the tent of meeting, or tabernacle. In addition, each tribe was supposed to "camp *facing* the tent of meeting" (Num 2:2, emphasis mine). The Levites, tasked with disassembling, transporting, and reassembling the tabernacle, camped even closer to the tabernacle. They formed an inner "circle," as it were, with groups of Levites on each side of the tabernacle.

---

[11]It is interesting to notice the prominence of Judah among the tribes, indicated by being named first and by its location east of the tabernacle, opposite the entrance.

This arrangement makes it abundantly clear that the tabernacle was situated in the very center of the camp. The entire community of Israel was oriented around it *and* toward it, making God the focal point of their communal life. Now that *is* interesting. It speaks volumes about divine presence and relationship. God dwells in the very midst of the people! The physical arrangement of their camp demonstrates this. It reminds them that God is near and that God goes with them as they embark on this new chapter of their journey.

Noticing the *centrality* of the tabernacle, rather than getting lost in all the details, can stimulate our own thinking and reflection. Do we live with an awareness of God's presence in our midst? To what extent are our lives oriented around God and toward God? Is God at the very center of our best thoughts and deepest affections? Viewing Numbers 2 through this "big picture" lens allows us to reflect on important questions like these. This, in turn, enhances our ability to appreciate a much-neglected text—and perhaps even enjoy it.

Look for unexpected treasures "hidden" in the boring parts. I have found there are often "hidden" treasures waiting to be discovered even in those portions of Scripture that seem most uninteresting. By "hidden" I do *not* mean intentionally concealed; these treasures tend to be sitting out there in plain sight. They just go unnoticed by most people for reasons already discussed. We read these parts too quickly, if at all, and our expectations are so low that our belief they will yield little or nothing of value becomes a self-fulfilling prophecy. Yet "hidden" among genealogies, census lists, purity laws, and the like, are brief stories, comments, and other information that is routinely ignored *but should not be*. These largely unknown treasures of the Old Testament can be quite rewarding to explore. Indeed, they often seem like a breath of fresh air when discovered. We just need to slow down and look.

To illustrate this, let's return for a moment to the tabernacle details recorded in the final third of the book of Exodus. We discussed this briefly in chapter six, noting how the repetition of these details emphasized Israel's obedience to God. They construct the tabernacle exactly as specified. The structure of the final portion of the book of Exodus can be presented as follows:

Exodus 25–31 Building a Tabernacle from A to Z

Exodus 32–34 The Golden Calf Debacle and Its Aftermath

Exodus 35–40 Building a Tabernacle to Exact Specifications

As we observed, many details in Exodus 25–31 are repeated—sometimes verbatim—in Exodus 35–40. That might tempt you to think you won't miss anything if you skim over the final chapters of Exodus. But that is not true. You would actually miss quite a lot. Exodus 35–40 doesn't *only* repeat earlier building instructions. There is new information here as well.

To be specific, there is a lot to learn about the nature of giving in this section, particularly in Exodus 35–36.[12] For example, we discover that giving is a communal activity open to everyone. "Both men and woman" make contributions for the construction of the tabernacle (Ex 35:22). We also learn that the people who gave did so willingly. "And they came, everyone whose heart was stirred, and everyone whose spirit was willing, and brought the LORD's offering to be used for the tent of meeting" (Ex 35:21). This reminds us that giving should be done freely and voluntarily (cf. 2 Cor 9:7). In addition, we notice that giving takes different forms: some contributed possessions such as jewelry (Ex 35:22) or things made by hand such as fine linens (Ex 35:25), while others gave of their time and skill. Israelite artisans cut stones, carved wood, and embroidered cloth for the tabernacle and its furnishings (Ex 35:30-35). This too was an act of giving, one that reminds us that giving encompasses writing a check *as well as* volunteering time and talents for the sake of others.

What makes this story especially intriguing is the end result. The people brought more than was needed. Their generous giving resulted in an *over*abundance of resources. In fact, they brought so much that Moses had to tell them to stop.

---

[12]I am indebted to Dr. Terry Brensinger for first suggesting this line of inquiry to me.

So Moses gave command, and word was proclaimed throughout the camp: "No man or woman is to make anything else as an offering for the sanctuary." So the people were restrained from bringing; for what they had already brought was more than enough to do all the work. (Ex 36:6-7)

It is a marvelous example of what can happen when people work together toward a common goal, with willing hearts and open hands. You get so much that you have to tell people to stop giving. These insights about the nature of giving are both instructive and inspiring and have all sorts of contemporary and practical applications.

While more could be said, I hope this is enough to encourage you to be on the lookout for "hidden" treasures as you make your way through some of the more arduous parts of the Old Testament. These treasures await your discovery and make a closer reading of the boring parts well worth the effort.

Get help from the experts. I realize that most people do not have, or use, many secondary sources when reading the Bible. That is part of the reason I have been so intentional about offering suggestions for engaging the Old Testament that do not require them. That said, if you continue to struggle with some of the less-inviting parts of the Old Testament and want more ways to appreciate them, I would encourage you to get a little help from the experts, particularly from biblical scholars who have written about these things. For example, if you really, really don't like genealogies, and can't for the life of you figure out any good reason why they were included in the Old Testament, consult a Bible dictionary.[13] Read an article about genealogies. Where do they appear in the Old Testament? What kind of information do they contain? What are some of the ways genealogies function in the Bible? See if this enhances your appreciation of them in some way.

Or maybe you find the purity laws in Leviticus confusing and even offensive at times. If you want to make more sense of these laws, read the

---

[13]The *Anchor Bible Dictionary* has a helpful entry on "genealogy, genealogies." See the appendix for bibliographic information on this multivolume resource.

work of biblical scholars and commentators who can help you better understand what Israel meant by categories such as clean, unclean, holy, and profane.[14] How were these used to classify people, places, and things? Does this answer some of your questions about these laws? Does it make them more interesting? Admittedly, this kind of inquiry takes some effort and intentionality. But it may be the key to helping you gain a greater appreciation for some of the most challenging sections of the Old Testament. It is certainly worth a try.

BUT WHAT IF THE BORING PARTS ARE STILL BORING?

My goal in this chapter has been to demonstrate that even some of the most notoriously boring parts of the Old Testament *can* be interesting. Old Testament laws that seem completely irrelevant sometimes contain general principles that are still widely applicable. Instructions about sacrifices—which are not part of Christian worship today—can be used to reflect more deeply on our own contemporary worship practices. And a chapter full of mind-numbing details about Israelite encampments around the tabernacle might inspire us to consider what is central in our lives and how we should orient ourselves.

I sincerely hope this chapter has encouraged you to take a second look at those parts of the Bible you find least enticing. I really do believe there are ways to enjoy the boring parts of the Old Testament—I wouldn't have written this chapter otherwise. Still, I am realistic. The truth of the matter is that despite your best efforts to delight in the Old Testament, some portions of it are likely to remain uninteresting. That's okay. Not every Old Testament passage yields profound spiritual truths no matter how many ways you look at it or what you try to do with it. Not even the most skilled biblical scholars and theologians can make every passage interesting. At the end of the day, some parts remain boring.

Try not to be discouraged by this. Instead, do what you can to appreciate these parts and move on. Don't get stuck there, and don't beat

---

[14]See, e.g., Wenham, *Book of Leviticus*, 18-25.

yourself up for not having a great time with these passages. As discussed earlier, enjoying the Old Testament requires realistic expectations. Expecting every part of the Old Testament to be equally fascinating and theologically bountiful is just not realistic. Thankfully, the Old Testament is a huge collection of sacred texts. If you find yourself having a really hard time finding value in one part of it, try another.

In addition, always remember that a portion of Scripture that doesn't interest you at one point in life may be just what you need at another. You can always go back and revisit passages you previously found boring or irrelevant. Although the text stays the same, we don't. As *we* change, and as the circumstances of our lives and our world change, we often see and hear biblical texts differently. Parts of the Old Testament that previously seemed of little value can take on new life and meaning. Someone who never cared much for prophetic literature might read a book like Amos with renewed interest after being awakened to the importance of doing justice. Or a person who never really appreciated the book of Job might suddenly connect with it in more profound ways after experiencing a personal tragedy. Our interests and needs change as we move through various seasons of life. This keeps open the possibility that texts once deemed "boring" might someday become more important to us than we ever thought possible. There is hope.

While "boring" passages present some real obstacles to enjoying the Old Testament, biblical passages we find offensive present an entirely different set of challenges. What should we do when we encounter Old Testament texts we find ethically, morally, or theologically troubling? Should we critique them? Try to find something good in them? Ignore them? Since troublesome texts like these have the potential to seriously hinder our enjoyment of the Old Testament—and have discouraged some from reading it at all—it is important to consider strategies for handling problematic passages in a way that keeps that from happening.

9

DEALING with MORALLY and THEOLOGICALLY TROUBLING TEXTS

One of the greatest barriers in the minds of people who try
to read the Old Testament is the sense that it consists basically
of a long narrative of cruel kings and barbarous battles, and
the worst of it is that God seems to sponsor these battles.

WILLIAM HOLLADAY, *LONG AGO GOD SPOKE*

MANY PEOPLE STRUGGLE WITH all the bloodshed and warfare in the pages of the Old Testament. They have little enthusiasm for all the violent portrayals of God in this part of the Bible, and they are dismayed by how often the Old Testament has been used to justify contemporary acts of violence toward others. Understandably, this turns off many readers. While one chapter is certainly not enough to fully address these concerns, my hope is that the following pages will provide you with the guidance you need to deal constructively with some of the more disagreeable parts of the Old Testament. Too many readers have been derailed by texts like these. It does not need to be this way.

THREE KINDS OF TROUBLING TEXTS

This chapter will focus on three kinds of texts that people find especially troubling: (1) texts that offend our moral sensibilities, (2) texts that conflict with our view of God, and (3) texts that have been used to harm others. Obviously, there is some overlap among these categories, since a text that conflicts with our view of God may also be one that offends our moral sensibilities and one that has been used to harm others. Still, these categories are useful for differentiating the different kinds of Old Testament texts that cause such consternation.

Texts that offend our moral sensibilities. There are many Old Testament texts that shock our moral sensibilities. Take the story of "the Levite's concubine" (Judg 19). It is the story of a woman who is gang raped throughout the night and left for dead. When found unresponsive the next morning, her husband (the Levite) dismembers her and sends parts of her body throughout the land of Israel. It is a truly horrifying tale.

In addition to stories like this one, other texts that offend our moral sensibilities include those which condone slavery, promote patriarchy, and sanction genocide. The presence of such morally troubling texts is one of the main reasons many people do not enjoy the Old Testament. They simply cannot get past all the violence and killing it contains.

Texts that conflict with our view of God. Throughout the Old Testament, God is frequently portrayed as smiting, slaying, and slaughtering people, sometimes by the tens of thousands. Old Testament passages that describe God flooding the planet (Gen 7:17-24), leveling cities in fiery conflagrations (Gen 19:24-25), and instantly annihilating countless individuals (Ex 12:29-30; 2 Kings 19:35) have caused no end of trouble for thoughtful readers throughout the centuries. Even when God is not directly responsible for killing others, the Old Testament often claims that God initiates and sanctions acts of lethal violence that leave many dead. Commands to "show them no mercy" (Deut 7:2) and to kill everything that breathes (Deut 20:16) are especially chilling, particularly when you realize that women, children, and other noncombatants are among the slain.

Many believers find it extremely difficult to reconcile God's violent behavior in such passages with their understanding of God's goodness, mercy, and love. This makes it difficult to value these parts of the Old Testament.

Texts that have been used to harm others. Some Old Testament texts
have been read and interpreted in ways that promote injustice, oppression, and violence against others. This represents yet another category of troubling Old Testament texts. For example, passages like
Genesis 9:20-27 and Leviticus 25:44-46 were routinely used to justify
slavery in nineteenth-century America. Other texts, like Genesis 3, have
become burdened with all sorts of misogynistic interpretations resulting
in enormous harm to women. Verses like Leviticus 18:22 and Leviticus
20:13 have been interpreted in ugly and hateful ways and have caused
severe pain and suffering to members of the LGBTQ community. Texts
that have an oppressive history of interpretation are very difficult to
enjoy. This is especially true if you yourself have been harmed by the way
these passages (and others) have been used against you.

SHOULD WE EXPECT TO "ENJOY" TROUBLING TEXTS?

Given the difficulties such texts raise and the harm they have often done,
it is fair to ask whether we should even try to enjoy them. Is it even appropriate to take pleasure from passages that endorse slavery, portray
women as inferior, or describe God behaving in terribly violent ways?
This is an important question, especially in a book named *Enjoying the
Old Testament*.

A number of things can be said here. First, I do *not* believe we should
ever *enjoy* reading about someone else being harmed. There is nothing
attractive about human suffering and misery. Stories of oppression and
injustice should disturb us, not delight us. We should take no pleasure
in the death and destruction of others in the pages of Scripture, even
when those "others" are regarded as enemies of Israel. Rather than celebrating the killing of Canaanites, Amalekites, or Philistines, we should
grieve their deaths.

Second, I don't think it is reasonable to expect people to treasure texts
that have been used to oppress them.[1] I'm reminded of a story Howard

---

[1] I am indebted to Emerson B. Powery and Rodney S. Sadler, Jr., *The Genesis of Liberation: Biblical
Interpretation in the Antebellum Narratives of the Enslaved* (Louisville, KY: Westminster John
Knox, 2016), 113-14, for what follows.

Thurman told about his grandmother, Nancy Ambrose. Nancy was born enslaved and later emancipated. Since she was unable to read or write, she would have her grandson read to her from the Bible. But Nancy never permitted Howard to read to her from the letters of Paul, with the occasional exception of 1 Corinthians 13. Why?

> "During the days of slavery," she said, "the master's minister would occasionally hold services for the slaves. Old man McGhee was so mean that he would not let a Negro minister preach to his slaves. Always the white minister used as his text something from Paul. At least three or four times a year he used as a text: 'Slaves, be obedient to them that are your masters . . . , as unto Christ.' Then he would go on to show how it was God's will that we were slaves and how, if we were good and happy slaves, God would bless us. I promised my Maker that if I ever learned to read and if freedom ever came, I would not read that part of the Bible."[2]

Verses that have an oppressive history will always be troubling, especially to those who have been abused by them. For example, Native Americans and other indigenous groups are unlikely to celebrate the conquest narrative in Joshua 6–11 since they are more likely to identify with the Canaanites living in the land than with the Israelite invaders coming in from the outside. Also, I highly doubt members of the LGBTQ community, or their allies, will ever truly "enjoy" passages like Leviticus 18:22 or Leviticus 20:13. Nor are you likely to hear African Americans quoting Genesis 9:25 as their "life verse" or see women lining up to have Genesis 3:16 tattooed on their arm. These passages have done too much harm for too long to be cherished by those directly affected by them. Perhaps the best we can do with some problematic passages is attempt to limit their negative influence by finding ways to read them more honestly and responsibly.

Third, though there may be some troublesome texts we never truly enjoy, I believe it is still possible to find value in many disagreeable parts of the Old Testament. Even violent verses can reveal truth. As we will see,

---

[2]Howard Thurman, *Jesus and the Disinherited* (Boston: Beacon, 1996), 20. Cited in Powery and Sadler, *Genesis of Liberation*, 114.

there are positive ways to use these texts. In fact, it seems imperative to use them constructively if for no other reason than to counter oppressive readings that are still too common today.

Thus, when I talk about enjoying the Old Testament, I am *not* talking about taking pleasure in violence or in other people's pain. Instead, I am talking about ways we can read the Old Testament—even those parts that are most disagreeable—in constructive, generative, and life-giving ways. There are valuable things we can learn from these disturbing passages, even if we do not particularly savor reading some of them.

DEALING WITH THE DISAGREEABLE
PARTS OF THE OLD TESTAMENT

Although the following suggestions won't remove all the difficulties you may have with certain problem passages, they should enable you to have more positive encounters with some of the most difficult parts of the Bible.

Be honest about what bothers you. As discussed in chapter five, enjoying the Old Testament involves being honest with it. As with any healthy human relationship, honesty is absolutely crucial. As the Trappist monk Thomas Merton reminds us:

> It is of the very nature of the Bible to affront, perplex and astonish the human mind. Hence the reader who opens the Bible must be prepared for disorientation, confusion, incomprehension, perhaps outrage.[3]

In other words, Merton is saying that some of this stuff is going to get under your skin. That's okay. It would be strange if it didn't. As Robert Carroll sardonically quipped, "If reading the Bible does *not* raise profound problems for you as a modern reader, then check with your doctor and enquire about the symptoms of brain death."[4] If you want to stay engaged with the Old Testament, you need the freedom to be honest with it and to ask questions about it.

---

[3]Thomas Merton, *Opening the Bible* (Collegeville, MN: Liturgical, 1986), 11.
[4]Robert P. Carroll, *The Bible as a Problem for Christianity* (Philadelphia: Trinity Press International, 1991), 2, emphasis original.

One of the reasons a number of young people are leaving the church is because they do not find it to be a welcome space for their questions and doubts about matters of faith. Instead, they are told to accept what they are taught and believe what they are told. Questions are discouraged, divergent views are suppressed, and outright disagreement is disallowed. All too often, this leads them to give up on church altogether.

Much the same happens with the Bible. People abandon the Bible when they feel there is no room for their sincere questions, understandable skepticism, and honest doubts. After all, what are people to do when they discover Old Testament passages that condone behaviors they condemn? If the Bible needs be accepted and endorsed "as is," then many people would rather abandon the Bible than violate their conscience.

But this is an unnecessary either/or. You don't need to agree with everything you read in the Old Testament. Just because the Old Testament sanctions war and regards women as second-class citizens does not mean you must do the same. You can critique these perspectives based on the teachings of Jesus, particularly the law of love (Mt 22:39).

For those who may worry about engaging the Old Testament this way, let me assure you that raising objections to certain things we encounter in the Old Testament is not a sign of disrespect to God or a rejection of biblical authority. On the contrary, as William Placher reminds us, "Our very commitment to the struggle is the sign of our faithfulness to this book."[5] Similarly, Peter Enns assures us it is quite permissible to ask questions and raise objections: "You are not being disloyal to God or 'rebelling' if you have trouble accepting, for example, that God would command his people to commit genocide."[6] Rather, you are standing in a long line of faithful individuals who protested divine activity that seemed out of line with God's character. People like Abraham, Moses, Job, the prophet Habakkuk, and many of the psalmists freely raised their

---

[5]William C. Placher, "Struggling with Scripture," in *Struggling with Scripture*, by Walter Brueggemann, William C. Placher, and Brian K. Blount (Louisville, KY: Westminster John Knox, 2002), 49.
[6]Peter Enns, *The Bible Tells Me So: Why Defending Scripture Has Made Us Unable to Read It* (New York: HarperOne, 2014), 22.

voices in protest when questions about God's justice were at stake. Yet their struggle with God was not seen as an act of defiance or disobedience. On the contrary, their engagement with God represented an act of profound faithfulness. When they thought God was acting out of character, they said so. Shouldn't we do the same when we encounter Old Testament texts that are morally offensive or theologically problematic?[7]

Of course, each of us should carefully consider the basis on which we critique various ideas in the Old Testament. It is important to have principled standards to guide us lest our "critique" reflect nothing more than our personal preferences, embracing what we like and rejecting what we don't. I find the following three criteria especially helpful in this regard: the rule of love (Does this idea enhance our love for God and others?), a commitment to justice (Does it set things right?), and a consistent ethic of life (Does it value *all* people?).[8] For me, this serves as a useful guide in my efforts to read, evaluate, and apply the Old Testament responsibly.

Also, as I have argued elsewhere, not every portrayal of God in the Old Testament accurately reflects God's character.[9] Some do, but others reflect Israel's culturally conditioned understandings of God. To put it bluntly, Israel didn't always get God right. Sometimes they wrote about God in ways that made sense given their historical context but not in ways that ultimately reveal God's character. Therefore, if we want to use the Bible to help us learn more about God—which I do—we need to read these texts carefully, avoiding any simplistic equation between the way God is represented in the text and the true character of the living God. Here is where I believe the life and teachings of Jesus can be of great help to us.[10] If Jesus provides the fullest and clearest revelation of God's character,

---

[7]See Eric A. Seibert, *Disturbing Divine Behavior: Troubling Old Testament Images of God* (Minneapolis: Fortress, 2009), 225-26.

[8]See Eric A. Seibert, *The Violence of Scripture: Overcoming the Old Testament's Troubling Legacy* (Minneapolis: Fortress, 2012), 67-69.

[9]See Seibert, *Disturbing Divine Behavior*, 169-81 and throughout.

[10]For more on the idea that the God Jesus revealed should be the standard by which we judge Old Testament portrayals of God, see C. S. Cowles, "The Case for Radical Discontinuity," in *Show Them No Mercy: Four Views on God and Canaanite Genocide*, by C. S. Cowles et al. (Grand Rapids, MI: Zondervan, 2003), 13-44; Seibert, *Disturbing Divine Behavior*, 183-207; Brian Zahnd, *Sinners in the Hands of a Loving God: The Scandalous Truth of the Very Good News* (Colorado

then it stands to reason that Old Testament portrayals most in line with the God Jesus reveals are most accurate. To put it another way, we know an Old Testament depiction of God accurately reflects God's character when it aligns with the life and teachings of Jesus. Portrayals that do not align well with the God Jesus reveals are likely to say more about the cultural context in which they emerged than they do about the God of whom they speak. Knowing this can help us work through some of the most difficult passages of the Old Testament more responsibly.

Remain convinced these texts are worth the effort (don't let them go until they bless you). Professor Ellen Davis was once asked, "Is there any text you would reject?"[11] The question was posed after she had just finished delivering a paper on the near-sacrifice of Isaac, a disturbing story in which God ostensibly commands Abraham to offer his beloved son as a burnt offering (Gen 22). Davis recognizes this as a potentially "haunting" question, one that has come back to her "periodically" when facing "an uncongenial, even repellant text."[12] Still, for Davis the answer is a resounding "No." She writes: "No biblical text may be safely repudiated as a potential source of edification for the Church."[13] Davis continues, "When we think we have reached the point of zero-edification, then that perception indicates that we are not reading deeply enough; we have not probed the layers of the text with sufficient care."[14] I agree. We should never throw up our hands and proclaim this or that text to be utterly devoid of all spiritual or theological value, regardless of how problematic we believe it to be. Instead, while acknowledging the difficulties, we should look for constructive ways to use even the most troubling texts.

Jacqueline Lapsley advocates the same approach in her book *Whispering the Word*. She is particularly concerned about "the patriarchal nature" of the Old Testament, and she recognizes the problems such texts

---

Springs: Waterbrook, 2017), 48-75; Gregory A. Boyd, *Cross Vision: How the Crucifixion of Jesus Makes Sense of Old Testament Violence* (Minneapolis: Fortress, 2017).

[11]Ellen F. Davis, "Critical Traditioning: Seeking an Inner Biblical Hermeneutic," *Anglican Theological Review* 82 (2000): 733.

[12]Davis, "Critical Traditioning," 733.

[13]Davis, "Critical Traditioning," 734.

[14]Davis, "Critical Traditioning," 734.

create for modern readers, especially when the values of a patriarchal culture are regarded as normative today.[15] Still, Lapsley is not willing to give up on these texts since she believes there is something more to them. As Lapsley expresses it:

> The difficulties posed by these disturbing aspects of the Bible do not mean that readers of biblical narratives must reductively conclude their interpretations with the lament that "this is a patriarchal text," as though this were the end result of interpretation or the only responsible interpretation. Many texts are patriarchal in some respects, and are *still about something else as well.*[16]

Precisely. Even if we find *certain aspects* of a text problematic, offensive, and unsalvageable, that is not the end of it. The text is "still about something else as well." Enjoying the Old Testament requires us to look for "something else," something of value.

This will take some hard work and struggle, especially for the most unsavory passages in the Old Testament. But it's worth the effort. As Professor Phyllis Trible counsels: "Do not abandon the Bible to the bashers [those who disparage the Bible] and thumpers [those who use the Bible to harm others]. Take back the text. *Do not let go until it blesses you.*"[17] Trible is borrowing language from the story of Jacob wrestling with God in Genesis 32. Jacob informs his nocturnal opponent that he won't let him go until he receives a blessing (Gen 32:26). Trible calls us to engage in the same kind of persistent, tenacious struggle with troublesome biblical texts. We should wrestle with these texts and not let them go until we find something of value in them. Rather than becoming paralyzed by the problems these texts raise, we should remain convinced that even the most troublesome texts can be of spiritual and theological value when read responsibly.

Find ways to use troublesome texts constructively. So what kind of "blessings" might we expect from troublesome texts? What is that

---

[15]Jacqueline E. Lapsley, *Whispering the Word: Hearing Women's Stories in the Old Testament* (Louisville, KY: Westminster John Knox, 2005), 7.

[16]Lapsley, *Whispering the Word*, 7, emphasis original.

[17]Phyllis Trible, "Take Back the Bible," *Review and Expositor* 97 (Fall 2000): 431, emphasis mine.

"something else" we are looking for, and how do we find it? In short, how can we use these texts more constructively?[18] In what follows, I'll offer two suggestions I find particularly useful in this regard. Although neither of these is likely to make you "fall in love" with the disagreeable parts of the Old Testament, they will provide some guidance for using these texts more profitably.

Learn by negative example. Sometimes troublesome texts are beneficial because they show us how *not* to live. "Some texts teach by negative example," writes John Collins, "and function as scripture by exhibiting attitudes that we must now condemn."[19] This is certainly true of texts that sanction violence against women. As Carol Hess sees it, "Some of the most difficult texts to deal with are those that portray, and do not seem to condemn, violence against women."[20] As an example, she mentions the horrifying story of the Levite's "concubine" (Judg 19) cited at the beginning of this chapter. What can be done with a story that describes the gang rape, murder, and dismemberment of a young woman yet never explicitly condemns these acts?[21] When we encounter passages like this, Hess suggests we should "name the violence as sin, mourn for the victims, and identify where the same terror is brought upon women today."[22] Even if the *text* does not explicitly condemn the violence it contains, *we* certainly can. When we do, troublesome texts become very useful for beginning important conversations about topics such as rape, misogyny, and patriarchy.

Another passage that provides ample opportunity to learn by way of negative example is 2 Samuel 11, the story of David and Bathsheba. David's behavior throughout this narrative is reprehensible. And in this

---

[18]For a book length treatment exploring how violent verses can be used constructively in the church, see my forthcoming book provisionally titled, *Do No Harm: How to Use Violent Biblical Texts Creatively and Responsibly in Church* (Louisville, KY: Westminster John Knox).

[19]John J. Collins, foreword to *The Human Faces of God: What Scripture Reveals When It Gets God Wrong (and Why Inerrancy Tries to Hide It)*, by Thom Stark (Eugene, OR: Wipf and Stock, 2011), xiv.

[20]Carol Lakey Hess, *Caretakers of Our Common House: Women's Development in Communities of Faith* (Nashville: Abingdon, 1997), 200.

[21]Lapsley (*Whispering the Word*, 35-67) argues that the narrator tells the story in a way that invites questions and even a critique of the violence on display in Judg 19–21. This may be true, but unfortunately most readers will not recognize this since there is no *explicit* critique in the text.

[22]Hess, *Caretakers*, 201.

case, the narrator explicitly says so: "But the thing that David had done displeased the LORD" (2 Sam 11:27). We should be outraged by David's selfish behavior. His actions cause great harm to Bathsheba, resulting in the death of her husband and the child she conceived by David.

At one level, this story illustrates the simple truth that sin has consequences. David's poor choices have ripple effects that affect many, many people. But there is more. The narrative also dramatically demonstrates how *one sin leads to another*. David's lust leads to adultery. This, in turn, leads to his abuse of power and ultimately to murder. When Bathsheba reveals she is pregnant, David desperately tries to cover his tracks. He recalls Bathsheba's husband Uriah from the battlefield under false pretenses in a desperate attempt to get him to sleep with her. When this plan fails, David sends Uriah back to the battlefield with a death warrant in his hand. He instructs Joab to put Uriah on the frontlines and to withdraw from him when the fighting gets fierce, all in an effort to make it look like Uriah was "innocently" killed in battle. Though David does not "pull the trigger," he has blood on his hands.

Moving from lust, to adultery, to abuse of power, and finally to murder by proxy, this story clearly illustrates how one sin leads to another. As such, it illustrates what we should *not* do, teaching by negative example.

Look for positive insights and explore key questions raised by troubling texts. Another way to use troublesome texts constructively is to explore some of the central questions they raise and to look for positive insights. As you work through the text, see if you can identify some of the main issues that are addressed. Jacqueline Lapsley observes how the gruesome story of the Levite's "concubine" in Judges 19 illustrates the truism that violence results in more violence.[23] More specifically, she notes how this story highlights the way violence against one woman leads to larger societal violence. The rape, death, and dismemberment of this unnamed woman precipitates a civil war in which the tribe of Benjamin is almost completely decimated (Judg 20). As Lapsley observes, that same pattern of violence against one woman leading to further acts of violence is also

---

[23]Lapsley, *Whispering the Word*, 64-65.

evident in two other rape stories in the Old Testament, the rape of Dinah (Gen 34) and the rape of Tamar (2 Sam 13).

When we read these stories, we *should* be appalled at the violence against women described there, and we should condemn it. But that's not all there is to be said. The way these stories link violence against one woman to widespread violence against others raises important questions for us to explore. As Lapsley writes, "The way the story [of the Levite's 'concubine'] is told encourages readers to ask what *we* might learn from this ancient story about how *we* respond to violence."[24] That is a *very* important question, especially in a culture like ours that routinely regards violence as an appropriate response to violence. When someone commits an act of violence, should we respond in kind, or are there better ways to deal with the situation? Lapsley believes this is the very question the narrator is raising based on the way the story is told.[25] We do well to explore this question and to consider what alternatives to violence we have at our disposal.[26]

For another example of how to use troublesome texts in this way, we can briefly return to the story of the near-sacrifice of Isaac.[27] This harrowing story, which portrays God commanding Abraham to offer his son Isaac as a burnt offering, has bothered readers for centuries. The terrifying divine command in Genesis 22 appears cruel and unloving, and it clashes with some of our most fundamental convictions about God's goodness, compassion, and kindness. It clearly stands at odds with the life and teachings of Jesus, a person who welcomed children and said the kingdom of God belongs to such as these. Therefore, it stands to reason that this portrayal of God in Genesis 22 says more about its cultural context than it does about the true nature and character of God. But coming to this conclusion does not mean we should dismiss the passage

---

[24]Lapsley, *Whispering the Word*, 66, emphasis mine.

[25]"We are led to wonder if there might have been other, more appropriate responses to the tragic fate of the Levite's wife." Lapsley, *Whispering the Word*, 66.

[26]For a wide-ranging discussion of nonviolent options in various contexts, see Eric A. Seibert, *Disarming the Church: Why Christians Must Forsake Violence to Follow Jesus and Change the World* (Eugene, OR: Cascade, 2018), especially chapters 9–17.

[27]Adapted from Seibert, *Disturbing Divine Behavior*, 217-20.

out of hand. There are other things going on in this text that are well worth our consideration, such as the way this text encourages us to examine our own lives and reflect on whether we are fully committed to God. Does God have *our* ultimate loyalty, or are there other priorities in our lives—work, possessions, relationships—that usurp our allegiance to God? Although God doesn't ask people to literally sacrifice their children, this passage still reminds us of the importance of putting God first. That is a positive insight and an important question to explore in an otherwise very troubling text.

Learning from negative examples and finding positive insights in problematic passages enables us to use them more constructively. This, in turn, makes our reading of the Old Testament more enjoyable.

BUT I'M STILL REALLY TROUBLED BY THESE TEXTS

While I am hopeful that these suggestions will help you find better ways to handle some of the most disagreeable parts of the Old Testament, I am keenly aware that for some readers they will not be enough. What can you do if you try some of these suggestions and still find it extremely difficult to deal with the most troublesome portions of the Old Testament? My advice would be to do some further reading. Pastors, scholars, and theologians have grappled with these challenging passages for years. See if the "solutions" they offer resolve some of your own struggles with these troubling texts.

For example, if you are struggling with violent portrayals of God in the Old Testament, take a look at Greg Boyd's book *Cross Vision: How the Crucifixion of Jesus Makes Sense of Old Testament Violence*, or my book *Disturbing Divine Behavior: Troubling Old Testament Images of God*, or Christopher Wright's book *The God I Don't Understand: Reflections on Tough Questions of Faith* (particularly the section on the slaughter of Canaanites).[28] While each one of us tackles this problem differently, reading books like these gives you options to consider.

---

[28]Christopher J. H. Wright, *The God I Don't Understand: Reflections on Tough Questions of Faith* (Grand Rapids, MI: Zondervan, 2008).

Or suppose you continue to be troubled by the way women are routinely portrayed in the Old Testament. Look at some of the different ways biblical scholars have dealt with this. What approaches have they used? Here you could explore Eryl Davies's fine book, *The Dissenting Reader: Feminist Approaches to the Hebrew Bible.*[29] Or you may appreciate reading Susanne Scholz's wide-ranging treatment of the issues in her book titled *Introducing the Women's Hebrew Bible: Feminism, Gender Justice, and the Study of the Old Testament* (2nd ed.).[30] You might also consider looking through *The Women's Bible Commentary* (3rd ed.), edited by Carol A. Newsom, Sharon H. Ringe, and Jacqueline E. Lapsley.[31] This excellent work covers the entire canon, Old and New Testament, and gives special attention to biblical passages that are particularly troubling and problematic for women.

Exploring resources like these can help a great deal. They reassure you that you are not alone. Others have struggled with the same texts you do. They also raise your awareness of the range of possibilities for addressing some of the most objectionable parts of the Bible. While none of these books will remove all the difficulties, and may in fact raise new questions, they will give you important tools that will help you work your way through these difficult passages.

Regaining Some Perspective

Before bringing this chapter to a close, I want to offer two additional suggestions that may lessen some of the distress caused by these problematic passages. Again, while neither of these suggestions "solves" the problem, they do provide some perspective and serve as a reminder that there is a lot of great material to enjoy in the Old Testament.

---

[29]Eryl Davies, *The Dissenting Reader: Feminist Approaches to the Hebrew Bible* (Burlington, VT: Ashgate, 2003).

[30]Susanne Scholz, *Introducing the Women's Hebrew Bible: Feminism, Gender Justice, and the Study of the Old Testament*, 2nd ed. (New York: Bloomsbury, 2017).

[31]Carol A. Newsom, Sharon H. Ringe, and Jacqueline E. Lapsley, *The Women's Bible Commentary*, 3rd ed. (Louisville, KY: Westminster John Knox, 2012).

*Bring troublesome texts into conversation with texts that are unprob-
lematic.* One of the inherent risks of focusing on troublesome texts is
that it may cause us to forget about all the other parts of the Old Testament that are not problematic. This is one of the weaknesses of the New
Atheists' relentless critique of the Old Testament.[32] While they are certainly right to argue that the Old Testament contains many morally problematic passages, their analysis is disappointingly one-sided. They give
the impression that violent and morally deficient passages are the sum
total of the Old Testament. They are not. There is much more to the Old
Testament than problem passages.[33]

One way to keep things in perspective is to bring some of the most
problematic Old Testament passages into conversation with other Old
Testament texts that present an alternate point of view. Before you conclude God is merciless based on your reading of Deuteronomy 7:2 and
Joshua 11:20, you must first consider verses like Exodus 34:6 and Lam-
entations 3:22-23:

> The LORD, the LORD,
> a God merciful and gracious,
> slow to anger,
> and abounding in steadfast love and faithfulness. (Ex 34:6)
> The steadfast love of the LORD never ceases,
> his mercies never come to an end;
> they are new every morning. (Lam 3:22-23)

Or rather than deciding God is hopelessly ethnocentric based on your
reading of Numbers 25 or Ezra 10, consider what Ruth 4:13-17 and 2
Kings 5:1-19 have to say. There you witness God's grace toward foreigners.
God blesses Ruth, a Moabite woman, with a child. And God heals
Naaman, an Aramean army commander, of leprosy.

---

[32]The New Atheists include individuals such as Dan Barker, Richard Dawkins, Sam Harris, and
Christopher Hitchens.

[33]For a recent, extensive critique of the New Atheists along these lines, see Katharine Dell, *Who
Needs the Old Testament? Its Enduring Appeal and Why the New Atheists Don't Get It* (Eugene,
OR: Cascade, 2017).

All this should remind you of an important point noted earlier, namely, that the Bible does not speak with one voice. Rather, it offers competing viewpoints for our consideration.[34] While bringing troublesome texts into conversation with other texts that are not problematic does not resolve all the difficulties, it can mitigate some of their more harmful effects.

Take a temporary break from the disagreeable parts of the Old Testament. If you are really feeling troubled by all the bloodshed and killing in the Old Testament and nothing else seems to help, then consider taking a *temporary* break from reading those kinds of passages. Instead, focus on parts of the Old Testament that you find encouraging and uplifting. Return to biblical passages that have been most meaningful and spiritually edifying to you in times past. It is better to do this than to abandon the Old Testament completely.

This is an especially good idea if you are going through a particularly difficult season of life. Depending on your circumstances, you may not have the time or energy to wrestle deeply with troubling Old Testament passages. Maybe in this moment you need texts that are familiar, safe, and reassuring. If so, revisit verses that remind you of God's presence amid the chaos of life. Reread passages that speak of God's great love and faithfulness. If you don't have the mental space to tackle some of the more disagreeable parts of the Old Testament right now, then take a break, turn to your "comfort texts," and regain your equilibrium. Once you are in a better place, you can then venture back out into the less hospitable parts of the Old Testament with renewed hope and determination.

Relatedly, you might consider reading books that focus primarily on positive passages in the Old Testament,[35] or that approach the Old Testament very appreciatively, in spite of some of its difficulties.[36]

---

[34]For more on this point, see Matthew Richard Schlimm, *This Strange and Sacred Scripture: Wrestling with the Old Testament and Its Oddities* (Grand Rapids, MI: Baker Academic, 2015), 139-59, and Mark McEntire, *The Internal Conversation of the Old Testament* (Macon, GA: Smyth & Helwys, 2018).
[35]See, e.g., David A. Leiter, *Neglected Voices: Peace in the Old Testament* (Scottdale, PA: Herald, 2007).
[36]See, e.g., Davis, *Getting Involved with God*, and Schlimm, *This Strange and Sacred Scripture*.

Books like these can be very encouraging and helpful. They can reenergize you and give you a renewed appreciation for this part of the Bible.

CONCLUSION

Problematic passages in the Old Testament can be tough, but there are ways to have positive encounters with them. Hopefully, enough has been said to demonstrate how you can find value in some of the most morally and theologically challenging parts of the Old Testament. While some of these texts will continue to be a struggle, and some will undoubtedly still bother you to varying degrees, that should not dissuade us from exploring these difficult parts of the Bible.

PART THREE

ENCOUNTERING *the* OLD TESTAMENT *in* NEW WAYS

10

EXPLORING DIFFERENT
PERSPECTIVES *and*
MAKING NEW DISCOVERIES

*Any serious reading of the Bible means
personal involvement in it, not simply mental
agreement with abstract propositions.*

Thomas Merton, *Opening the Bible*

ONE OF THE MAIN CLAIMS I have made in this book is that enjoying the Old Testament requires getting actively involved with it. Just reading is not enough, at least not over the long haul. Rather, it is necessary to find ways to engage these texts *and* to be engaged by them. While we have already made various suggestions in this regard, they have been interspersed throughout a number of different chapters. Here, in the final section of this book, we will give concentrated attention to many additional ways to encounter the Old Testament. Unlike previous suggestions, these are not typically tied to a particular section of the Old Testament but apply more generally to the whole.

While the present chapter and the next describe over twenty different ways to encounter the Old Testament, chapter twelve focuses on a single approach, namely, a method for exploring individual books of the Old Testament one at a time.

While there is no strict logic behind the order in which suggestions are made in these next two chapters, I have grouped them into several categories that should provide some sense of coherence. As you read through these chapters, I'm sure some ideas and activities will be more attractive than others. See what jumps out at you and try these first as you seek to get more involved with the Old Testament.

BECOME FAMILIAR WITH THE BASIC
CONTENT OF THE OLD TESTAMENT

Part of what makes the Old Testament so formidable to many people is its length. The sheer size sometimes scares off potential readers. Don't let this deter you. If you feel overwhelmed by the Old Testament or are less familiar with it than you would like, consider trying one of these approaches. Remember, the better you get to know the Old Testament, the more satisfying your experience will likely be.

Read the Old Testament from cover to cover in a year. If you have never read the Old Testament in its entirety, set a goal to read through it in a year. This is an especially helpful way to get the "lay of the land." Since there are 929 chapters in the Old Testament, you would need to read approximately two and a half chapters each day to make your way from Genesis to Malachi in a year.[1]

Part of what makes this year long journey through the Old Testament so rewarding is that it enables you to cover so much ground in such a relatively short amount of time. Most of us rarely take the time to read large swaths of the Old Testament. This exercise allows you to do precisely that. Along the way, note intriguing passages, troublesome texts, curious customs, inspiring verses, and other items of interest you want to explore further. You can always return to these later.

Mark up the Old Testament. Whenever I read a book, I like to underline important parts and write things in the margins. It's my way of actively engaging what I am reading. You might find it beneficial to do the same kind of thing with the Old Testament.[2] Marking up the biblical

---

[1] A basic online search will yield various ways of reading through the Old Testament (or the entire Bible) in a year.

[2] My thanks to Emily Cowser for this suggestion.

text is an excellent way to interact with it and to see things you might otherwise miss.

One way to do this would be to make notes and observations in the Bible you typically read. Yet most Bibles don't have a lot of extra space in the margins and some people are hesitant about writing in their Bible. So here is an alternative. Consider cutting and pasting portions of the Bible from a site like biblegateway.com. Select a specific passage or an entire book of the Old Testament you want to explore. Then cut and paste this text into your word processing program of choice. There, you can custom design the text by choosing the font style and size you prefer and by altering the spacing. Once you have made these choices, being sure to leave ample space around the margins and between lines of text, go ahead and print it. (You could also work with it digitally, if you prefer.)

You are now ready to mark up the printout you have created, and you can do this any way you choose. Use colors, pictures, pens, pencils, crayons—whatever works for you. You can circle recurring words and phrases, underline difficult or confusing items, and divide the text into major units and subunits.[3] You might also wish to note further questions to explore, thoughts about applications, and ways you may have sensed God speaking to you. There are no rules here, so feel free to mark up the text in whatever way seems most useful.

Actively engaging the Old Testament like this allows you to see it differently than you might when reading it straight out of the Bible. It also provides you with a written record of your interaction with the text. You might find it helpful to come back to this later, and you can certainly build on your work in the future if you desire. Marking up the Old Testament in this way helps you become more familiar with it and encourages you to keep digging deeper.

Create your own personalized study tools. Another way to deepen your engagement with the biblical text while increasing your knowledge

---

[3]For guidance on making these divisions, see chapter twelve.

of the Old Testament is to create your own personalized study tools such as maps, charts, and timelines. While many of these aides can be found in study Bibles and other reference works, there is real benefit to making them yourself. Doing so gets you more directly involved with the biblical text and allows you to personalize these tools in ways that are most helpful to you. It also increases your chances of remembering the key content of these resources since you are the one who created them.

Obviously, there are all sorts of personalized study tools you could create. What follows are just a few examples to get you started.

Draw a map. Knowing where places are located can greatly enhance your enjoyment of the Old Testament. It can also help you understand the Bible in ways not possible otherwise. Earlier, we discussed the importance of knowing where Joppa, Nineveh, and Tarshish are located when reading the book of Jonah. Drawing a map that includes these locations makes it unmistakably clear how determined Jonah was to flee from God's presence.

Make a chart. Charts are helpful for organizing large amounts of information in a relatively small space. They are also quite useful for allowing you to see patterns and make connections that might otherwise go undetected.

For example, let's suppose you are studying the book of Judges. The book is often divided into three sections: Judges 1:1–3:6; 3:7–16:31; 17:1–21:25. The middle (and longest) section provides an account of each of the six major "judges" who appear in the book. Each account is structured the same way, albeit with significant variations in content. The "Judges Cycle," as this recurring pattern is commonly called, contains the following basic elements:

1. Israel sins.

2. The Lord delivers the Israelites into the hand of foreign oppressors.

3. The Israelites cry out to the Lord for help.

4. The Lord raises up a deliverer (judge).

5. The deliverer (judge) frees Israel from oppression.

6. The land has rest, the judge dies, and then the cycle repeats itself.

A chart would be a very helpful way to organize the material in Judges 3:7–16:31. You could begin your chart by creating two columns, one to list the major judges and one to identify the biblical texts in which their stories appear. Additional columns could be added that correspond to various parts of the Judges Cycle. The result would be a chart that looks something like table 10.1.

As you make your way through Judges 3:7–16:31, fill in the relevant information on the chart. Once you are finished, look closely at the information you have collected. Did any patterns emerge? What happens to the Judges Cycle as you move from Othniel to Samson, and what do you think all this implies about Israel's spiritual well-being?

A chart could also be very helpful for working through 1–2 Kings. These oft-neglected books of the Old Testament describe the reigns of numerous kings, and it is exceedingly difficult to keep them all straight. To provide some order, you could produce two charts, one for kings in the north (Israel), and one for kings in the south (Judah). Begin by listing the kings in the order they reigned. Then create columns for such things as (1) their family/dynastic connections, (2) their most notable achievements, (3) their interaction with prophets (if any), (4) their evaluation by the writer, and (5) the circumstances of their death. Creating a resource like this would serve as a helpful reference as you read and study this part of the Old Testament.

Create a family tree. A family tree is another helpful tool. It is particularly useful for figuring out who is related to whom—and how. If you are reading through the book of Genesis and have difficulty remembering how people are connected to one another, try creating a family tree. Start with Abram (Abraham) and Sarai (Sarah) in Genesis 11, and trace their descendants through the book of Genesis, ending with Joseph and his sons. Having something like this at hand can help you make better sense of some aspects of the story, such as why Jacob favored Joseph and why

Table 10.1. The Judges Cycle

JUDGE	REFERENCE	ISRAEL'S SIN	THE OPPRESSOR	DESCRIPTION OF THE OPPRESSION	YEARS OF ISRAEL'S BONDAGE	ISRAEL'S RESPONSE	THE JUDGE'S OUTSTANDING DEEDS	YEARS THE LAND HAS REST
1. OTHNIEL								
2. EHUD								
3. DEBORAH AND BARAK								
4. GIDEON								
5. JEPHTHAH								
6. SAMSON								

Joseph favored Benjamin. It also helps explain why Joseph imprisons Simeon rather than Reuben after his brothers' first visit to Egypt.

Produce a pictorial "biblical timeline" for parts of the Old Testament. For some parts of the Old Testament, it is relatively easy to keep track of people and events. This is especially true of shorter books like Ruth and Jonah. But for longer books, especially less-familiar ones like Numbers or 2 Samuel, it becomes much more difficult. For books like these, you might consider producing a pictorial "biblical timeline" that enables you to organize key events in sequential order.

The reason I put "biblical timeline" in quotes is that, unlike an actual timeline, the purpose of this one is *not* to identify specific dates for particular events.[4] Rather, you'll design your timeline to help you get a handle on the order of events as they appear in the Bible. Sometimes the biblical order and the actual order of things coincide (e.g., Saul comes before David, David comes before Solomon, etc.), but other times things are displaced (e.g., some Minor Prophets that appear at the end of the Old Testament were active during the reigns of kings described in the books of 1–2 Kings, which appear much earlier in the Old Testament). The "biblical timeline" I am envisioning enables you to acquire a grasp of the basic sequence of the *biblical* story by determining what comes first, what comes next, and so forth.

To create this, you need to decide how extensive you would like your timeline to be. Which Old Testament book, or books, will you include? (Alternatively, you might decide to make a biblical timeline of a particular person in the Old Testament such as Sarah, Moses, David, or Esther.) Once you determine the scope of your timeline, identify the key events you wish to include on it. Describe each event in a few words, and include a picture or symbol that represents it. You can draw these if you like, or you can use a digital image or something cut out of a magazine

---

[4]When reading certain parts of the Old Testament, like prophetic literature, it is quite helpful to have a *historical* timeline to consult so you have some idea of where these individuals fit into Israel's larger story. These can easily be found online, though there is considerable difference of opinion about when some prophets were active.

or newspaper. Line these up from left to right and you will have a pictorial biblical timeline that represents the key people and events of the portion of the Old Testament you have selected.

To keep this within manageable proportions, it is probably best not to have more than one item on your timeline for each chapter, even if the chapter contains a number of significant events. And in some cases, one description and picture will suffice for multiple chapters if they are related to the same event. For instance, in the book of Exodus, you could easily group Exodus 14–15 together since both chapters deal with the story of Israel's dramatic crossing of the Red Sea. It is not difficult to think of many pictures that could be used to represent the deliverance of the Israelites and the devastation of the Egyptians.

Being able to see the overall structure and narrative arc of a book through pictures makes it more vivid and memorable. Moreover, creating something like this forces you to read the text more closely and requires you to make choices about what you think is most significant. All this has the potential to enhance your enjoyment of the Old Testament as your knowledge increases through your active involvement with this part of the Bible.

Memorize key Old Testament passages and verses. Another way to get to know the Old Testament (or at least specific parts of it) really well is Scripture memory. As children, many of us memorized key verses and passages from both the Old and New Testament. If you grew up in church or went to a private Christian school, you may have memorized such things as the Ten Commandments (Ex 20:1-17) or the "Shepherd's Psalm" (Ps 23). When I was very young, my mom encouraged me to memorize verses from a book designed for that very purpose.[5] The book literally went from A to Z. The first memory verse began with the letter A, the next with the letter B, and so forth. Though I don't think I ever made it all the way through the book—and I couldn't recall what they did with letters like X or Z—I still remember some of the verses all these years

---

[5]N. A. Woychuk, *The ABC Memory Plan: In Stages One, Two and Three* (Saint Louis: Bible Memory Association, n.d.).

later—A: "All we like sheep have gone astray; we have turned every one to his own way" (Is 53:6 KJV); C: "Children, obey your parents in the Lord: for this is right" (Eph 6:1 KJV).[6]

There are many advantages of committing verses from the Bible to memory. Scripture memory forces us to pay attention to *every* word. This slows us down and helps us notice things we often miss, deepening our appreciation of the text. It also makes the Old Testament portable. The verses we memorize travel with us wherever we go, regardless of whether or not we have a copy of the Bible in hand. Being able to recall verses at a moment's notice is quite helpful when we need a word of encouragement or when temptation comes our way. As the psalmist puts it, "I treasure your word in my heart, so that I may not sin against you" (Ps 119:11). Jesus used verses from Deuteronomy very effectively to resist temptation in the wilderness (see Mt 4:1-11 and Deut 8:3; 6:16; 10:20). It is not unusual for God to bring to mind verses we have committed to memory.

The great thing about Scripture memorization is that it can be done anytime, anywhere, even if you only have a couple minutes to devote to it. You can memorize Scripture as you are commuting to work, riding the bus to school, working in the garden, making dinner, folding laundry, shopping for groceries, exercising—the list goes on. Consider writing a verse or two on an index card that you can look at throughout the day. Or put these verses on a sticky note that you post on your computer screen, in the bathroom, or above the microwave.

To encourage you in this endeavor, find friends and family members who are willing to memorize the same verses. You might even propose a noncompetitive challenge to your family: if we collectively memorize fifteen verses by the end of the summer, we get to go out for ice cream! Be creative and have fun with this. It is a great way to get to know and love the Old Testament.

---

[6]Since my mom still has this book, I looked to see what they did for *X* and *Z*. While there were no memory verses for these letters, they had a page that said "X is for eXodus" and another that said "Z is for Zacchaeus."

ENCOUNTER THE OLD TESTAMENT DIFFERENTLY

One of the wonderful things about the Bible is that there are many different ways to encounter it. So rather than reading and experiencing the Old Testament the same way all the time, try mixing things up. This can revitalize your interest in this part of the Bible and increase your enjoyment of it. Let me encourage you to give some of the following suggestions a try and see what happens.

Read the Old Testament in a variety of different versions. Many Christians prefer a particular version of the Bible and read that version almost exclusively. Whether it is the New Revised Standard Version, the New International Version, the Common English Bible, The Message, or some other version or paraphrase, we are creatures of habit and tend to stick with what we know. Of course, there is nothing wrong with this. In fact, there is much to commend it. Consistently reading one translation enables us to develop a sense of familiarity with it. We learn to appreciate its unique phrasing and cadence, and memorization becomes easier if we routinely encounter the same text over and over again.

Yet, as the saying goes, familiarity breeds contempt. It is possible to become *so* accustomed to the way laws, stories, proverbs, and prophetic pronouncements are worded in a particular version of the Bible that it becomes increasingly difficult to "hear" these biblical texts in fresh, new ways. They no longer have the same impact on us because we are so familiar with them.

Reading the Old Testament in a different version than the one you customarily use can be helpful in this regard. It can enable you to experience the Old Testament in exciting new ways. For example, when you read a familiar verse or well-known story that is worded differently than what you are accustomed to, you might notice things you previously overlooked. It might rekindle your interest to dig deeper, especially if you find some significant differences between versions. For example, consider how both the New International Version and the New Revised Standard Version render Jonah 3:10:

When God saw what they did and how they turned from their evil ways, he relented and did not bring on them the destruction he had threatened. (NIV)

When God saw what they did, how they turned from their evil ways, God changed his mind about the calamity that he had said he would bring upon them; and he did not do it. (NRSV)

What is the difference between the NIV speaking of God relenting and the NRSV speaking of God's mind changing? How do other translations render this verse? What do you think is going on here?

Another thing you will discover when comparing translations is that some include more material than others. This happens when translations incorporate readings from manuscript discoveries like the Dead Sea Scrolls.[7] Suppose you are reading about David's response to the rape of his daughter Tamar in 2 Samuel 13. The New International Version reads as follows: "When King David heard all this, he was furious" (2 Sam 13:21).[8] But David doesn't punish his son Amnon for committing this egregious act of violence. Why? The NRSV supplies the answer by drawing on the Dead Sea Scrolls as well as the Septuagint, an ancient Greek translation of the Old Testament: "When King David heard of all these things, he became very angry, *but he would not punish his son Amnon, because he loved him, for he was his firstborn*" (2 Sam 13:21, emphasis mine).

The portion of the verse in italics no longer appears in the Hebrew Bible. But based on the Dead Sea Scrolls and the Septuagint, it seems to have been there originally. Apparently, it was inadvertently omitted at some point in the process of textual transmission.[9] Bringing this back

---

[7]For a helpful discussion of the Dead Sea Scrolls, see James C. VanderKam, *The Dead Sea Scrolls Today*, 2nd ed. (Grand Rapids, MI: Eerdmans, 2010).

[8]So also the English Standard Version: "When King David heard of all these things, he was very angry."

[9]This omission from the Hebrew Bible appears to be a classic case of haplography, the act of inadvertently skipping letters or words when hand-copying a manuscript. For a discussion of scribal errors and the process by which textual critics attempt to determine which readings are closest to the original, see Ellis R. Brotzman and Eric J. Tully, *Old Testament Textual Criticism: A Practical Introduction*, 2nd ed. (Grand Rapids, MI: Baker Academic, 2016).

into the story helps us understand the rationale behind David's behavior, though it certainly does not excuse his failure to act.

Another interesting example is found in 1 Sam 10:27. Here, an entire paragraph that is not present in the NIV has been included in the NRSV. It comes from the Dead Sea Scrolls and also has support from the writings of the Jewish historian Josephus. This paragraph provides some important backstory—albeit rather gruesome—to the conflict between the Ammonites and the Israelites reported in 1 Samuel 11.

> Now Nahash, king of the Ammonites, had been grievously oppressing the Gadites and the Reubenites. He would gouge out the right eye of each of them and would not grant Israel a deliverer. No one was left of the Israelites across the Jordan whose right eye Nahash, king of the Ammonites, had not gouged out. But there were seven thousand men who had escaped from the Ammonites and had entered Jabesh-gilead.

Whether you discover "new" information like this or simply hear familiar texts translated differently, reading a version of the Bible other than the one you are accustomed to will help you experience the Old Testament in new ways and can enhance your appreciation for it. If you are looking for a convenient site to read many different English versions of the Bible, check out biblegateway.com.[10]

Listen to the Old Testament audibly. For a number of years, I "commuted" from Erie, Pennsylvania to Grantham, Pennsylvania. For those of you unfamiliar with Pennsylvanian geography, Erie is in the far northwest corner of the state. Grantham is in southcentral Pennsylvania. It's about three hundred miles one way, a five-hour trip. At the time, my wife, Elisa, was working on her PhD in Counseling Psychology at Gannon University in Erie and I was teaching at Messiah University (then College) in Grantham. I would leave Erie *very* early Tuesday morning so I could arrive at Messiah in time to teach a 10:30 a.m. class, my first of the day. After teaching classes on Tuesday, I then drove to my parents' home

---

[10]This site also allows you to do searches within a particular translation (e.g., find all occurrences of the word "forgiveness") and to set different versions side-by-side so you can read and compare them verse-by-verse.

about thirty minutes away. I would stay there two nights and then return to Messiah to teach classes on Thursday before making my three-hundred-mile return trip to Erie.

Needless to say, those trips back and forth gave me lots of "alone time" in the car. Since one can only listen to so much National Public Radio (NPR), I would sometimes pass the time listening to chapter after chapter of the Old Testament from an audible reading of the New International Version. This enabled me to hear the Old Testament in a new way. You pick up on different things when you *hear* Scripture aloud rather than read it silently. This can be rewarding and can rekindle your desire to dive into this part of the Bible.

In addition to hearing the Old Testament read aloud, you might try reading the Bible aloud yourself. Feel free to read it dramatically—and loudly—if you like. Just don't do it at 2:00 a.m. when everyone else is asleep! You might choose to invite some friends to join you. As Michelle Curtis proposes, "Another really fun exercise is to read one whole Old Testament book aloud with friends in one sitting. Get tea and snacks. Hearing the whole thing together really helps you hear the story and it's actually quite a fun event."[11]

Hearing Scripture read aloud, whether in your own voice or someone else's, can be beneficial and pleasurable. It helps you notice overlooked details, seldom-read stories, and long-neglected insights, things we often miss by reading the Old Testament silently and selectively. As John Burgess observes,

> When we read Scripture aloud, we are challenged to read thoughtfully and carefully, so that the sounds help interpret the text, to lift up its nuances, and to impress it more firmly on our memory. . . . Scripture reading takes on the character of an event, not merely of a private, mental exercise. It shapes an encounter with God.[12]

In the ancient world, it was customary to hear sacred texts audibly. Given very low levels of literacy and the relative scarcity of handwritten

---

[11]This is taken from Michelle Curtis's comments on a draft of this book. Used by permission.
[12]John P. Burgess, *Why Scripture Matters: Reading the Bible in a Time of Church Conflict* (Louisville, KY: Westminster John Knox, 1998), 61.

manuscripts, this was the only way most people had access to biblical texts. The Bible contains numerous examples of people hearing Scripture read to them.[13] One of the most fascinating accounts is tucked away in the book of Nehemiah. In this particular instance, we are told that "all the people" gathered together in a central location where they instructed Ezra, the scribe, "to bring the book of the law of Moses" (Neh 8:1). Ezra starts reading aloud at the beginning of the day and does not stop until noon, reading "from early morning until midday" (Neh 8:3). There are Levites in the crowd who help the Israelites understand what they are hearing, and this affects the people deeply. They weep because they feel so convicted, presumably about their failure to keep the law. But the Levites tell them not to grieve. The words they heard were intended to encourage them, not condemn them. As a result, everyone "went their way to eat and drink . . . and to make great rejoicing, because they had understood the words that were declared to them" (Neh 8:12).

Hearing Scripture read aloud can have a powerful impact on you. It is an ancient practice we do well to reclaim.[14]

Read a familiar Old Testament story from a different perspective. One way to get reengaged with the Old Testament, particularly with familiar stories you have heard so often that you don't really pay attention to them anymore, is to read them from a different perspective. For example, try reading the flood narrative from the perspective of those *outside* the ark (Gen 6–7). As beautiful images of colorful animals aboard a floating zoo fade away, a much more desperate scene emerges. Or read the conquest narrative in the book of Joshua through the eyes of the indigenous population (Josh 6–11). How would Canaanites living in the land have viewed the invading Israelites and their merciless God? Or reread the story of David and Goliath from the Philistines' perspective (1 Sam 17). How would this story sound differently if a Philistine told it?

---

[13]For some examples of people reading Scripture aloud, or being instructed to do so, see Ex 24:7; Deut 31:11; Josh 8:34-35; 2 Kings 22:10; 23:2; Jer 36:10; Lk 4:16-21; Acts 8:30.

[14]For more on reading the Bible out loud, see Burgess, *Why Scripture Matters*, 59-62, 70-72.

Doing this involves using some imagination. It requires you to take a different point of view than the one taken by the biblical writer. When you do so, you invariably see these texts in a new light. This can help rekindle your interest in Old Testament stories you may have grown tired of hearing.

Reading Old Testament stories from a different angle of vision is especially beneficial when you read from the perspective of those who are victims of violence in the text.[15] Reading the flood narrative from the perspective of those outside the ark, for example, or reading the conquest narrative from the perspective of those inside the city walls, humanizes the countless people slain in these accounts of divine destruction. It helps us to develop compassion for these individuals. This is crucial lest we view the enemies of Israel with disdain and contempt. Canaanites and Philistines were created in God's image just like Israelites. These "foreigners" were not disposable, and we should take no delight in their demise in the pages of Scripture. Reading from *their* perspective reminds us of their humanity and cautions us against demonizing the "other," whether in the pages of the Old Testament or in the world around us.

MAKE NEW DISCOVERIES IN OLD TEXTS

Part of what draws many people back to the Bible time and again is the joy of discovery. It is rewarding and often deeply satisfying to see things in the Bible you never noticed before, especially when you make these discoveries on your own. If you are eager to explore the Old Testament to see what "hidden" treasures it contains, try some of these approaches and see where they lead.[16]

Look in neglected places. Another creative way to approach this part of the Bible, and one that can yield some unexpected rewards, is to spend some time examining a portion of the Old Testament that is unfamiliar

---

[15]For more on reading from this perspective, see Eric A. Seibert, *The Violence of Scripture: Overcoming the Old Testament's Troubling Legacy* (Minneapolis: Fortress, 2012), 81-85, 100-101, 121-22.

[16]See also the discussion in chapter eight about finding hidden treasures in the boring parts of the Bible.

to you. Who knows what you will find there? It is sort of like exploring an attic that has been untouched for years. There is something exciting about rummaging through boxes of stuff long forgotten. While some discoveries will be rather mundane, others will be real treasures: an old diary from a long lost relative; a jar of rare coins; a photograph album with pictures of family and friends; a family heirloom thought to be lost, and so forth. Likewise, there are some real gems waiting to be discovered in the neglected places of the Old Testament, in the books and passages rarely mentioned in church. Venture onto the side streets and back alleys of the Old Testament and see what you find in these seldom traveled places.

To get you started on this quest, let me suggest you start with a book like 2 Kings, or some part of it. Read the dramatic story of Elisha bringing the Shunammite woman's son back to life (2 Kings 4:32-37). Witness the honorable actions of four lucky lepers who happen upon enormous wealth and prosperity (2 Kings 7:1-20). Be inspired by the bold and daring actions of Jehosheba whose quick thinking saves her one-year-old nephew from certain death (2 Kings 11:1-3). Look at what King Hezekiah does to recover from his illness and get a fifteen-year extension on his life (2 Kings 20:1-11). This is just a brief sampling of the treasures waiting to be found when exploring some of the more neglected parts of the Old Testament. So go ahead, look in the nooks and crannies. Spend some time in the forgotten places and see what you can find. You may be delightfully surprised.

Search for the rest of the story. There are times when a story told in one part of the Old Testament is continued elsewhere. On these occasions, when there is more information to be had, it is worth taking the time to discover "the rest of the story," as Paul Harvey used to say.

To take one rather peculiar example, consider this passage at the very end of the book of Genesis:

> Then Joseph said to his brothers, "I am about to die; but God will surely come to you, and bring you up out of this land to the land that he swore

to Abraham, to Isaac, and to Jacob." So Joseph made the Israelites swear, saying, "When God comes to you, you shall carry up my bones from here." And Joseph died, being one hundred ten years old; he was embalmed and placed in a coffin in Egypt. (Gen 50:24-26)

So whatever happened to the bones of Joseph? Did his brothers honor his request? Genesis 50:26, the last verse of the book, seems to suggest they did not. Does the Old Testament have more to say about Joseph's request, or is this all we have?

If you do a quick search for the word *bones* in the Bible, you will find two additional references to the bones of Joseph in the Old Testament, one in Exodus and one in Joshua. The reference in Exodus follows the ten plagues and occurs about four hundred years after the death of Joseph. As the recently freed Hebrew people are making their way out of Egypt toward the Red Sea, we read:

And Moses took with him the bones of Joseph who had required a solemn oath of the Israelites, saying, "God will surely take notice of you, and then you must carry my bones with you from here." (Ex 13:19)

Then, over forty years after that, the story comes to its final conclusion when the Israelites are settled in Canaan.

The bones of Joseph, which the Israelites had brought up from Egypt, were buried at Shechem, in the portion of ground that Jacob had bought from the children of Hamor, the father of Shechem, for one hundred pieces of money; it became an inheritance of the descendants of Joseph. (Josh 24:32)

Following this story through to the end is rewarding at a number of levels. There is something very satisfying about discovering more of the story. It's like going on a treasure hunt and finding the treasure. Finding the rest of the story can also open up interesting lines of inquiry for reflection and application. Setting aside questions of historicity for the moment, and just working with this story as a story, it is fascinating to imagine Israelites toting a bone box around with them for over forty years while they traveled from Egypt to Canaan. What's even more intriguing is the fact that later generations followed through on a commitment their distant ancestors made *hundreds* of years prior. That's impressive, to say the least. And it makes me wonder what kind of responsibility we have to fulfill promises made by those who came before us.

Suppose you have a close relative who promises her two teenage children that she will use the money in her savings account for their college education. Yet, tragically, she dies before they enter college. She was an only parent and you have been appointed as the legal guardian of her children. All her assets—including the aforementioned savings account—have been transferred to you. Do you have an obligation to keep the promise she made to her children about using her savings to fund their education? Or, to put this in the language of the Joseph story, must you carry the bones of Joseph out of Egypt even though *you* were not the one who promised to do so? These are interesting questions to consider, and they emerge most clearly when looking at the narrative arc of the story in its entirety.

Regardless of how you might answer these questions, my point here is to emphasize the value and pleasure of discovering the rest of the story when it is available. So, when you read a story about a person or event in one part of the Old Testament, let me encourage you to look for more of the story. A searchable online Bible, like those found at biblegateway.com, can help you in this regard. Just type in some key words from the story you think would appear elsewhere and see what you find.

Explore one chapter of the Old Testament for an entire week. Earlier I suggested reading through the Old Testament in a year, an approach that privileges distance over depth. As an alternative to that, try spending an entire week with just one chapter from the Old Testament. Select whatever chapter you like and read it each day throughout the week. Linger over it to see what you can find. The longer you look, the more you are likely to notice. What new insights and questions emerge as you move from day to day? Be sure to record your observations daily to remind you of things already discovered and to encourage you to keep looking for new insights.

One way to help you dig deeper as you move throughout the week is to explore what the chapter has to offer on specific topics. What does this chapter of the Old Testament reveal about temptation, for example? About justice? About peace? What can I learn here about God, or humanity, or creation? This probably works best if you focus on just one question at a time.

To illustrate, let's consider what the writer says about God in Jonah chapter one. Here is a sampling of what you will find:

1. God communicates with certain individuals.

   "The word of the LORD came to Jonah son of Amittai, saying, . . ." (Jon 1:1)

2. God is aware of human sinfulness and takes decisive action to deal with it.

   "Go at once to Nineveh, that great city, and cry out against it; for their wickedness has come up before me." (Jon 1:2)

3. God controls the natural world and uses extreme weather for divine purposes.

   "The LORD hurled a great wind upon the sea." (Jon 1:4)

4. God created the world.

   "I worship the LORD, . . . who made the sea and the dry land." (Jon 1:9)

5. God's presence is unescapable.

   Jonah unsuccessfully tries to flee "from the presence of the LORD." (Jon 1:3-4)

6. God answers prayer, even when offered by "pagans."

   "Then they [the sailors] cried out to the LORD, 'Please, O LORD, we pray, do not let us perish on account of this man's life. Do not make us guilty of innocent blood; for you, O LORD, have done as it pleased you.' So they picked Jonah up and threw him into the sea; and the sea ceased from its raging." (Jon 1:14-16)

7. God can use large aquatic animals to do what God desires.

   "The LORD provided a large fish to swallow up Jonah." (Jon 1:17)

After you have finished making these observations, you might find it interesting to determine how closely they coincide with your own views about God. For instance, while you might readily affirm that God is the Creator of the world (#4), you might be less comfortable with the notion that God uses extreme weather for divine purposes (#3). This process of evaluation can help you sharpen and develop your personal beliefs in conversation with these texts.

Once you think you have exhausted all there is to discover about God in Jonah 1, select another category and repeat the same process. For example, what can be learned from Jonah 1 about the importance of obedience or the danger of running from God? Asking questions like these can help you see things that might have otherwise gone unnoticed. Devoting an entire week to a single chapter will help you make new discoveries as you slow down and read more carefully.

Learn more about the Old Testament from the experts. Finally, to reiterate a point touched on previously, a great way to make new discoveries is by learning from experts in the field: authors, speakers, teachers, and others. You can enhance your enjoyment of the Old Testament by learning more about it from people who have spent their lives studying it. Consider taking, or auditing, a course on the Old Testament from a nearby college or seminary. If that is not feasible, you could take an online course or watch lectures on DVD.[17] Or purchase some good books on the Old Testament that will expand your knowledge of it. Read Old Testament introductions, commentaries, and other books of interest in the field of biblical studies.[18] This will take some time and intentionality, but it has the potential to rejuvenate your interest in this part of the Bible. The more you learn about the Old Testament, the better you will be able to read, understand, and enjoy it.

---

[17]One example would be Amy Jill-Levine's lectures on the Old Testament (The Great Courses), which can be streamed at no charge from some public libraries.
[18]See the appendix for some suggestions.

CONCLUSION

This chapter has demonstrated many different ways to approach the Old Testament. Each one has the potential to increase your attraction to this part of the Bible. Since these are only suggestions, you are free to try the ones that look most appealing while ignoring those that seem less attractive. Part of the reason I have offered so many ideas here—with more to come in the next chapter—is to give you options, not to overwhelm you. I do not expect anyone to do everything in this chapter. If you experiment with one of the ideas mentioned here and discover it's just not working for you, set it aside and try something else. There's no need to feel bad about that. It may take a few tries to find a good fit. And keep in mind, what works well for you today may not work as well a month or a year from now. So it is good to be flexible and to have multiple options at your disposal.

I'll say more about how to implement some of these ideas later, but first we need to look at some additional ways to creatively encounter the Old Testament.

11

TOPICALLY MOTIVATED, ARTISTICALLY ORIENTED, *and* PERSONALLY REFLECTIVE APPROACHES

*The Bible may be likened to an artesian well whose supply
is inexhaustible, regardless of how much we drink of it.*

Robert A. Traina,
Methodical Bible Study

Though we considered nearly a dozen different ways to engage the Old Testament in the previous chapter, these just scratch the surface. There are many other possibilities. The purpose of this chapter is to present more options for getting actively involved with this part of the Bible.

The additional approaches offered here have been grouped into three categories. Some promote reading and studying the Old Testament topically; others allow for significant creativity and artistic expression; and some are primarily related to personal reflection and introspection. All are beneficial for spiritual formation, and all have the potential to deepen our relationship with God.

Topically Motivated Approaches to the Old Testament

The Old Testament touches on a wide range of topics and themes. While some receive only passing mention (e.g., fishing), others occur with great frequency and occupy a considerable amount of space (e.g., warfare).

The two approaches mentioned below illustrate a couple different ways you can interact with the Old Testament topically.

Use the Old Testament to explore a topic of interest. One way to get started would be to select a topic that interests you and then see what the Old Testament says about it. Maybe you want to learn more about forgiveness, or perhaps you are curious about Old Testament perspectives on the poor and needy. Whatever topic you choose, allow this to guide your investigation.

Once you have a topic in mind, use a concordance or a searchable online Bible to find verses and passages in the Old Testament that relate to it. If you want to know what the Old Testament says about forgiveness, you could look for every occurrence of the word *forgiveness*, along with words like *forgive, forgave, forgiven*, and so on. Once you have identified these passages, read them carefully and contextually to see what light they might shed on the topic you are studying.

Depending on your topic, a keyword may not yield many results. For example, suppose you want to discover what the Old Testament says about favoritism. You do a quick search of the word *favoritism* only to discover it appears just once in the Bible, and it's not even an Old Testament reference! The only time the word *favoritism* occurs in the New Revised Standard Version of the Bible is in James 2:1. While this verse is part of an important passage about favoritism in the Bible, you know the Bible has more to offer on this topic than what you find in James 2. From your recent study of Genesis, you remember that Rebekah favored Jacob (Gen 25:27-28). You also recall that when Jacob grew up and had children, he favored his son Joseph and made a special garment for him. You suspect there may be other stories about favoritism like this in the Old Testament but struggle to bring them to mind.

This is where a topical Bible comes in very handy. It is a bit of a misnomer to refer to this as a topical *Bible* since this resource is not really a Bible at all. Rather, it is a reference work that identifies a large number of topics related to material in the Bible. The topics are arranged alphabetically, and under each entry you will find Bible verses that directly relate to the topic you have chosen. *Nave's Topical Bible* is one of the most popular topical Bibles. It can be purchased very inexpensively or used freely online.[1] Sometimes it is bundled with certain Bible software programs.

When you open *Nave's Topical Bible* to the word *favoritism*, this is what you find:

Favoritism

INSTANCES OF

- Jacob, for Rachel
  Genesis 29:30, Genesis 29:34

- Elkanah, for Hannah
  1 Samuel 1:4, 1 Samuel 1:5

- Rebekah, for Jacob
  Genesis 27:6-17

- Jacob, for Joseph
  Genesis 37:3, Genesis 37:4

- Joseph, for Benjamin
  Genesis 43:34

- Forbidden in parents
  Deuteronomy 21:15-17

- See PARTIALITY[2]

This entry identifies five Old Testament stories about people showing favoritism. It also cites a passage in Deuteronomy containing legislation that prohibits showing favoritism in a particular case. Finally, it indicates another entry ("partiality") where you can find more passages related to this topic.

---

[1]Orville J. Nave, *Nave's Topical Bible: A Comprehensive Digest of over 20,000 Topics and Subtopics with More Than 10,000 Associated Scripture References* (Nashville: Thomas Nelson, 2002). Online at www.biblestudytools.com/concordances/naves-topical-bible/.

[2]*Nave's Topical Bible*, s.v. "Favoritism," accessed January 30, 2021, www.biblestudytools.com /concordances/naves-topical-bible/favoritism.html.

While lists like these are not exhaustive—one might also add Isaac's favoritism for Esau (Gen 25:28)—they do provide a great starting point for studying a particular topic in the Old Testament. This approach to the Old Testament can be invigorating and is quite beneficial for personal enrichment. It is also very useful when preparing a devotional or Bible study to use with a small group or Sunday school class.

Select one Old Testament book and see what it says about a topic. Another way to encounter the Bible topically that involves a slight variation to the previous approach is to limit your exploration to one particular book, or part, of the Old Testament. This can be really helpful if you are dealing with a topic that occurs frequently in the pages of the Old Testament since it is more manageable to focus on just one book rather than all thirty-nine.

To illustrate how this works, let's consider what the book of Proverbs has to say about the importance of proper speech.[3] Since a keyword search would probably miss many important references in this case, it is probably best to read through the entire book and note all the verses that deal with speech in one way or another. This could be completed over several days and is quite doable since it is limited to just one book of the Bible.

Once you have gathered all the relevant verses, read through them carefully. What do you learn? One thing you will quickly notice is that proverbs about speech tend to fall into one of two broad categories: speech to avoid and speech to practice. Some types of speech to avoid include gossip, boasting, talkativeness, and interference in another person's quarrel. Here is a sampling:

When words are many, transgression is not lacking,
but the prudent are restrained in speech. (Prov 10:19)

A gossip goes about telling secrets,
but one who is trustworthy in spirit keeps a confidence. (Prov 11:13)

Like somebody who takes a passing dog by the ears
is one who meddles in the quarrel of another. (Prov 26:17)

---

[3] I am indebted to Terry Brensinger for the suggestion to select a topic and then to explore all the verses in Proverbs that pertain to that particular topic.

Let another praise you, and not your own mouth—
a stranger, and not your own lips. (Prov 27:2)

Types of speech to practice include gentle speech, gracious speech, and well-timed speech.

A gentle tongue is a tree of life,
but perverseness in it breaks the spirit. (Prov 15:4)

Those who love a pure heart and are gracious in speech
will have the king as a friend. (Prov 22:11)

Words spoken at the right time
are like gold apples in a silver setting [i.e., something very beautiful].
        (Prov 25:11 CEB)

Once you have collected these, consider how well they apply in today's world. You will discover that many of these proverbs are just as applicable today as they were thousands of years ago. As Christians, we still believe gossip is harmful, and we discourage people from boasting. Also, most people would agree it is beautiful to observe someone saying just the right thing at just the right time as Proverbs 25:11 asserts.

Yet some proverbs don't work quite as well in the modern world, especially if they are interpreted too literally or too broadly. For example, is "transgression" *always* associated with many words? (Are college professors perennially sinful?) Or is it *always* dangerous to get involved in other people's disputes? (What about the valuable role of mediators?) Questions like these remind us to be wise about how we interpret and apply these proverbs to current day situations.

Once you have reflected on the contemporary relevance of these sayings, consider extending your study beyond the book of Proverbs. How do other passages of Scripture confirm or contradict what you learned about "proper speech" from the book of Proverbs? A passage like James 3:1-12, which also emphasizes the need to use our words carefully, would be an excellent place to begin.

There would be many useful takeaways from a study like this. First and foremost, it reminds us that what we say really matters. Careless words can have serious consequences. They sometimes result in ruined friendships, damaged reputations, and lost jobs. On the other hand, prudent speech can do an enormous amount of good. It can build people up and remind them of their inherent value and worth. Consider how you feel when someone pays you a compliment or expresses gratitude for something you have done. These words stick with you and can encourage you for a long time. There is tremendous power in our tongue. No wonder so many proverbs counsel us to use it wisely.

Using a book of the Bible to collect and analyze verses related to a certain theme or idea provides focus and can yield some rather profound insights. Dig in and give it a try.

Use humor to enhance your enjoyment of the Old Testament. A somewhat different way to approach the Old Testament topically is to look at it through a particular lens, in this case, through humor. Although most people do not regard the Old Testament as being particularly funny, some texts were clearly designed to amuse.[4] Take the ark narrative in 1 Sam 4:1–7:1, for example. After defeating the Israelites in two successive battles, the Philistines capture the ark of the covenant (gasp!). They take this war trophy home and promptly place it in the temple of their god Dagon. As the story goes, very unusual things begin to happen. The following morning, Dagon is found lying prostrate in front of the ark as though worshiping Yahweh. The same thing happens again the next morning, but this time only Dagon's torso is there. His head and hands, mysteriously severed during the night, are lying on the threshold of the temple. Israelite audiences would have found this a hoot. And this is just the beginning.

Reading further, we learn that the presence of the ark not only afflicts Dagon, it afflicts the Philistines as well. While the ark is stationed in Ashdod, the Philistines are "struck . . . with tumors" (1 Sam 5:6). As John Goldingay comments:

> The NRSV coyly tells us that the effect was that the Philistines grew tumours. . . . The tumours were actually something like haemorrhoids and

---

[4]See Mark E. Biddle, *A Time to Laugh: Humor in the Bible* (Macon, GA: Smyth & Helwys, 2013).

they seem to have issued from having diarrhoea. This is the stuff of situation comedy and no doubt the Israelites were intended to laugh at the idea of the Philistines queuing to use the lavatory.[5]

When the Ashdodites transfer the ark to Gath, the same thing happens to the Philistines there. Then, when the people of Gath unload the ark on the inhabitants of Ekron, the people cry out, "Why have they brought around to us the ark of the God of Israel to kill us and our people?" (1 Sam 5:10). The ark of the covenant is like a ticking time bomb that people cannot get rid of fast enough. The Israelites must have relished telling this story, one that affirms the superiority of their God at the expense of the Philistines and their lackluster deity Dagon.[6]

Finding humor in the Old Testament often requires us to look at texts from an unconventional perspective or imagine certain details that are not present. This is what cartoonists and stand-up comedians do all the time. For some examples of this as it applies to the Old Testament, see the cartoon strip *Frank & Ernest* by Thaves which contains many cartoons related to Old Testament people and ideas.[7] Or check out *The Creation Chronicles*, a theatrical production by Ted and Lee that can be purchased on DVD.[8] The comedian Ken Davis also has a great video about the call of Moses titled, *A Wimpy Prophet: A Butane Bush and No Excuses*.[9] Watching things like these is not only entertaining; it helps us stay interested in the Old Testament. Seeing the Old Testament in new and humorous ways that help us laugh will keep us coming back for more.

[5]John Goldingay, *Men Behaving Badly* (Carlisle, Cumbria: Paternoster, 2000), 43.

[6]Obviously, a story like this raises questions about the propriety of ridiculing other religions, something most Christians today would frown upon. While this is an important conversation to have, it should not obscure the fact that for ancient Israelites, this was a funny story.

[7]These can be found at http://frankandernest.com. Use the search box to type in names like Noah, Moses, David, etc., and see what you find.

[8]Downloads of the script and videos of this performance, along with other resources, are available at www.tedandcompany.com/store.

[9]Ken Davis, *A Wimpy Prophet, a Butane Bush, and No Excuses*, dir. Dan Marlow (Crown Video, 2013), DVD. A CD of this show is also available at http://store.kendavis.com/a-wimpy-prophet-cd-by-ken-davis.

Artistically Oriented Approaches
to the Old Testament

Another way to experience the Old Testament from a new perspective is to engage it artistically in some fashion. The next few suggestions explore various ways to do precisely that. Some involve creating art yourself, while others invite you to experience the Old Testament through various forms of art created by others such as pictures, movies, novels, and songs.

Create a work of art related to a person, passage, event, or theme in the Old Testament. If you are the type of person who enjoys making art, consider merging your artistic interests with the Old Testament. Create a drawing, sculpture, or painting that relates to something you have encountered in the Old Testament. Or try making a collage, writing a poem, creating a musical composition, or producing a short video based on an Old Testament passage, character, or event. Creative projects like these deepen your engagement with the Old Testament and allow you to interact with it in fresh new ways. And this is not just for accomplished artists. Whatever your skill level, simply choose a medium you like and go for it!

Though the possibilities are myriad, I'll suggest a few just by way of example. If you enjoy painting, paint a scene from the Old Testament that feels particularly meaningful to you such as Jacob's nocturnal wrestling match with a "man" at the Jabbok (Gen 32:22-32), Moses' divine call at the burning bush (Ex 3), Israel's miraculous manna provided daily in the wilderness (Ex 16), Hannah's fervent prayer for a son (1 Sam 1), Isaiah's dramatic vision of the Lord (Is 6), or Daniel's deliverance from the lion's den (Dan 6).

If you are musically inclined, create a musical composition about Israel's deliverance from slavery (Ex 14–15) or Israel's return from exile (Ezra 1–2). Or try writing a song about reconciliation, based on the reunion of Jacob and Esau after twenty years of estrangement (Gen 33), or about forgiveness, based on Joseph's treatment of his brothers in Egypt (Gen 45:1-15; 50:15-21).

Then again, maybe sculpting is your thing. Get some clay, wood, metal or other material, and try making a sculpture, or carving, of an important person or object from the Old Testament. An olive wood carving of Moses sits on my computer desk at work. It was made in Israel and given to me by a close friend. The carving is over a foot high, and features Moses with the Ten Commandments in one hand and his staff in the other. What biblical figure would you carve or sculpt? And what—if anything—would you put in that person's hands?

If you enjoy writing poetry, try writing a poem that explores the feelings of the midwives who save Hebrew baby boys (Ex 1), or the feelings of Naomi who experiences great loss (Ruth 1). Powerful poems could also be written about really difficult texts like the rape of Dinah (Gen 34) or the rape of Tamar (2 Sam 13). Or, on a lighter note, you might use poetry to explore the love between Jacob and Rachel (Gen 29, esp. Gen 29:20), or the friendship between David and Jonathan (1 Sam 18).

After you have completed a work of art related to the Old Testament, I would encourage you to spend a little time writing about it. Describe what you made and why you made it. Say a little bit about how your artwork deepened your appreciation of the biblical text(s) that inspired it. If you are so inclined, show your artistic creation to someone else. You might even consider encouraging family members and friends to produce their own artistic creations. Or, if you *really* want to have a blast, throw an Old Testament art party. Think of how much fun you could have creating Old Testament themed art with others. Since people of all ages from the very young to the very old can make art, no one would be excluded.

There are countless ways to engage the Old Testament creatively, and there is a long and rich history of people who have done so. The creative possibilities are truly endless, restricted only by the limits of our imagination. So pick up your paintbrush, pencil set, or sculpting tools and join in!

Write the rest of the story. Creative writing is another excellent way to interact with the Bible. In chapter ten, we talked about trying to find the rest of the story in the Bible. But many Old Testament narratives begin storylines they do not finish. When you encounter one of these, consider writing the rest of the story.

For example, at the end of the first chapter of the book of Jonah, the prophet is in the belly of a really big fish and the sailors are left on a badly damaged boat. We know what Jonah does next, but what about the sailors? Do they try to recover some of the cargo they had just thrown overboard? Do they return to Joppa and put the boat in dry dock for repairs? Do they eventually make it to Tarshish? And what of their newfound fear of the Lord (see Jon 1:16)? Do they continue to worship Yahweh, the God of Israel, or was this just a momentary act of desperate piety? How would you complete the sailors' story? What would you write?

At the other end of this short prophetic book, we are left with what is arguably its most significant unfinished storyline. In chapter four, Jonah is angry about two things: (1) God's mercy on the Ninevites and (2) the death of a bush that had given him shade. In the final verses of the book, God asks the prophet an important question that goes unanswered and leaves us hanging:

> Then the LORD said, "You are concerned about the bush, for which you did not labor and which you did not grow; it came into being in a night and perished in a night. And should I not be concerned about Nineveh, that great city, in which there are more than a hundred and twenty thousand persons who do not know their right hand from their left, and also many animals?" (Jon 4:10-11)

Now imagine you have been commissioned to write Jonah 5:1-15. What would you say? Does Jonah finally get it? Does he realize it was right for God to show mercy on Nineveh? Or does Jonah travel back to Israel, angry and bitter that God would be gracious toward people he despised? How would you finish the story? Why? Engaging in creative writing like this prompts deeper reflection on the biblical text and gets you more personally involved with the story.

Write (or read) "fuller" Old Testament stories in the first person. Another way to enrich your engagement with Scripture, and one closely related to what has just been said, is to write (or read) Old Testament stories in the first person. Considering how little space is devoted to even the best-known people in the Bible, you quickly realize there is much more to their lives than what has been preserved. One way to fill out their stories is to "allow" them to speak about their experiences in the first person. Obviously, this takes some imagination and creativity.

This approach is especially useful for people in the Old Testament who often hover on the margins of the biblical text like women and children. They are part of the story—sometimes mentioned by name, sometimes not—but we often know very little about them. Not much, if anything, is said about their thoughts and feelings, and we typically hear much less from them than we do from their male counterparts. How can we recover their voices and bring them out of the shadows?

One way to do this is to write a creative first-person account that provides a window into their lives and experiences. Once you have selected an individual from the Old Testament, take the biblical text as your starting point, but then go beyond it. Supply a backstory, provide some interior monologue, and create some additional conversations. Have the person share their attitude about other family members, city officials, or foreigners. Allow them to express some of their hopes, dreams, and fears. Giving this person a voice allows you to dive deeper into the text and enables you to explore what abides in its gaps, silences, and ambiguities. This can be quite illuminating and may help you connect with the Old Testament in new and interesting ways.

There are many examples of this kind of writing in both Jewish and Christian tradition, and you might find some of these stories stirring, even if you don't wish to write your own.[10] To provide just one brief example of what this can look like, consider how Clara Garnier-Amouroux ends her first-person retelling of the story of Leah, Rachel's *older* sister.[11] As you

---

[10]For a recent and very accessible collection of examples, see Julie Faith Parker, ed., *My So-Called Biblical Life: Imagined Stories from the World's Best-Selling Book* (Eugene, OR: Wipf and Stock, 2017).

[11]Clara Garnier-Amouroux, "What about Me? The Tale of the Forgotten Sister," in *My So-Called Biblical Life: Imagined Stories from the World's Best-Selling Book*, ed. Julie Faith Parker (Eugene, OR: Wipf and Stock, 2017), 12-21.

may recall, Jacob is tricked on his wedding night. Laban had promised to give Jacob his daughter Rachel, whom Jacob loved. But Jacob is given Leah instead. The next morning, when Jacob wakes up with Leah by his side, he storms out to confront Laban. Meanwhile, Leah is left alone. Nothing is said about what she is thinking and feeling at that moment. Here is the way Garnier-Amouroux has Leah express her predicament:

> As much as I could not bear the thought of facing anyone in my family, I couldn't stay in the tent forever. Still, I remained there throughout the day, fasting, praying, begging for mercy. Might the gods bestow sons upon me, that I could find some redemption in motherhood?
>
> When the light of day had nearly faded, I readied myself and walked to the house. Rachel was there, her anger still fresh. I had no idea what I could say, but I did not need to worry for she did all the talking. Apparently some negotiations had taken place while I was in the tent. "I will wed him too," Rachel said in a low, angry voice. "Jacob must work longer for Father, but I will marry my husband." She almost spit the words at me.
>
> We had all been cheated. Rachel did not have the husband she wanted. Jacob did not have the wife he wanted. I was the wife who had the husband who did not want me. But Jacob and Rachel's situations would be set right when they wed, and mine would never be. Who was cheated the most? What about me?[12]

Encounter the Old Testament outside of the Old Testament. Another way to engage the Old Testament creatively is to encounter it through a variety of artistic renderings. For example, after reading a portion of the Old Testament, see what kind of visual art you can find related to it: paintings, etchings, carvings, and the like. In addition to books containing these images,[13] there are numerous online sites that enable you

---

[12]Garnier-Amouroux, "What about Me?," 20-21.
[13]See, e.g., Chiara de Capoa and Stefano Zuffi, eds., *Old Testament Figures in Art* (Los Angeles: J. Paul Getty Museum, 2003), a book that provides some discussion of the artwork depicted. For a creative and thought-provoking look at Old Testament texts, see Brendan Powell Smith, *The Brick Testament: A New Spin on the Old Testament* (New York: Skyhorse, 2011). For a sober rendering of many Old Testament stories, see Gustave Doré, *The Doré Bible Illustrations* (Mineola, NY: Dover, 1974).

to find these rather easily.[14] As you view these images, consider what part of the story or passage the artist emphasizes. Why do you think the artist focused on *that* part of the story, and how does the artist's interpretation of the text enhance your own understanding of it?

For an animated audio-visual stroll through the Old Testament that is very nicely done, check out BibleProject (bibleproject.com). This free online resource retells the story of the Bible in short videos. Each video focuses on a book (or part of a book) of the Old Testament. These videos explore the content of the book by emphasizing key themes and ideas and discussing the book's structure. Words and pictures are drawn to accompany the narration, making it easier to comprehend and remember what is being discussed.[15]

You might also consider watching films that retell various portions of the Old Testament. These range from classics like Cecil B. DeMille's *The Ten Commandments* (1956), starring Charlton Heston, to more recent blockbusters like Darren Aronofsky's *Noah* (2014), starring Russell Crowe, and *Exodus: Gods and Kings*, starring Christian Bale (2014). They also include animated pictures such as *The Prince of Egypt* (1998). Rent or stream these. Or consider purchasing inexpensive used copies you can watch and then lend to friends or church members so they can benefit from them as well.

In addition, there have been numerous dramatic retellings of the Old and New Testament produced for television. One series produced mainly in the 1990s by TNT can conveniently be purchased as a set of twelve DVDs titled *The Bible Stories Collection*. The Old Testament portion of the series covers the early chapters of Genesis as well as the lives of Abraham, Jacob, Joseph, Moses, David, Solomon, Samson and Delilah, Esther, and Jeremiah. More recently, *The Bible: The Epic Miniseries*, aired the first of ten episodes on March 3, 2013. The first half of the miniseries

---

[14]See, e.g., www.biblical-art.com and www.artbible.info/bible/old-testament.html.

[15]There are many other helpful resources at bibleproject.com, such as podcasts; animated videos on things such as key words, themes in the Bible, and guidelines for reading the Bible; and much more.

is based on the Old Testament.[16] For children, teens, and those who are young at heart, there are also a host of Veggie Tales videos retelling well-known Old Testament stories like the Battle of Jericho (*Josh and the Big Wall!*) and the story of David and Goliath (*Dave and the Giant Pickle*).

As you might suspect, film and television adaptations of the Old Testament are of varying quality and need to be used wisely (more on that momentarily). Still, they can be valuable resources and have the potential to increase your appreciation of the Old Testament.

Music is still another way to enhance your enjoyment of the Old Testament. You can find enormous pleasure listening to (and singing) songs related to this part of the Bible. Classics like Handel's *Messiah* can bring Old Testament texts to life. And singer-songwriter Michael Card's marvelous trilogy based on the Old Testament—*The Beginning, The Way of Wisdom*, and *The Word*—illuminates important parts of the Old Testament story.[17] Many more recent Christian songs and praise choruses take their inspiration—if not their lyrics—from the Old Testament (e.g., "We Will Feast in the House of Zion" by Sandra McCracken, and "Oh Give Thanks" by Wendell Kimbough). More broadly, you can find all sorts of Old Testament references in a variety of popular songs as Mark McEntire and Joel Emerson so helpfully demonstrate in their book *Raising Cain, Fleeing Egypt, and Fighting Philistines: The Old Testament in Popular Music*.[18]

So rather than limiting yourself to words on a page, branch out and engage the Old Testament through various artistic renditions. View artwork, watch movies, and listen to music related to the Old Testament from time to time. Creative alternatives like these will keep your engagement with the Old Testament fresh and interesting.

Before leaving this point, I want to say a little bit more about how to make good use of these artistic representations and retellings of the Old

---

[16]The entire series is inexpensive and readily available.
[17]This is available as a two-CD set titled *The Ancient Faith*.
[18]Mark McEntire and Joel Emerson, *Raising Cain, Fleeing Egypt, and Fighting Philistines: The Old Testament in Popular Music* (Macon, GA: Smyth & Helwys, 2006).

Testament. An illustration from the classroom should help here. Each semester, the students in my introductory Bible class spend a couple weeks reading and studying the book of Jonah. At one point, I take some time to read aloud several children's books that retell the story of Jonah. While some books stick very closely to the basic storyline, others take considerable poetic license. After I finish reading a number of these in a row, I ask the class to use their imagination. I want them to imagine it is a rainy afternoon, and they are responsible for watching a young child for the next several hours. All the children's books I have just read are available to them. Here's what I want to know: Which would they consider reading to the child in their care, and which would they shove under the couch because the books are so poorly done?

Pondering this scenario helps students think through a number of very significant questions. How much does it matter whether or not the children's book actually follows the storyline of the book of Jonah? Is a book that covers the entire story—all four chapters—inherently superior to a book that stops at the end of chapter three? How important are the illustrations in the book? And what do you do with misinformation in children's books, like the one pop-up book which claims the fish spit Jonah out near Nineveh, a feat that would require the fish to hurl Jonah hundreds of miles!

I want students to consider these kinds of questions for a couple different reasons. First, I really do want them to be thoughtful about what "Bible storybooks" they read to children. When I read several of these to the class in rapid succession, it becomes abundantly clear that not all children's books are created equal. Some are more accurate, engaging, and memorable than others. We should be intentional about selecting high-quality, age-appropriate, theologically responsible books to read to children.

But I also want students to reflect on these questions to demonstrate the value of experiencing the Old Testament outside of the Old Testament. There is something really beneficial about encountering the Old Testament through artwork, movies, novels, comic strips, and yes, even children's books. Encounters like these should prompt us to ask if the book or song or artistic creation faithfully represents what is found in the biblical text. This should then encourage us to return to the Old Testament with renewed interest and enthusiasm as we seek to discover what the Bible *really* says. For example, one of the books I read suggests that Jonah was going to the city of Nineveh to proclaim God's love. Was that Jonah's message? No, it was not. Another book I read says Jonah got upset when God spared the Ninevites. Is that the way the Bible describes it? Yes, that's exactly what happens (Jon 4:1-3).

We can ask these same kinds of questions with other retellings of the biblical story, such as those dramatized in movies and television programs. The TNT production of Jacob shows him kissing Rachel the first time they met. Really? Is that the way the Bible describes it? Actually, it is (Gen 29:11). The recent blockbuster about Noah portrays him speaking with the people of the land who are destroyed by the floodwaters. Does that happen in the biblical account? No, it does not.

Experiencing the Old Testament outside of the Old Testament helps us think more carefully and critically about the biblical text.[19] What parts of the biblical story are missing from this children's book or that movie? What extra material has been added? Why do you think the author or producer made those choices? Exploring questions like these encourages us to read the Bible more closely. This, in turn, enables us to gain clarity and see things often overlooked, ultimately making our experience with the Old Testament more fruitful and rewarding.

PERSONALLY REFLECTIVE APPROACHES TO THE OLD TESTAMENT

In addition to topically oriented and artistically motivated approaches, another way to enjoy the Old Testament is through what I call "personally reflective" approaches. These approaches involve a significant

---

[19]Another way to do this is to examine the way the Bible appears in news stories. See, e.g., Leonard J. Greenspoon, *The Bible in the News: How the Popular Press Relates, Conflates, and Updates Sacred Writ* (Washington, DC: Biblical Archaeological Society, 2012).

degree of self-reflection, and they are especially beneficial for spiritual formation and growth.

Use selected Old Testament passages for personal reflection and self-examination. One particularly helpful way to use the Old Testament for personal reflection involves focusing on one passage of Scripture at a time and using it for self-examination and introspection. While not every passage is equally useful for this task, some are especially beneficial in this regard.

To illustrate, let's return to the book of Jonah and consider Nineveh's remarkable repentance described in Jonah 3:5-9. As the story goes, Jonah is only partway through the city ("a day's walk") when he preaches the world's shortest sermon (only five Hebrew words) with amazing results. The entire city repents! The Ninevites respond immediately and appropriately, just as they should given their sinful past and precarious future. They believe God, proclaim a fast, and wear sackcloth (Jon 3:5).[20] Likewise, when the king gets word of Jonah's message, he gets off his throne, lays aside his robe, puts on sackcloth, and sits in ashes (Jon 3:6). He then mandates additional acts of repentance for everyone in the city—including animals. He decrees an absolute fast (no food *or* water) and orders everyone to wear sackcloth. In addition, the people of Nineveh are told to cry out to God and to give up evil and violence (Jon 3:8). The Ninevites comply, repenting in dramatic fashion in the hopes that God will be merciful and spare the city. The people of Nineveh take every conceivable step to demonstrate their humility and contrition before God. It is a picture-perfect example of genuine repentance. Any Israelite hearing this story would have immediately recognized this.

So how can we use a passage like this for self-reflection? How might it help us on our own spiritual journey? One thing we might do is to focus on a key question that emerges by way of analogy, namely, How do

---

[20]Sackcloth was a coarse garment, often made of goat's hair, traditionally worn by people when in distress.

I respond when confronted by my own sinful behavior?[21] Do I deny it, like Gehazi, Elisha's servant (2 Kings 5:19-27)? Do I try to cover it up, like David (2 Sam 11:6-25)? Do I blame others for it, like Adam (Gen 3:12) or Aaron (Ex 32:21-24)? Or do I engage in appropriate acts of repentance like the people of Nineveh? How *do* I respond when confronted by my own sinful behavior? This strikes me as a really, really important question, one worth sitting with and reflecting upon.

This question implicitly raises another important question: What does genuine repentance look like today? Though many people of faith fast, most Christians do not wear sackcloth or sit in ashes. What kind of attitudes, practices, and behaviors characterize repentance in the twenty-first century? Rather than viewing the Old Testament as just a collection of ancient stories, using it to reflect on significant questions like these reminds us of its ongoing applicability to our lives. This makes it much more relevant and encourages us to keep reading.

Connect your story with others in the Old Testament. Another way to use the Old Testament self-reflectively is to consider how various aspects of your story connect with the stories of people in the pages of the Old Testament. Conrad L'Heureux does this in his book, *Life Journey and the Old Testament*. Reflecting on the story of Abraham, he writes:

> The patriarch set out on a journey to a land he knew nothing about except that it had been promised to him by the God who called him. In my own life, I have sometimes felt that I was making a new beginning which required that I leave behind much of my past. Sometimes I saw these new beginnings as a response to a call from God, while at other times they seemed to be simple practical decisions which I had reached after weighing the pros and cons. Either way, in many of these situations, I had little understanding of what would lie ahead for me. I learned from the story of Abraham that I needed to trust that by answering the call, I was

---

[21]This same question could be prompted by a number of other Old Testament passages such as 2 Sam 12:1-15 (Nathan's confrontation of David after the Bathsheba-Uriah debacle), 1 Kings 21:17-29 (Elijah's confrontation of Ahab after the king wrongly appropriated Naboth's vineyard), and 2 Kings 22:3-20 (Josiah's reaction to hearing the words of the "lost" book, which prompted him to realize that the people have not been faithful to God's commands).

moving in a direction of growth, journeying towards what was for me the land of promise. I derived support and encouragement by looking at the model provided by Abraham in his journey. By looking at that model, I was able to move on, in spite of uncertainty and fear.[22]

L'Heureux drew important parallels between his story and Abraham's, and this enabled him to use the Old Testament in relevant and edifying ways. As L'Heureux sees it, "The key . . . to making the Old Testament significant for us today lies in establishing connections between the stories of ancient Israel and our own personal stories."[23]

Obviously, Abraham is not a perfect model. He makes mistakes along the way. Then again, so do we. Part of the reason we are able to make connections with these individuals is because they are *not* perfect. We see our own shortcomings and weaknesses in theirs. Sometimes we behave like Esau, wanting instant gratification so badly that we are willing to trade our birthright for a bowl of bean soup (Gen 25:29-34). Other times we feel like Moses, overextended and completely exhausted (Ex 18). We need the wise counsel of someone like Jethro to speak into our lives and say, "What you are doing is not good. You will surely wear yourself out. . . . For the task is too heavy for you; you cannot do it alone" (Ex 18:17-18).[24]

When we make personal connections with people in the Old Testament, it allows this part of the Bible to come alive and creates a greater desire to read and study it. Our stories begin to mingle with theirs, and we realize how much we can learn from the "cloud of witnesses" that has gone before us (Heb 12:1).

Practice lectio divina. For centuries, Christians have practiced a form of Bible reading referred to as *lectio divina,* or spiritual reading. This provides yet another way to use the Old Testament for our spiritual growth and development. Richard Foster claims that this approach to

---

[22]Conrad E. L'Heureux, *Life Journey and the Old Testament: An Experiential Approach to the Bible and Personal Transformation* (New York: Paulist, 1986), 2-3.

[23]L'Heureux, *Life Journey and the Old Testament,* 5.

[24]After leaving Egypt, Moses spent his days settling legal disputes from morning till evening: a classic case of overfunctioning (Ex 18). Moses needed to learn the art of delegation.

Scripture "is the primary mode of reading the Bible for transformation."[25] It is an ancient practice that consists of four parts, what Foster identifies as *"listening, reflecting, praying,* and *obeying."*[26] The purpose of this approach is to open our hearts *to* God and to connect *with* God in a very real way. This keeps our engagement with the Old Testament from being just a cognitive exercise.

To practice this approach, read a small portion of the Old Testament, paying attention to any words or phrases that seem to stand out to you. You might want to have paper and pencil close by so you can make note of these. After you have read the passage a number of times this way, review the items that struck you and consider which of these God might be inviting you to reflect on more deeply.

Using the New Testament passage in which Mary encounters the resurrected Christ, Richard Foster describes what this practice might look like for someone using this approach.

> Suppose we are reflecting on the risen Christ's appearance to Mary, and we have been drawn to the one word that changes her ability to see Jesus: the sound of him speaking her name. Our concern is not with the theological implications of this appearance. . . . Rather, our goal is imaginatively to take Mary's place. . . . What does "the stranger" look like before we recognize him? How do we feel physically when we hear the sound of his voice? What does our own name sound like on his lips? How would we describe the feelings now surging through us as we realize it is Jesus?[27]

Foster continues:

> As our minds are working through such details, our spirits are alert to what, if any, connections the Spirit may be revealing between this passage and the particulars of our own lives. Inwardly we are asking, *How are you revealing yourself to me, Lord? What am I to see and understand in this border territory where my life merges with yours?*[28]

---

[25]Richard J. Foster, *Life with God: Reading the Bible for Spiritual Transformation*, with Kathryn A. Helmers (New York: HarperOne, 2008), 62.
[26]Foster, *Life with God*, 63, emphasis original.
[27]Foster, *Life with God*, 66.
[28]Foster, *Life with God*, 66, emphasis original.

This kind of reflection should lead us to prayer, allowing us to offer words of "gratitude, confession, lament, relief, or praise."[29] Finally, we prepare to take whatever steps of obedience we sense are necessary in light of what God has revealed to us through this process. As Foster puts it:

> Now is the time to seek divine wisdom for carrying this precious gift into the flow of our life with God as it spills over into our life in the world—relationships with loved ones, interaction with friends, chance encounters with acquaintances, crossed paths with strangers. For example, we may find that the tenderness of Christ's word to Mary urges us to do a double take in offering a kind word of attention to those we might have overlooked, even to merely speak their name. We may feel so strengthened by God's awareness of us that we seek out a loved one to make sure that he or she is aware of our love and gratitude.[30]

This way of reading Scripture can make a significant impact on us, especially if we tend to read the Bible very cerebrally. *Lectio divina* engages us at the deepest levels and creates space for God's Spirit to transform us. There are any number of Old Testament texts that could be profitably explored this way. So give it a try, especially if you are inclined to get stuck in your head and want to connect more with your heart.

Keep a journal about your experience with the Old Testament. Finally, one of the easiest and most helpful ways to reflect on the Old Testament is to keep a journal. Your journal does not need to be anything fancy or formal. A simple notebook will do. Many people find writing by hand particularly useful for journaling since it helps them process their thoughts and feelings differently than typing on a keyboard. Of course, typing is perfectly fine if that works better for you. Your writing does not need to be polished, and you need not be preoccupied with issues of spelling and grammar. It is the content rather than the form that is most important here.

---

[29]Foster, *Life with God*, 68.
[30]Foster, *Life with God*, 69.

While you can include whatever you like in your journal, here are some suggestions to get you started. To begin, it is helpful to date your entries and to record what passage(s) you have read. As you reflect on the biblical text, you could discuss what you found most helpful and unhelpful about it. What new insights did you gain, and what questions do you have? How did your reading connect with current events or your own personal life? If the experience was frustrating, or if you felt like you didn't "get anything out of" the text, write about that. If you feel like jotting down a prayer, do it. If you want to explore some tangential rabbit trail, go for it. If you were offended by something in the text, talk about it. If you are convicted by what you read, confess it. This is *your* journal, for your eyes alone. Make it work for you. Nobody is grading you or telling you what you have to say. You and you alone control what you write here. There is no right or wrong way to do it.

One of the many benefits of keeping a journal like this is that it encourages you to do more than just read words on a page. It requires you to reflect on what you have read and to interact with it in some way. This gets you more deeply involved with Scripture and makes your experience more satisfying. Journaling also provides an outlet for your feelings and helps clarify your thinking. Indeed, sometimes the very process of writing itself is what allows our thoughts to come into focus.

Keeping a journal is also useful because it provides you with a written record of your experience with the Old Testament, one you can return to time and again. You can look through your journal and find entries that are inspiring, hopeful, and challenging. You can see the way God has been at work in your life and can revisit these entries when you need to be encouraged or reminded of God's presence in your life. If you ever need ideas to share with others, perhaps for a brief devotional or meditation, you can return to entries you feel were particularly insightful and find useful material there. Consistent journaling also enables you to look back and evaluate how your Old Testament reading is going. If you notice a lot of bland entries in a row, perhaps that is an indication that you need to find some new ways to read and engage this part of the Bible.

Jane Herring believes that writing about the Old Testament can transform our relationship with it. She makes this point in a helpful book that invites us to interact with Scripture through creative writing. As she puts it, "Scripture did not really speak to me until one day I wrote back."[31] Herring was introduced to this idea by one of her professors at Vanderbilt Divinity School. After instructing a small group of students to read and silently reflect on a portion of Scripture, Herring says she and others were told "to take up pen and write back to scripture in whatever form inspired us: poetry, lists, story, letter, and so on."[32] This practice transformed her encounter with the Bible.

> When I began interacting with scripture through writing, a new relationship unfolded. I copied scripture word for word, questioning it, prodding the text to uncover what had not been said, speaking back to it about what I found confusing, too good to be true, too hard, too easy, and sometimes trying to rewrite it with details from contemporary life. In this way, I entered into a relationship with scripture.[33]

Writing gets us more actively involved with the Old Testament. This not only benefits us spiritually, it also helps us appreciate the Old Testament more fully.

For all these reasons, I strongly encourage you to give journaling a try. Your journal entries need not be long and will undoubtedly vary in length from day to day. Some days, just a sentence or two may be all you want to write—or have time to write. Other days, a few pages will not seem to be enough space to write all that is in your heart and mind. Again, there are no rules here. Do what seems helpful for you, and enjoy.[34]

A brief word of guidance about using the Old Testament for personal reflection. For some people, the kind of personal reflection and introspection I have been suggesting here comes easily and naturally. For

---

[31]Jane Herring, *One Day I Wrote Back: Interacting with Scripture through Creative Writing* (Nashville: Upper Room, 2015), 10.

[32]Herring, *One Day I Wrote Back*, 10.

[33]Herring, *One Day I Wrote Back*, 10.

[34]Herring's book has many helpful ideas and suggestions to help you get started and to enhance your engagement with the Bible.

others, not so much. If this is something you find difficult, let me encourage you to try it in small doses. Like athletic conditioning, the more you do it, the better you get at it. And the better you get at it, the more likely you are to enjoy it.

To take your experience with the Old Testament to another level, consider inviting a Christian friend to engage in some of these practices with you. For example, one week you might both decide to use a particular Old Testament passage for personal reflection and self-examination. Or perhaps you might both do some journaling on your encounters with the Old Testament over a given period of time. That way, by engaging in similar practices, you can talk about what is working well and what is not, and you can learn from each other. You may find it especially beneficial to journey with someone who is a bit more experienced with some of these approaches so you can benefit from their accumulated wisdom along the way.

CONCLUSION

The more options you have for encountering the Old Testament, the more likely you are to stick with it. That is why so many practical suggestions appear in this chapter and the previous one. As noted earlier, these options are not meant to overwhelm you but to equip you with many different ways to engage this part of the Bible. Try out some of the suggestions that interest you and set aside those that do not. Just be sure to open the Old Testament. There is fun waiting to be had, and there are riches waiting to be found.

12

READING *the* OLD TESTAMENT ONE BOOK *at a* TIME

*One of the great needs among Christians today is
simply the reading of large portions of Scripture.*

RICHARD J. FOSTER, *CELEBRATION OF DISCIPLINE*

*No matter how good the textbook, no matter how responsible the
information it contains, it can never replace reading the Bible itself.*

MICHAEL R. COSBY, *PORTRAITS OF JESUS*

THE PREVIOUS TWO CHAPTERS considered a wide range of different approaches to encountering and enjoying the Old Testament. In this chapter, we focus on just one: doing a book survey. This approach involves surveying individual books of the Old Testament one at a time. Since the Old Testament is technically not a book, but rather a *collection* of books, it makes sense to focus on individual books within the Old Testament as one way to explore this part of the Bible.

THE PURPOSE OF SURVEYING BOOKS IN THE OLD TESTAMENT

The primary purpose of surveying a particular book of the Old Testament is to gain a rudimentary grasp of both its content (what's actually in the book) and its structure (how that content is arranged). As your knowledge of the Old Testament increases and your confidence grows, this part of the Bible becomes much less formidable and much more enjoyable.

Often, people who venture into the Old Testament read it piecemeal—a snippet here, a snippet there. Sometimes, this is due to the way daily devotionals are designed.[1] One day you might be directed to read a few verses from the book of Genesis, the next day a passage from the Gospel of Matthew, and the day after that something from the book of Ecclesiastes. While there is nothing wrong with reading around the Bible this way, if it constitutes the sum total of your engagement with the Old Testament, your experience will be rather disjointed and fragmented. It is difficult to get a handle on the basic content and structure of a particular Old Testament book if you are constantly jumping around from one passage to another. Doing a book survey is a helpful remedy to this.

When you survey a book of the Old Testament, your goal is to get an overview of the book, the "big picture" as it were. Perhaps this image will help. Imagine yourself flying around the country in a plane, not a 747, but a smaller craft like a Piper Cub. Since you are only about five thousand feet or so above the surface, when you look out the window you can see a river to the east, a range of hills on the horizon, and a medium-sized town in the distance. But at that altitude, you are not going to be able to spot small wildlife or identify all the different kinds of trees in the forest below. Instead, you get a general lay of the land without seeing everything in high definition. That is what doing a book survey is all about. It gives you a general feel for some of the major features of the book without getting tangled in the weeds.

THE BOOK SURVEY METHOD: GENERAL PROCEDURES

While there are a variety of ways to complete a book survey, I would suggest including at least these six steps.[2]

---

[1] It is also due to the simple fact that people tend to read what is familiar. When we open the Bible, many of us naturally gravitate toward texts we know and love.

[2] I am indebted to Terry Brensinger for first introducing me to the inductive Bible study method generally, and the book survey process specifically. The following discussion of the book survey process largely reflects how I learned it under Dr. Brensinger at Messiah University (then College) and later at Asbury Theological Seminary. For more on the inductive Bible study method, see Robert A. Traina, *Methodical Bible Study* (Grand Rapids, MI: Francis Asbury, 1985) and David L. Thompson, *Bible Study that Works* (Nappanee, IN: Evangel, 1994).

1. Read the entire book in one sitting.

2. Provide a title for each chapter.

3. Identify the predominant type of material in the book.

4. Divide the book into major units and subunits and label these.

5. Select and discuss strategic passages.

6. Record miscellaneous comments and questions.

In what follows, I will discuss each of these steps in more detail, providing numerous examples along the way. Even though there are a number of steps to this process, the book survey method is actually quite easy to learn, and you are likely to get the hang of it very quickly. In fact, once you have done a couple of these, it will become second nature to you.

Read the entire book in one sitting. The first step of the process is to read through the entire book you have selected from beginning to end all at once. The length of time it will take to complete this will vary depending on the book you have chosen. A book like Genesis, with fifty chapters, may take you a couple hours to read, whereas a book like Jonah—all of four chapters—might only take about ten minutes. Either way, set aside enough time to read the whole thing in one sitting so you can get a good feel for the book as a whole. If doing this is simply not practical for you, at least try to read it in a few big chunks, as close together as possible.

As you read, pay attention to big ideas and major movements within the book. You may want to have a paper and pencil close by so that you can write down some of your observations as you read. If you do make some notes, keep them very brief at this point. Don't get bogged down in details. This is *especially* important when you are working with books that are relatively long. You need to keep moving or you'll never get finished.

At this stage in the process, resist the temptation to chase rabbit trails. For example, if you are surveying a book like Exodus, don't worry about what kind of bush was burning (Ex 3:2), or why God reportedly tried to kill Moses (Ex 4:24-26), or what is meant by the recurring references to

Pharaoh's hard heart in the plague narrative (Ex 7–12). You can make note of these questions and always come back to them later if you like. Remember, the goal of the book survey is to familiarize yourself with the *major* features of the book, not to pursue specific detailed questions at this point.

Provide a title for each chapter. After you have read the entire book (or as you are reading it), provide a title for each chapter. Creating chapter titles forces you to pay close attention to what you are reading since you have to summarize what you just read in a few words. If your Bible already has chapter titles, do your best to ignore them for now so they do not bias your thinking.

As you create your own chapter titles, work at making them brief, descriptive, creative, and memorable. First, in terms of making them brief, aim for five words or less. This is *very* important because it helps you remember them. Second, try to describe as much of the chapter as you can in as few words as possible. Obviously, you won't be able to summarize the entire chapter in five words or less, but do your best to capture the main thrust of it. Third, be as creative as possible with your chapter titles. Here is where you can really have fun. It is far better to produce chapter titles that are unique, and perhaps a bit quirky, than to create titles that are theologically sophisticated but boring.

Let's suppose you are doing a book survey of Exodus and you are working on a chapter title for Exodus 14. Rather than going with something like "Israel Crosses the Red Sea," which is brief and descriptive but not very creative, try something like "Walls of Water" or "Pharaoh's Last Stand." Creative titles like these are far more memorable. Using alliteration or other literary techniques is also a great way to facilitate easy recall. Consider my chapter titles for the book of Jonah:

- 1—Jonah the *Perishing* Prophet
- 2—Jonah the *Praying* Prophet
- 3—Jonah the *Preaching* Prophet
- 4—Jonah the *Pouting* Prophet

By remembering just a few words—actually, just the four in italics—I have instant recall to the basic content of the entire book of Jonah.

- *Perishing*—That's when Jonah is on the run and gets thrown overboard.

- *Praying*—That's where Jonah is in the belly of the fish.

- *Preaching*—That's when Jonah goes to Nineveh and preaches.

- *Pouting*—That's where Jonah gets angry because God spared Nineveh.

While Jonah is a very short book by Old Testament standards, it would not be difficult to memorize chapter titles like these for considerably longer books as well. This is helpful because it gives you a general sense of what these books contain and where things are located.

Many people find creating chapter titles both enjoyable *and* beneficial. So give it a try and see what happens.

Identify the predominant type of material in the book. The third step in the process is to identify what *type* of material predominates throughout the book. Is this book primarily about events (*historical*), people (*biographical*), ideas (*ideological*), or places (*geographical*).[3] Obviously, many Old Testament books contain all of these to one degree or another. Your job is to choose the one you think is most representative of the material *in* the book, and to support that choice with material *from* the book.

For example, if you think the book of Exodus is primarily about events, identify some of those: Pharaoh's failed attempts to limit the Hebrew population (Ex 1), the birth of Moses (Ex 2), God's call of Moses through a burning bush (Ex 3), the ten plagues (Ex 7–12), the Red Sea crossing (Ex 14–15), and so forth. If you conclude a book like Esther is primarily about people, then identify some of the main characters: Esther (the Jew who becomes a Persian queen), Mordecai (her cousin), King Ahasuerus (the Persian King), Haman the Agagite (the enemy of the Jews), and others. Unlike Exodus or Esther, Leviticus has very few big "events" and even fewer main characters (primarily just

---

[3]Traina, *Methodical Bible Study*, 55-56

Moses and Aaron). But it has *lots* of big ideas. It explores the role of priests, emphasizes the importance of sacrifices and offerings, and draws crucial distinctions between that which is holy and profane, clean and unclean. While geography it not particularly important in the book of Leviticus (the people of Israel are parked at Mount Sinai the entire time), it is very important in a book like Joshua which is, after all, a story about Israel occupying the Promised Land. The first part of the book discusses the military campaign in three phases based on where the battles are located geographically: in the central part of the land (Josh 6–8), in the south (Josh 9–10), and in the north (Josh 11). And a significant portion of the second half of the book describes the boundaries of the land for the various tribes (Josh 13–19).

Again, your task here is to choose whichever of these four options you think best represents the predominant material in the book, keeping in mind that you are likely to find many different types of material in any given book. Remember, the goal of this is to get a general feel for the nature of the book you are surveying. Don't be overly concerned about choosing the "right" type of material. Rather, choose the one that makes the most sense to you and then provide some support for your choice.

Divide the book into major units and subunits and label these. Dividing a book into major units and subunits is one of the most important parts of the book survey process since it helps you "see" how the book is structured. In some ways, this step is analogous to the way a play is divided into acts and scenes. Many plays have two or three major acts that may be differentiated by time, place, characters, or major events. Within each act, there are often numerous scenes which further demarcate different segments of the play. By way of analogy, acts are like major units, and scenes are like subunits.

You task is to divide the book you are surveying into *no more than four* major units. Major units tend to be organized around common themes, people, places, or events and should have some sense of coherence. As you make divisions, pay close attention to major shifts in these areas. Or, to return to the theater analogy, think about where you would envision the curtain rising and falling if you were watching a dramatic production of the Old Testament book you are reading. Once you have identified these major units, provide a title for each one using the same guidelines given above for creating chapter titles. You should also clearly identify where each major unit begins and ends by providing the appropriate chapter and verse references.

Once you have settled on some major units, divide them into subunits, limiting yourself to no more than *four* subunits for each major unit. Remember, the point of doing a book survey is to get the general lay of the land, not to create a highly detailed, fifty-point outline of the book. Just like major units, subunits should be titled and should include specific chapter and verse references indicating where they begin and end.

Since all this makes a whole lot more sense when you actually see it applied, let's look at a couple examples using the rather short book of Jonah and the considerably longer book of Exodus.

The book of Jonah can be divided into two major units: Jonah 1:1–2:10 and Jonah 3:1–4:11

JONAH DISOBEYS AND PRAYS	JONAH PREACHES AND POUTS
1:1 2:10	3:1 4:11

Figure 12.1. Jonah's two major literary units

Each major unit begins with God's call to the prophet:

Jonah 1:1 Now the word of the LORD came to Jonah son of Amittai . . .

Jonah 3:1 The word of the LORD came to Jonah a second time . . .

The first major unit describes Jonah's (failed) attempt to run from God's presence, resulting in a three-day, three-night fish ride. The second major unit describes Jonah's proclamation of doom to the Ninevites, resulting in their repentance and Jonah's annoyance at God's decision to be merciful to them.

Each of these major units can be subdivided as follows:

JONAH DISOBEYS AND PRAYS			JONAH PREACHES AND POUTS		
1:1		**2:10**	**3:1**		**4:11**
God calls Jonah	Jonah runs away	Jonah needs to pray	Jonah preaches	Nineveh repents —God relents	Jonah pouts
1:1-2	1:3-16	1:17–2:10	3:1-4	3:5-10	4:1-11

Figure 12.2. Jonah's two major literary units with subdivisions

The subunits in the first major unit describe Jonah's reception of God's word (Jon 1:1-2), his experience aboard the ship (Jon 1:3-16), and his encounter with the fish (Jon 1:17–2:10). The subunits in the second major unit include Jonah's journey to Nineveh (Jon 3:1-4), the Ninevites' dramatic repentance (Jon 3:5-10), and Jonah's severe displeasure over God's decision to spare them from destruction (Jon 4:1-11).

This same process of dividing books into major units and subunits can also be applied to much longer books, such as the book of Exodus. Like Jonah, the book of Exodus can be divided into two major sections:

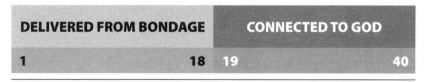

DELIVERED FROM BONDAGE		CONNECTED TO GOD	
1	**18**	**19**	**40**

Figure 12.3. Exodus's two major literary units

The first major unit (Ex 1–18) tells the dramatic story of God's deliverance of the Hebrew people from Egyptian bondage. The second major unit (Ex 19–40) describes the relationship established between the people and God, primarily through the giving of the law and the construction of the tabernacle. The first major unit is fast paced, adventurous, and filled with the miraculous, whereas the second major unit is quite a bit slower, less dramatic, and more mundane. Whereas the first unit is primarily Hebrew narrative (story), the second contains mostly laws and priestly materials. The setting of each of these units is also different. Chapters 1–18 are set in Egypt and the wilderness; chapters 19–40 take place at Mount Sinai.[4]

Some possible subdivisions of the book would be as follows:

DELIVERED FROM BONDAGE			CONNECTED TO GOD	
1		18	19	40
Oppressed in Egypt	Ten terrible plagues	Across the sea toward Sinai	Receiving the Law	Building a Tabernacle
1:1–7:13	7:14–13:16	13:17–18:27	19–24	25–40

Figure 12.4. Exodus's two major literary units with subdivisions

The first subunit, Exodus 1:1–7:13, recounts the Hebrew people's oppression in the land of Egypt. God sees this and responds to it by calling Moses to deliver them, though Moses' initial efforts only result in greater oppression. The second subunit, Exodus 7:14–13:16, describes ten plagues sent upon Egypt, culminating in the death of the firstborn and the institution of Passover. The final subunit in this section, Exodus 13:17–18:27, describes the people's safe passage through the Red Sea and their journey south toward Sinai amid various hardships.

The second major unit has two subunits. The first subunit, Exodus 19–24, is primarily concerned with Israel receiving the Ten Commandments and the book of the covenant, and the second subunit, Exodus 25–40, is primarily concerned with the construction of a tabernacle which God indwells at the climactic ending of the book.

Obviously, these major units and subunits represent very broad brushstrokes. Still, they enable us to gain a rudimentary grasp of the basic content and structure of the book of Exodus. It provides a general orientation to the book that serves as a helpful starting point for digging deeper.

As you identify major units and subunits, do not feel constrained by the chapter divisions in your Bible. These divisions were not there

---

[4]Focusing on the setting would be another way to divide the book of Exodus into major units: Israel in Egypt (Ex 1:1–12:36); Israel on the Road (Ex 12:37–18:27); Israel in Sinai (Ex 19:1–40:38).

originally but were added much later during the Middle Ages. While these chapter divisions can be helpful and often do signal significant transitions, this is not always the case. It is perfectly acceptable—and sometimes best—to note major unit divisions within chapters rather than between them. Likewise, try not to be unduly influenced by the way many English translations often subdivide chapters into smaller segments. Again, you can certainly follow these divisions if that seems useful, but you are completely free to deviate from them if you like. These divisions, and the section headings that typically accompany them, represent modern editorial efforts to make the Bible more readable. Part of the purpose of doing a book survey is to decide these things for yourself. Then you can compare your work with the choices made by the editors of your Bible to see where you agree or disagree.

Finally, I would encourage you to represent your major unit and subunit divisions visually in some way. As illustrated above, I like to use a simple chart. But there are many other ways this could be done. You could put your major units and subunits in outline form, or you might try using pictures, colors, or both to identify different sections of the book. Doing this enhances your ability to "see" and remember the basic structure and content of the book you are surveying.

Select and discuss strategic passages. The fifth step in the book survey process is to select and discuss key, or strategic, passages. A strategic passage is a relatively short passage of Scripture you think is essential to the book you are surveying. It often helps you make sense of what came before the passage and what comes after it. Without this passage, the book would be much more difficult to understand or perhaps not make any sense at all.

Most books typically have only a few key passages. For the book of Jonah, I would consider Jonah 4:1-3 to be a key passage.

> But this was very displeasing to Jonah, and he became angry. He prayed to the LORD and said, "O LORD! Is not this what I said while I was still in my own country? That is why I fled to Tarshish at the beginning; for I knew that you are a gracious God and merciful, slow to anger, and

abounding in steadfast love, and ready to relent from punishing. And now, O Lord, please take my life from me, for it is better for me to die than to live."

For the first time, we learn *why* Jonah tried to run away. Although we knew Jonah was trying to get away from God's presence (Jon 1:3, 10), we did not know why. This strategic passage supplies the reason. Jonah wanted to get away from God because he knew God was merciful. He was worried that if he went to Nineveh and told the people what God was planning to do, they might repent and God might show mercy on the dreaded Ninevites (heaven forbid!). Jonah wanted no part of that.

This strategic passage not only helps us understand Jonah's behavior at the beginning of the book, it also helps us make sense of his behavior at the end. After the Ninevites respond positively to Jonah's message and God spares the city, Jonah sits outside the city and pouts. He is angry—angry enough to die. And, based on Jonah 4:1-3, we know why. Jonah was furious with God for behaving graciously toward his enemies. If you read between the lines, you can almost hear Jonah accusing God, saying, "You just couldn't help yourself, could you? You had to be gracious to the Ninevites. Well, don't expect me to like it!" Without this passage, we would be left in the dark, speculating about why Jonah bolts in chapter one and pouts in chapter four.

To consider another example, let's return to the book of Exodus. If you were to survey this book, you might identify Exodus 19:1-6 as a strategic passage.

> On the third new moon after the Israelites had gone out of the land of Egypt, on that very day, they came into the wilderness of Sinai. They had journeyed from Rephidim, entered the wilderness of Sinai, and camped in the wilderness; Israel camped there in front of the mountain. Then Moses went up to God; the Lord called to him from the mountain, saying, "Thus you shall say to the house of Jacob, and tell the Israelites: You have seen what I did to the Egyptians, and how I bore you on eagles' wings and brought you to myself. Now therefore, if you obey my voice and keep my covenant, you shall be my treasured possession out of all the peoples.

> Indeed, the whole earth is mine, but you shall be for me a priestly kingdom and a holy nation. These are the words that you shall speak to the Israelites."

This passage marks time based on Israel's exodus from Egypt ("On the third new moon after the Israelites had gone out of the land of Egypt") and recalls God's deliverance of the people ("You have seen what I did to the Egyptians, and how I bore you on eagles' wings and brought you to myself"). Themes of exodus and deliverance have been central to the first half of the book and this strategic passage captures these concisely.

But the passage also looks forward to what lies ahead, namely, the relationship God is about to formalize with the people. If Israel will obey God, the people will enjoy a unique covenant relationship with God. They will be God's "treasured possession" (Ex 19:5). They will also be a "priestly kingdom" and a "holy nation" (Ex 19:6). This is a pivotal moment in the life of Israel and this passage is strategically situated just before they receive the Ten Commandments (Ex 20:1-17) and enter into that binding covenantal relationship with God (Ex 24).

Looking for strategic passages like these helps you consider what is most central about the book you are surveying. It enables you to discern key ideas and concerns, which further enhances your ability to see the big picture and get the lay of the land.

Record miscellaneous comments and questions. This final step in the book survey process is rather wide open and provides you with an opportunity to record some things that might not fit elsewhere in your survey. For example, as you survey a book, you are likely to make some interesting discoveries that deserve further exploration. This is a good place to write these down so you don't forget them and can return to them later. This is also a good place to make note of questions that have arisen along the way. You can sort through them later to determine which feel most important and are worth pursuing further. In addition, you might also identify major themes and ideas you encountered in your survey and note them here. Use this final step to record whatever you think will be most beneficial to you at this stage of the process as you work to develop a general overview of the book you are surveying.

Conclusion (and Some Final Guidelines)

Doing a book survey is a great way to learn more about the Old Testament. These surveys help you get a basic sense of the content and structure of Old Testament books, and they serve as an excellent starting point for further study and exploration.

Obviously, you are free to survey any Old (or New) Testament book you choose. But if you have never done a book survey before, I would recommend beginning with a book that is primarily narrative. Start with something short like the book of Ruth. Then try something a bit longer like Joshua or Judges and eventually work your way up to Genesis or Exodus.

While it is certainly possible to do a book survey "in your head," I would encourage you to consider writing it out. The process of writing will help clarify your thinking and will provide you with a written record of your discoveries. You can handwrite your survey or type it on the computer. Just find some way to preserve your findings so you can benefit from them in the future.

Completing a book survey is not the kind of thing most people sit down and crank out all at once—unless it's an assignment that's due the next day! So give yourself plenty of time. You can spread it out over multiple days or even weeks if need be. There is no rush.

Finally, though it goes without saying, you should feel free to use the book survey method any way you like. Nobody is looking over your shoulder or grading you. Feel free to modify and adapt the six-step process I have described in ways that are most helpful to you. Enjoy!

13

SOME FINAL WORDS *of* ENCOURAGEMENT *and* ADVICE

The rewards offered by the Old Testament do not come easily, I admit. Learning to feel at home in its pages will take time and effort. All achievements—climbing mountains, mastering the guitar, competing in a triathlon—require a similar process of hard work; we persevere because we believe rewards will come.

PHILIP YANCEY, THE *BIBLE JESUS READ*

JULIA O'BRIEN, a professor of Old Testament at Lancaster Theological Seminary, says one of her "primary goals" in teaching the first part of the Bible is

> to help people value, *even enjoy*, the Old Testament and move beyond negative stereotypes of this collection as difficult, nasty, or just plain boring. I long for readers to quit saying, "Why do I have to read the Old Testament, anyway?" and to experience for themselves the fascination and power of these texts.[1]

That is my goal as well. I really do want people to enjoy the Old Testament. I especially want people to encounter God in the pages of Scripture and to find ways to read these texts that deepen their faith. In

---

[1]Julia M. O'Brien, *Challenging Prophetic Metaphor: Theology and Ideology in the Prophets* (Louisville, KY: Westminster John Knox, 2008), xi, emphasis mine. O'Brien states her other primary goal "is to challenge readers to acknowledge the violence, sexism, and other 'problems' of the Old Testament and of the Bible as a whole" (xi). This too is a concern of mine and has been the focus of much of my scholarship.

this way, having fun with the Old Testament is not an end in and of itself. Rather, it helps us stay engaged with these texts, texts that have the power to help us grow spiritually and to strengthen our relationship to God.

I am hopeful that the practical suggestions offered throughout this book *have* helped you—and *will* help you—connect with the Old Testament in meaningful and deeply satisfying ways. I am also hopeful that they will lead you into profound encounters with the living God. What remains to be said are a few parting words of advice and encouragement for the journey.

FOUR WORDS TO THE WISE: HOW TO USE ALL THESE SUGGESTIONS

While I have offered many suggestions for encountering the Old Testament, especially in the final section of this book, I have not yet provided much guidance for how to implement and incorporate these into a regular routine of reading and studying this part of the Bible. What follows should be especially helpful in that regard.

Be intentional (design a plan). One of the most significant things I would encourage you to do—sooner rather than later—is develop a plan for how you intend to use the Old Testament in the coming days and weeks. Ignoring the Old Testament is undesirable, and engaging the Old Testament haphazardly is not very satisfying. Developing a plan provides some focus and gives you direction for moving forward more effectively.

The kind of "plan" I'm envisioning does *not* need to be extensive or elaborate. You do not need to create a ten-year plan or even a one-year plan. Instead, it could be something as simple as a one-month plan or even just a one-week plan. The point is to give some intentional thought about what you are going to do with the Old Testament for a particular period of time. Develop some sort of plan, and then try to stick to it. Maybe you want to survey a book of the Old Testament you have never spent much time reading. Or perhaps you will decide to read the same chapter of the Old Testament for an entire week to see what new insights emerge each day. Maybe you are interested in doing a topical study on peacemaking in the Old Testament to see what you can learn. Whatever you decide, be clear about *what* you plan to do and for *how long*. This will give you something to aim for and will prevent you from roaming aimlessly through the Old Testament, randomly bouncing from one text to the next.

Be flexible (use various approaches). In addition to developing a plan for how you intend to use the Old Testament in the short term, I would suggest trying out a variety of *different* approaches over time. If you do the same thing with the Bible day in and day out, sooner or later you are likely to get bored. Even if what you are doing with the Bible is good and beneficial, the very repetitiveness of it all may eventually become tiresome. But here's the good news: we don't need to do the same thing with the Bible each and every day. If this book has demonstrated anything, it is that there are many ways to read and encounter the Old Testament. *We have options.* There are a whole host of approaches at our fingertips, and we should take advantage of these. This can prevent us from getting stuck in a rut or disengaging from the Old Testament altogether.

When you find a way to interact with the Old Testament that works well for you, count your blessings and keep at it. But if you sense your reading of the Old Testament growing stale, or if you find it difficult to engage the text in meaningful ways, or if you realize that what you are doing with the Old Testament is just not working, *try something else.* Utilize some of the suggestions in this book. Pick the ones that seem most promising and experiment with them. Mixing things up and trying different approaches is one of the best ways to keep your encounters with the Old Testament interesting and pleasurable.

Part of the reason I suggested developing a simple plan for a short period of time is because I am keenly aware that something we find helpful one month may be less so the next—hence the need for flexibility. If one week you decide to read some familiar Old Testament stories from an alternate perspective and you really like it, try it again the next week. If your enthusiasm wanes by the third week, then try something new. Maybe it's time to create some art related to the Old Testament, or to practice *lectio divina,* or to journal. Be flexible as you engage the Old Testament and explore multiple approaches along the way. This is key to enjoying this part of the Bible.

Be balanced (read different parts of the Bible). Rather than *only* reading from one place in the Old Testament for an extended period of time, you might want to augment that by spending at least some time reading from other parts of the Bible as well. Churches that follow the lectionary will often have three Scripture readings during the service: one from the Old Testament, one from the book of Psalms, and one from the New Testament. This public practice of reading from multiple places in the Bible is a helpful model to follow. It is especially beneficial if you are making your way through some of the more challenging portions of the Old Testament.

For example, suppose you decide to embark on a three-month study of 1 and 2 Chronicles. Rather than reading nothing but Chronicles for the next three months, you may want to dip into some other parts of the Old Testament like the book of Psalms or the marvelous collection of salvation oracles in Isaiah 40–55. You might also wish to supplement your study of Chronicles with some reading from the New Testament. While the majority of your time would be devoted to Chronicles, reading other portions of Scripture will add some variety and will be especially welcome on days when you are slogging through genealogies.

Be a preservationist (write down key insights and questions). In various ways, this book has stressed the importance of engaging the Old Testament through writing. As you read the Old Testament, preserve your insights, questions, and reflections by writing them down. Doing this will help you remember what you just read and will give you space to make connections with your life and the world around you. Preserving your thoughts in writing also makes it easier to access later. At some point, you might want to expand on some of these ideas or share them with others.

If you like to write things out by hand, consider keeping a file folder for each book of the Old Testament, or at least for each major section of it. You could also use a series of loose-leaf notebooks to collect what you have studied and learned from various parts of the Old Testament. Start with one and then expand outward as you gain more material. Or, if you prefer keeping things electronically, create a system of computer files for this purpose. However you choose to do it, be sure to find some way to preserve the key insights, questions, and reflections that your encounter with the Old Testament generates. You will thank yourself later.

Developing the Right Atmosphere and Connecting with Others

In addition to what has already been mentioned, here are some relatively simple things you can do to make your experience with the Old Testament more enjoyable.

Create a pleasant environment. While you can encounter the Old Testament anytime, anywhere—and I encourage all such encounters—there is something to be said for having a designated time and space for reading and studying this part of the Bible. Consider setting aside a special place in your home that you can use for this purpose. Make this space as welcoming as possible. Be sure to have a comfortable chair and good lighting. If you prefer listening to music while you read, consider having some playing in the background. A cup of coffee or tea, along with some fruit or snacks can also enhance the environment. The point is to make this the kind of space you are eager to enter. If it is, you will have a greater incentive to read the Old Testament in the first place and will be more inclined to come back to it time and time again.

It is also a good idea to have your most extensive engagements with the Old Testament during a time when you can be uninterrupted (I realize this is a real challenge for parents of young children). It is best to enter this time as well-rested and undistracted as possible (unplug if you can). This will also increase your chances of having a meaningful and satisfying experience with the Old Testament.

Surround yourself with good resources. As I have repeatedly emphasized, many of the suggestions in this book can be implemented without the need for secondary sources. Still, it is wise to surround yourself with good resources. These can significantly enhance your reading and enjoyment of the Old Testament. Even just a few key resources can go a long way toward helping you have a more positive experience with this part of the Bible. A good study Bible, a single volume Bible commentary, or a Bible dictionary will provide you with a wealth of information that will enable you to dig deeper and understand more of the Old Testament story. A standard introduction to the Old Testament is also quite valuable in this regard. Specific suggestions for these resources, and others, can be found in a very brief appendix at the end of this book.

If finances are an issue, consider putting some of these books on your birthday or holiday wish list, or see what books you can borrow from your church library or from your local Christian college or seminary. There are also a number of good resources online for free.[2] Just remember that the quality of what you will find online will vary greatly, as it also does in books. Some free resources are excellent; others are very poor.

Read the Old Testament with others. While it is good to carve out some "alone time" to read the Old Testament, reading the Old Testament should not be something we *only* do alone. It is also important to have opportunities to talk about the Old Testament with others. Some people claim their best encounters with the Bible have happened when reading and discussing it with other people. This can take place in various ways: in a college classroom, a small group setting, a Sunday school class, an online forum, and so forth. There is real value in having interpersonal interaction around the text. It provides an opportunity for us to articulate our own thoughts and feelings about a passage, and it allows us to hear different perspectives. This enables us to see things we may have missed and sometimes challenges the way we have been reading and interpreting certain passages.

---

[2]See the appendix.

One of the benefits of reading in community is that it provides a series of checks and balances. For example, if no one else in the group sees the passage the way you do, it does not necessarily mean your interpretation is "wrong" or misguided. But it should cause you to do some further investigation. Have other Christians past or present understood the passage this way? If not, why not? If so, how closely does their interpretation align with yours? Where are points of similarity and difference? This kind of engagement with the larger Christian community, which is also a form of reading with others, can sharpen your thinking and deepen your understanding of the text.

Another benefit of reading with others is that it provides some accountability. If you know you are going to be meeting with a small group to discuss a particular passage of Scripture or to work through a certain book of the Bible, you will probably be more likely to read and reflect on the passage before you arrive, so you have something to share. At the very least, reading in community ensures you are getting some steady exposure to these tantalizing texts.

So grab your Bible, find some friends, and spend some time reading the Old Testament together. You will be glad you did.

Look for opportunities to have more frequent encounters with the Old Testament. Given how little most of us are naturally exposed to the Old Testament, it's a good idea to be intentional about seeking out opportunities to encounter it. Consider attending a Sunday school class at your church that focuses on the Old Testament. If there is none, and you feel up to the task, volunteer to lead one. Or consider starting a Bible study on a book of the Old Testament with your friends or family. If your minister does not give much attention to the Old Testament in sermons or homilies, ask him or her to preach from it more often. You might also gently encourage your pastor, priest, or worship leader to incorporate more Old Testament readings into the order of service. If you live near a Christian college or university, consider sitting in on a class related to the Old Testament. In short, do what you can to have more frequent encounters with this part of the Bible.

ENJOY THE JOURNEY

Before bringing this chapter to a close, I want to make some final comments of a more pastoral nature relating to our expectations and attitudes. Since we already devoted an entire chapter to what we should expect from the Old Testament (chapter four) and to the kind of attitude we should bring to the Old Testament (chapter five), a few brief remarks will suffice here.

Don't become paralyzed by expectations to get the "right" meaning. Some church circles and theological traditions place enormous pressure on people to get their theology straight and have all the right answers. While I certainly affirm the need to think rigorously and responsibly about matters of faith, ethics, and Scripture, the way this is framed sometimes places an unnecessary burden on Christians. To counter that, my counsel is simply this: When you read the Old Testament, don't become paralyzed by a need to read it "the right way" or to get "the right meaning" out of the text. These expectations hinder our enjoyment of the Old Testament. More to the point, these expectations are based on faulty assumptions about the nature of the biblical text and the interpretive process. They wrongly assume there is only one "right way" to interpret a biblical text. There are many ways to approach the Old Testament, and biblical texts can be understood from a variety of different perspectives. The dynamic interplay between text and reader generates multiple possible meanings and no single interpretation or interpretive approach exhausts all the richness any particular text has to offer.

This is not to deny that there are bad interpretations, or that biblical texts can never be misinterpreted and abused. Unfortunately, such misuse and abuse happens all too often. When the Old Testament is used to sanction violence, or when people are otherwise harmed because of the way these texts are read and interpreted, we should confront such abuse swiftly and directly. As I have argued elsewhere at length, the Bible should never be used to harm people.[3]

---

[3]Eric A. Seibert, *The Violence of Scripture: Overcoming the Old Testament's Troubling Legacy* (Minneapolis: Fortress, 2012), 1-26, and throughout.

But that is not what I am talking about here. Rather, I'm talking about letting go of the mistaken notion that there is only one correct way to interpret a text, a notion that creates unnecessary anxiety when reading the Bible. Rather than getting tied up in knots about whether or not you have arrived at the "right" interpretation, ask yourself whether your interpretation increases your love for God and others, promotes justice, and values all people.[4] If it does, then you can rest assured you are reading the Old Testament responsibly and faithfully. Instead of being uptight about getting it "just right"—whatever that even means—give yourself permission to have fun with the Bible even as you do your best to read and interpret it as responsibly as possible.

Be eager to learn and open to God. A lot of enjoying the Old Testament comes down to our attitude. If we expect our encounter with the Old Testament to be boring and uneventful, it probably will be. But if we go into the text open and expectant, ready to learn and grow from the experience, chances are we will have a much more positive encounter. Attitude plays a crucial role in how we experience things in life, and this is no less true when it comes to reading the Old Testament.

Earlier, we talked about cultivating an attitude of "hopeful expectancy."[5] As people of faith, we regard the Old Testament as Scripture. This should cause us to read it with genuine openness, ready to learn whatever we can about God, the world, and ourselves. Our basic posture should be one of gratitude and receptivity. We can pray, thanking God for the Scriptures and asking God to lead and guide us as we read. We can also ask God to help us apply what we learn in responsible ways.

Even when we struggle to appreciate the parts of the Old Testament we find boring, irrelevant, or morally offensive, we should still be open to receiving a word from God. God wants to be known and uses Scripture as a primary means of communication. If we approach the Old Testament this way, with open hands and expectant hearts, we stand a much greater chance of enjoying the experience and encountering God.

---

[4]For a brief discussion of these three guidelines, see Seibert, *Violence of Scripture*, 67-69.
[5]See chapter five.

Be patient with yourself and your progress. Finally, I would encourage you to be patient with yourself as you work your way back and
forth through the pages of the Old Testament. On the first day of my
introductory Bible course, I assign students a brief response paper that
is due the next class. The assignment is designed to get them thinking
about what the Bible is and how it functions in their lives. One of the
prompts asks the following questions: What role has the Bible played in
your life? Are you satisfied with your current relationship with the Bible?
And I ask students to explain their answer here.

Invariably, many students express dissatisfaction about their relationship with the Bible. Some bemoan the fact that they do not read it as
much as they think they should. Others are distressed by how little they
actually know about it. These feelings are certainly understandable, don't
beat yourself up about how little time you spend reading the Old Testament or how much you don't know about it. Instead, just recommit
yourself to engaging the Old Testament on a regular basis. If you realize
you have not read the Old Testament for months, don't be too hard on
yourself. Instead, give thanks to God for bringing this to mind and devise
a plan to start digging in.

As you reengage the Old Testament, keep in mind that not every encounter will be a mountaintop moment. On some days, your reading
may not seem to move you in the least. Yet on others, you may discover
something so wonderful that you will fall to your knees in prayer and
worship. Some encounters with the Old Testament will be so pleasurable
you'll wonder where the time went, while others will leave you frustrated
that you did not get more out of the text. This is all part of the process.
With a collection of texts as large and diverse as those we find in the Old
Testament, you are bound to find some portions exciting and energizing,
and other parts less so. Like beach glass hunting, there will be good days
and bad days. So be patient with yourself and with your progress. Insights will come. Greater understanding will develop. Fun will be had. So
settle in and enjoy the journey. Treasures await!

Appendix

ADDITIONAL RESOURCES *to*
ENHANCE YOUR ENJOYMENT
of the OLD TESTAMENT

OLD TESTAMENT INTRODUCTIONS

Birch, Bruce, et al. *A Theological Introduction to the Old Testament.* 2nd ed. Nashville: Abingdon, 2005.

Drane, John. *Introducing the Old Testament.* 3rd ed. Minneapolis: Fortress, 2011.

The Bible Project. https://thebibleproject.com/. (Short, well-told, animated videos on all books of the Old Testament plus much more.)

SEARCHABLE ONLINE BIBLES

Bible Gateway. www.biblegateway.com/.

COMMENTARIES (ONE VOLUME)

Barton, John, and John Muddiman, eds. *Oxford Bible Commentary.* Oxford: Oxford University Press, 2001.

Gaventa, Beverly Roberts, and David L. Petersen, eds. *The New Interpreter's® Bible One-Volume Commentary.* Nashville: Abingdon, 2011.

Mays, James L., ed. *HarperCollins Bible Commentary.* Rev. ed. San Francisco: HarperSanFrancisco, 2000.

BIBLE DICTIONARIES AND ENCYCLOPEDIAS

Freedman, David Noel, ed. *The Anchor Bible Dictionary.* 6 vols. New York: Doubleday, 1992.

———, ed. *Eerdmans Dictionary of the Bible.* Grand Rapids, MI: Eerdmans, 2000.

Powell, Mark Allen, ed. *HarperCollins Bible Dictionary.* 3rd ed. New York: HarperOne, 2011.

———, ed. *HarperCollins Bible Dictionary.* Abr. ed. New York: HarperOne, 2009. Online at www.bibleodyssey.org/tools/harper-collins-dictionary.

CULTURE OF ANCIENT ISRAEL

King, Philip J., and Lawrence E. Stager. *Life in Biblical Israel.* Louisville, KY: Westminster John Knox, 2001.

Matthews, Victor H. *The Cultural World of the Bible: An Illustrated Guide to Manners and Customs.* 4th ed. Grand Rapids, MI: Baker Academic, 2015.

BIBLE MAPS

Aharoni, Yohanan, et al. *The Macmillan Bible Atlas.* 3rd ed. New York: Macmillan, 1993.

StudyLight.org. www.studylight.org/pastoral-resources/bible-maps-archive.html.

STUDY BIBLES

Coogan, Michael D., ed. *The New Oxford Annotated Bible.* 5th ed. New York: Oxford University Press, 2018.

Harrelson, Walter. *The New Interpreter's® Study Bible.* Nashville: Abingdon, 2003.

MISCELLANEOUS STUDY TOOLS

Nave, Orville J. *Nave's Topical Bible: A Comprehensive Digest of over 20,000 Topics and Subtopics with More Than 10,000 Associated Scripture References.* Nashville: Thomas Nelson, 2002. Online at www.biblestudytools.com/concordances/naves-topical-bible.

BIBLIOGRAPHY

Achtemeier, Elizabeth. *Preaching from the Old Testament.* Louisville, KY: Westminster John Knox, 1989.

Achtemeier, Paul J., and Elizabeth Achtemeier. *The Old Testament Roots of Our Faith.* Rev. ed. Peabody, MA: Hendrickson, 1994.

Aharoni, Yohanan, et al. *The Macmillan Bible Atlas.* 3rd ed. New York: Macmillan, 1993.

Alter, Robert. *The Art of Biblical Narrative.* New York: Basic, 1981.

Amit, Yairah. *Reading Biblical Narratives: Literary Criticism and the Hebrew Bible.* Minneapolis: Fortress, 2001.

Ateek, Naim Stifan. *Justice and Only Justice: A Palestinian Theology of Liberation.* Maryknoll, NY: Orbis, 1989.

Baden, Joel. *The Historical David: The Real Life of an Invented Hero.* New York: HarperCollins, 2013.

Barton, John, and John Muddiman, eds. *Oxford Bible Commentary.* Oxford: Oxford University Press, 2001.

Beal, Timothy. *Biblical Literacy: The Essential Bible Stories Everyone Needs to Know.* New York: HarperCollins, 2009.

———. *The Rise and Fall of the Bible: The Unexpected History of an Accidental Book.* Boston: Houghton Mifflin Harcourt, 2011.

Beale, G. K., and D. A. Carson. *Commentary on the New Testament's Use of the Old Testament.* Grand Rapids, MI: Baker Academic, 2007.

Berlin, Adele. *Poetics and Interpretation of Biblical Literature.* Winona Lake, IN: Eisenbrauns, 1994.

Biddle, Mark E. *A Time to Laugh: Humor in the Bible.* Macon, GA: Smyth & Helwys, 2013.

Birch, Bruce, et al. *A Theological Introduction to the Old Testament.* 2nd ed. Nashville: Abingdon, 2005.

Boyd, Gregory A. *Cross Vision: How the Crucifixion of Jesus Makes Sense of Old Testament Violence.* Minneapolis: Fortress, 2017.

Brensinger, Terry L. "Compliance, Dissonance, and Amazement in Daniel 3." *Evangelical Journal* 20 (2002): 7-19.

———. *Simile and Prophetic Language in the Old Testament.* Mellon Biblical Press Series 43. Lewiston, NY: Edward Mellon, 1996.

Brotzman, Ellis R., and Eric J. Tully. *Old Testament Textual Criticism: A Practical Introduction.* 2nd ed. Grand Rapids, MI: Baker Academic, 2016.

Burgess, John P. *Why Scripture Matters: Reading the Bible in a Time of Church Conflict.* Louisville, KY: Westminster John Knox, 1998.

Carroll, Robert P. *The Bible as a Problem for Christianity.* Philadelphia: Trinity Press International, 1991.

Collins, John J. Foreword to *The Human Faces of God: What Scripture Reveals When It Gets God Wrong (and Why Inerrancy Tries to Hide It),* by Thom Stark, xiii-xiv. Eugene, OR: Wipf and Stock, 2011.

Coogan, Michael D., ed. *The New Oxford Annotated Bible.* 5th ed. New York: Oxford University Press, 2018.

Cosby, Michael R. *Interpreting Biblical Literature: An Introduction to Biblical Studies.* Grantham, PA: Stony Run Publishing, 2009.

———. *Portraits of Jesus: An Inductive Approach to the Gospels.* Louisville, KY: Westminster John Knox, 1999.

Cowles, C. S. "The Case for Radical Discontinuity." In *Show Them No Mercy: Four Views on God and Canaanite Genocide,* by C. S. Cowles, Eugene H. Merrill, Tremper Longman III, and Daniel L. Gard, 13-44. Grand Rapids, MI: Zondervan, 2003.

———. "A Response to Eugene H. Merrill." In C. S. Cowles et al., *Show Them No Mercy: Four Views on God and Canaanite Genocide,* by C. S. Cowles, Eugene H. Merrill, Tremper Longman III, and Daniel L. Gard, 97-101. Grand Rapids, MI: Zondervan, 2003.

Davies, Eryl. *The Dissenting Reader: Feminist Approaches to the Hebrew Bible.* Burlington, VT: Ashgate, 2003.

Davis, Ellen F. *Getting Involved with God: Rediscovering the Old Testament.* Cambridge, MA: Cowley, 2001.

———. "Losing a Friend: The Loss of the Old Testament to the Church." In *Jews, Christians, and the Theology of the Hebrew Scriptures,* edited by Alice Ogden Bellis and Joel S. Kaminsky, 83-94. SBL Symposium Series 8. Atlanta: Society of Biblical Literature, 2000.

———. "Critical Traditioning: Seeking an Inner Biblical Hermeneutic." *Anglican Theological Review* 82 (2000): 733-51.

de Capoa, Chiara, and Stefano Zuffi, eds. *Old Testament Figures in Art.* Los Angeles: J. Paul Getty Museum, 2003.

deSilva, David A. *Introducing the Apocrypha: Message, Context, and Significance.* Grand Rapids, MI: Baker Academic, 2002.

Dell, Katharine. *Who Needs the Old Testament? Its Enduring Appeal and Why the New Atheists Don't Get It.* Eugene, OR: Cascade, 2017.

Doré, Gustave. *The Doré Bible Illustrations.* Mineola, NY: Dover, 1974.

Drane, John. *Introducing the Old Testament.* 3rd ed. Minneapolis: Fortress, 2011.

Dutcher-Walls, Patricia. *Reading the Historical Books: A Student's Guide to Engaging the Biblical Text.* Grand Rapids, MI: Baker Academic, 2014.

Enns, Peter. *The Bible Tells Me So: Why Defending Scripture Has Made Us Unable to Read It.* New York: HarperOne, 2014.

Fee, Gordon D., and Douglas Stuart. *How to Read the Bible for All Its Worth.* 4th ed. Grand Rapids, MI: Zondervan, 2014.

Fokkelman, J. P. *Reading Biblical Narrative: An Introductory Guide.* Translated by Ineke Smit. Louisville, KY: Westminster John Knox, 1999.

Foster, Richard J. *Celebration of Discipline: The Path to Spiritual Growth.* Rev. ed. San Francisco: Harper & Row, 1988.

———. *Life with God: Reading the Bible for Spiritual Transformation.* With Kathryn A. Helmers. New York: HarperOne, 2008.

Freedman, David Noel, ed. *The Anchor Bible Dictionary.* 6 vols. New York: Doubleday, 1992.

———, ed. *Eerdmans Dictionary of the Bible.* Grand Rapids, MI: Eerdmans, 2000.

Fretheim, Terence E., and Karlfried Froehlich. *The Bible as Word of God: In a Postmodern Age.* Minneapolis: Fortress, 1998.

Garnier-Amouroux, Clara. "What about Me? The Tale of the Forgotten Sister." In *My So-Called Biblical Life: Imagined Stories from the World's Best-Selling Book*, edited by Julie Faith Parker, 12-21. Eugene, OR: Wipf and Stock, 2017.

Gaventa, Beverly Roberts, and David L. Petersen, eds. *The New Interpreter's® Bible One-Volume Commentary.* Nashville: Abingdon, 2011.

Goldingay, John. *Men Behaving Badly.* Carlisle, Cumbria: Paternoster, 2000.

Greenspoon, Leonard J. *The Bible in the News: How the Popular Press Relates, Conflates, and Updates Sacred Writ.* Washington, DC: Biblical Archaeological Society, 2012.

Gunn, David M., and Danna Nolan Fewell. *Narrative in the Hebrew Bible.* Oxford: Oxford University Press, 1993.

Harrelson, Walter. *The New Interpreter's® Study Bible.* Nashville: Abingdon, 2003.

Herring, Jane. *One Day I Wrote Back: Interacting with Scripture through Creative Writing.* Nashville: Upper Room, 2015.

Hess, Carol Lakey. *Caretakers of Our Common House: Women's Development in Communities of Faith.* Nashville: Abingdon, 1997.

Hess, Richard S., and Gordon J. Wenham, eds. *Make the Old Testament Live: From Curriculum to Classroom.* Grand Rapids, MI: Eerdmans, 1998.

Holladay, William L. *Long Ago God Spoke: How Christians May Hear the Old Testament Today.* Minneapolis: Fortress, 1995.

Jacobson, Rolf A., and Karl N. Jacobson. *Invitation to the Psalms: A Reader's Guide for Discovery and Engagement.* Grand Rapids, MI: Baker, 2013.

King, Philip J., and Lawrence E. Stager. *Life in Biblical Israel.* Louisville, KY: Westminster John Knox, 2001.

Kirsch, Jonathan. *King David: The Real Life of the Man Who Ruled Israel.* New York: Ballantine, 2001.

Klein, William W., Craig L. Blomberg, and Robert L. Hubbard, Jr. *Introduction to Biblical Interpretation.* Dallas: Word, 1993.

Lamb, David T. *God Behaving Badly: Is the God of the Old Testament Angry, Sexist, and Racist?* Downers Grove, IL: InterVarsity Press, 2011.

Lapsley, Jacqueline E. *Whispering the Word: Hearing Women's Stories in the Old Testament.* Louisville, KY: Westminster John Knox, 2005.

L'Heureux, Conrad E. *Life Journey and the Old Testament: An Experiential Approach to the Bible and Personal Transformation.* New York: Paulist, 1986.

Leiter, David A. *Neglected Voices: Peace in the Old Testament.* Scottdale, PA: Herald, 2007.

Long, Thomas G. "The Fall of the House of Uzzah . . . and Other Difficult Preaching Texts." *Journal for Preachers* 7.1 (1983): 13-19.

Mann, Thomas W. *The Book of the Torah: The Narrative Integrity of the Pentateuch.* Atlanta: John Knox, 1988.

Matthews, Victor H. *The Cultural World of the Bible: An Illustrated Guide to Manners and Customs.* 4th ed. Grand Rapids, MI: Baker Academic, 2015.

Mays, James L., ed. *HarperCollins Bible Commentary.* Rev. ed. San Francisco: HarperSanFrancisco, 2000.

Merton, Thomas. *Opening the Bible.* Collegeville, MN: Liturgical, 1986.

McEntire, Mark. *The Internal Conversation of the Old Testament.* Macon, GA: Smyth & Helwys, 2018.

McEntire, Mark, and Joel Emerson. *Raising Cain, Fleeing Egypt, and Fighting Philistines: The Old Testament in Popular Music.* Macon, GA: Smyth & Helwys, 2006.

McKenzie, Steven L. *How to Read the Bible: History, Prophecy, Literature—Why Modern Readers Need to Know the Difference and What It Means for Faith Today.* New York: Oxford University Press, 2005.

———. *King David: A Biography.* New York: Oxford University Press, 2000.

Nave, Orville J. *Nave's Topical Bible: A Comprehensive Digest of Over 20,000 Topics and Subtopics with More Than 10,000 Associated Scripture References.* Nashville: Thomas Nelson, 2002.

Newsom, Carol A., Sharon H. Ringe, and Jacqueline E. Lapsley. *The Women's Bible Commentary.* 3rd ed. Louisville, KY: Westminster John Knox, 2012.

Newsome, James D., Jr. *A Synoptic Harmony of Samuel, Kings, and Chronicles: With Related Passages from Psalms, Isaiah, Jeremiah, and Ezra.* Eugene, OR: Wipf and Stock, 2006.

O'Brien, Julia M. *Challenging Prophetic Metaphor: Theology and Ideology in the Prophets.* Louisville, KY: Westminster John Knox, 2008.

O'Connor, Kathleen M. "The Feminist Movement Meets the Old Testament: One Woman's Perspective." In *Engaging the Bible in a Gendered World: An Introduction to Feminist Biblical Interpretation in Honor of Katharine Doob Sakenfeld*, edited by Linda Day and Carolyn Pressler, 3-24. Louisville, KY: Westminster John Knox, 2006.

Parker, Julie Faith, ed. *My So-Called Biblical Life: Imagined Stories from the World's Best-Selling Book.* Eugene, OR: Wipf and Stock, 2017.

Peterson, Eugene H. *Eat This Book: A Conversation in the Art of Spiritual Reading.* Grand Rapids, MI: Eerdmans, 2006.

Placher, William C. "Struggling with Scripture." In *Struggling with Scripture,* by Walter Brueggemann, William C. Placher, and Brian K. Blount, 32-50. Louisville, KY: Westminster John Knox, 2002.

Powell, Mark Allen, ed. *HarperCollins Bible Dictionary.* 3rd ed. New York: HarperOne, 2011.

———, ed. *HarperCollins Bible Dictionary.* Abr. ed. New York: HarperOne, 2009.

Powery, Emerson B., and Rodney S. Sadler, Jr. *The Genesis of Liberation: Biblical Interpretation in the Antebellum Narratives of the Enslaved.* Louisville, KY: Westminster John Knox, 2016.

Schlimm, Matthew Richard. *This Strange and Sacred Scripture: Wrestling with the Old Testament and Its Oddities.* Grand Rapids, MI: Baker Academic, 2015.

Scholz, Susanne. *Introducing the Women's Hebrew Bible: Feminism, Gender Justice, and the Study of the Old Testament.* 2nd ed. New York: Bloomsbury, 2017.

———. *Sacred Witness: Rape in the Hebrew Bible.* Minneapolis: Fortress, 2010.

Seibert, Eric A. *Disturbing Divine Behavior: Troubling Old Testament Images of God.* Minneapolis: Fortress, 2009.

———. *Disarming the Church: Why Christians Must Forsake Violence to Follow Jesus and Change the World.* Eugene, OR: Cascade, 2018.

———. *Do No Harm: How to Use Violent Biblical Texts Creatively and Responsibly in Church* (provisional title). Louisville, KY: Westminster John Knox, forthcoming.

———. *Subversive Scribes and the Solomonic Narrative: A Rereading of 1 Kings 1–11.* Library of Hebrew Bible/Old Testament Studies 436. New York: T&T Clark, 2006.

———. *The Violence of Scripture: Overcoming the Old Testament's Troubling Legacy.* Minneapolis: Fortress, 2012.

Sharp, Carolyn J. *Old Testament Prophets for Today.* Louisville, KY: Westminster John Knox, 2009.

———. *The Prophetic Literature.* Nashville: Abingdon, 2019.

Smith, Brendan Powell. *The Brick Testament: A New Spin on the Old Testament.* New York: Skyhorse, 2011.

Smith, Christian. *The Bible Made Impossible: Why Biblicism Is Not a Truly Evangelical Reading of Scripture.* Grand Rapids, MI: Brazos, 2011.

Stetzer, Ed. "The Epidemic of Biblical Illiteracy in Our Churches." *The Exchange* (blog). *Christianity Today.* July 6, 2015. www.christianitytoday.com/edstetzer/2015/july /epidemic-of-bible-illiteracy-in-our-churches.html.

Stewart, Dorothy M., comp. *The Westminster Collection of Christian Prayers.* Louisville, KY: Westminster John Knox, 2002.

Strawn, Brent A. *The Old Testament Is Dying: A Diagnosis and Recommended Treatment.* Grand Rapids, MI: Baker Academic, 2017.

Thompson, David L. *Bible Study That Works.* Nappanee, IN: Evangel, 1994.

Thompson, Henry O. "Why Christians Should Bother with the Old Testament." *Bible Review* 5 (February 1989): 12-13.

Thurman, Howard. *Jesus and the Disinherited.* Boston: Beacon, 1996.

Traina, Robert A. *Methodical Bible Study.* Grand Rapids, MI: Francis Asbury, 1985.

Trible, Phyllis. "Take Back the Bible." *Review and Expositor* 97 (Fall 2000): 425-31.

VanderKam, James C. *The Dead Sea Scrolls Today.* 2nd ed. Grand Rapids, MI: Eerdmans, 2010.

Walsh, Jerome T. *Old Testament Narrative: A Guide to Interpretation.* Louisville, KY: Westminster John Knox, 2009.

Walvoord, John F. *Armageddon, Oil, and the Middle East Crisis: What the Bible Says About the Future of the Middle East and the End of Western Civilization.* Grand Rapids, MI: Zondervan, 1991.

Weber, Timothy P. *Living in the Shadow of the Second Coming: American Premillennialism, 1875-1982.* Rev. ed. Chicago: University of Chicago Press, 1987.

Wells, Steve. *Drunk with Blood: God's Killings in the Bible.* USA: Giordano Press, 2010.

Wenham, Gordon J. *The Book of Leviticus.* New International Commentary on the Old Testament. Grand Rapids, MI: Eerdmans, 1979.

Wood, John A. *Perspectives on War in the Bible.* Macon, GA: Mercer University Press, 1998.

Woychuk, N. A. *The ABC Memory Plan: In Stages One, Two and Three.* Saint Louis: Bible Memory Association, n.d.

Wright, Christopher J. H. *The God I Don't Understand: Reflections on Tough Questions of Faith.* Grand Rapids, MI: Zondervan, 2008.

———. *Old Testament Ethics for the People of God.* Downers Grove, IL: InterVarsity Press, 2004.

Yancey, Philip. *The Bible Jesus Read.* Grand Rapids, MI: Zondervan, 1999.

Zahnd, Brian. *Sinners in the Hands of a Loving God: The Scandalous Truth of the Very Good News.* Colorado Springs: Waterbrook, 2017.

AUTHOR INDEX

SCRIPTURE INDEX